# A BEGINNER'S GUIDE TO BEING MENTAL

D1042635

CALGARY PUBLIC LIBRARY

JAN     2019

# A BEGINNER'S GUIDE TO BEING MENTAL: AN A–Z FROM ANXIETY TO ZERO F**KS GIVEN

## NATASHA DEVON

### WITH ILLUSTRATIONS BY RUBYETC

bluebird
books for life

Some names in this book have been changed to protect identities.
This book is not intended as a substitute for medical or professional advice.

First published in the UK 2018 by Bluebird
an imprint of Pan Macmillan
20 New Wharf Road, London N1 9RR
Associated companies throughout the world
www.panmacmillan.com

ISBN 978-1-5098-8222-9

Copyright © Natasha Devon 2018
Illustrations copyright © Ruby Elliott 2018

The right of Natasha Devon to be identified as the
author of this work has been asserted by her in accordance
with the Copyright, Designs and Patents Act 1988.

All rights reserved. No part of this publication may be reproduced,
stored in a retrieval system, or transmitted, in any form, or by any means
(electronic, mechanical, photocopying, recording or otherwise)
without the prior written permission of the publisher.

Pan Macmillan does not have any control over, or any responsibility for,
any author or third party websites referred to in or on this book.

3 5 7 9 8 6 4 2

A CIP catalogue record for this book is available from
the British Library.

Printed and bound by CPI Group (UK) Ltd, Croydon, CR0 4YY

This book is sold subject to the condition that it shall not,
by way of trade or otherwise, be lent, hired out,
or otherwise circulated without the publisher's prior consent
in any form of binding or cover other than that in which
it is published and without a similar condition including this
condition being imposed on the subsequent purchaser.

Visit **www.panmacmillan.com** to read more about all our books and to buy them.
You will also find features, author interviews and news of any author events, and you can
sign up for e-newsletters so that you're always first to hear about our new releases.

For Marcus, my 'madness enabler'.

# CONTENTS

# BEING MENTAL, AN INTRODUCTION

**From the moment you were born it was acknowledged that you had a body and therefore a physical health. As you progressed through life, the chances are you were given information which helped you to identify when your physical health was waning and measures you could take that would assist with physical health maintenance. Most people had the importance of eating their vegetables drummed into them by the time they were five years old. As we progress though childhood we are made aware of the benefits of fresh air and exercise. Via this cumulative process, the majority of people have been primed to monitor their body both constantly and instinctually.**

When it comes to mental health, however, we tend to wait until an issue arises before giving it any consideration. We're told one in three people will experience symptoms of a mental illness during their lifetime and we fervently cross our fingers, hoping that we will dwell within the other two thirds.

My work as a campaigner is both broad and varied, but it can essentially be summarized as an attempt to make our social mental-health model more closely resemble its physical counterpart. For, whilst statistically one in three of the population will struggle with their mental wellbeing in a way that is recognized within the scope of medical diagnostic criteria, three in three people have a head with a brain in it.

We all exist somewhere within a spectrum of mental health. The options are not restricted to either 'mentally ill' or 'fine', there are infinite variables which exist in between the binaries. This book represents my attempt at a mind manual, designed for use by anyone with a brain. Which is everyone.

I don't know about you, but I find the notion of being alone in my own head to be simultaneously the most exhilarating and terrifying aspect of my existence on this topsy-turvy planet. I can create intimacy with other people in a variety of different ways, yet they will never truly understand what it is like for me to exist within the weird and wonderful confines of my mind, or vice versa.

Our neurological solitude can, in turn, make effective communication a tricky landscape to navigate. Even as you read this, thoughts which have exited my mind, with all its intricacies and peculiarities, and been committed to paper will pass through the filters of your values, beliefs and experiences and change shape, to take on new meanings. As a writer, the process of reader interpretation can be exciting. Sometimes people quote my work back at me in their own words and make it sound far more profound and important than it seemed when it was reverberating around my skull. At other times it can feel like a violation, like when I wrote an article about how 'the patriarchy' is not the same as 'men' and had all these terrifying alt-right types congratulating me on Twitter for articulating the failings of feminism as a movement and I felt how I imagined Nietzche must have when Hitler wrongly interpreted his work and used it to justify mass genocide. Although, obviously, on a much smaller scale.

The above challenges are never more pronounced than when we are using emotional vocabulary to describe our mental health. This is for two reasons. Firstly, English-speaking people have a very limited number of words with which to have conversations about feelings. This is despite the English language having more words overall than any other.

We have words which describe phenomena we're very unlikely to encounter on a day-to-day basis, yet here are just a few of the feelings I experience regularly which require (in my opinion) altogether too many words to convey:

- The feeling of YESSS when you arrive on a station platform to see the train you need pulling in and the fleeting, egotistical sensation that the universe has conspired in that moment to make your day as convenient as possible;

- The realization that you and a formerly close friend have outgrown each other and sadness at the loss, mingled with acceptance of your respective personal evolutions;

- The slight discomfort of having an entire Sunday stretched out ahead with no fixed plans, knowing that you ought to make the most of it before work on Monday and experiencing a niggling guilt at all the productive ways you could spend the time in the face of an overwhelming desire to sit on your arse and devour an entire series on Netflix whilst eating items of little to no nutritional value;

- The first time a new acquaintance who you think is *amaaaazing* does or says something distinctly less-than-amazing and you abruptly realize that you need to reconcile their true self with the constructed version of them you have built in your head;

• The energy it takes to suppress the urge to swear when in official/family-based or child-centred situations;

• Knowing something is bothering you but not being able to put your finger on what, precisely;

• The nanosecond when you know with absolute certainty that a panic attack is inevitable;

• The nanosecond when you know with absolute certainty that an orgasm is inevitable;

• The few blissful moments after you wake from sleep after a catastrophic life event, like the break-up of a relationship or a bereavement, when you have forgotten to feel sad;

• The terrible seconds that follow, when it all comes flooding back;

• The dual sensation of being desperate to know what happens next yet not wanting to finish a book because you're enjoying it too much.

Other languages don't have these sorts of problems. In Greek, for example, they have four different words to describe distinct types of love. The glorious German language has a word for absolutely everything, so much so that we've had to steal a few, like *schadenfreude*. Germans can also choose from fifteen words for different types of anger, which makes total sense to me: it doesn't feel the same every time I am angry.

My theory is that emotional and mental vocabulary in English is incredibly restricted as a direct result of the fact that English was first given to the world by British people, who are traditionally perceived not to have feelings and emotions, eschewing them in favour of a cup of tea and a stiff upper lip. This can render English a rather inadequate tool for having emotional and mental health-based conversations and means that there are often misunderstandings and miscommunications. Mental health is, quite rightly, forefront on our social agenda in 2018, but we're having this huge, transformative, international conversation at cross purposes.

For example, people regularly say they're 'depressed' or having a 'panic attack' when they are quite clearly neither and those who have experienced them as clinical conditions become (understandably) upset. But what if they aren't trying to diminish mental illness and are simply bewildered by all the conflicting information in the world, or stuck because the word for how they're feeling doesn't exist?

There has also been an inevitable public backlash, with some corners of the media accusing people who speak openly about their mental health of 'attention seeking', 'self-diagnosing' and celebrities of 'competing to see who is the most traumatized' (that last quote was from Katie Hopkins, who clearly could not see the irony). Throw into the mix the stigma surrounding mental illness and the net result is not only bafflement, but fear.

Equally, however, just because the plight of a person who is finding the pressure of their looming exams difficult to cope with isn't directly comparable with someone who is being treated in hospital following a suicide attempt, it doesn't mean they don't have a 'mental-health issue'. It certainly doesn't mean they aren't entitled to talk about it.

In an attempt to sprinkle some clarity on the subject, I have drawn on my own experience of living with an anxiety disorder, as well as my battle with and recovery from an eating disorder spanning seven years. I've used the knowledge I've gleaned working with tens of thousands of people in schools and at events throughout the world, as well as my brief (yet illuminating) time as an advisor to the Conservative UK government. I have called upon experts in the fields of psychology, neuroscience and anthropology and translated their smarts into more common vernacular to give what I hope will be a comprehensive yet easy-to-understand overview.

I don't think it's an exaggeration to say that the crisis in mental wellbeing threatens the future of our species. If climate change or capitalism don't cause the apocalypse first, it might very well be heralded by the collective loss of our minds. This book is therefore my attempt to save the world. No pressure, then . . .

The most important thing to acknowledge before we begin is this: I am mental. I am mental according to the most common understanding of the term, in that I have a mental illness. I am also mental in the sense that I am an intellectual and emotional being, in possession of a brain. To have a mind is to be 'mental'. And that, reader, means that you are mental, too.

# PROLOGUE

**When I was ten years old, my favourite thing to do was to pedal my bike to the top of the whacking great, mile-long hill that stretched between where I lived, in a picturesque village paradoxically called Ugley,* to nearby Henham and then freewheel down as fast as humanly possible whilst pretending I was She-Ra (and my bike her flying horse, Swiftwind).**

One glorious summer day in the six long weeks before my last year of primary school, I was riding past a field of the hideously named oilseed rape (a vivid yellow crop) when I began to struggle for breath. Unaccustomed as I was to feeling short on lung capacity, I opened my mouth wide and attempted to gulp in some oxygen. The next thing I knew, I'd keeled over sideways into a ditch. As I was a robust sort of child (and by 'robust' I mean 'incredibly clumsy and completely au fait with falling in ditches'), I quickly regained my composure and cycled home. It was only later, over a feast of my mum's infamous bean stew that I remembered what had happened.

The next day Mum took me to see our GP. Dr Phillips had grey tufts of hair above each ear with a gleaming dome of bald head in between, half-moon spectacles and a penchant for muttering 'good, good good good' in response to absolutely everything.

'Gosh, haven't you grown Natasha?' he said. He'd last seen me when I was nine, so I thought it would have been highly unusual and worrying if I hadn't grown during the intervening year. 'And how are you?'

'I'm fine, thanks,' I replied, because at that moment I was fine and also I am British and thus tend to respond in this way even when in distress/half dead. My mum raised her eyes to the ceiling and went on to explain that I'd had shortness of breath and a possible 'fainting episode' the day before.

'Good. Good good good,' said Dr Phillips. Then, for reasons which I will never fully understand, he asked me to step on some scales. My body mass index, he concluded, was slightly above average. Therefore the most likely explanation for what I had experienced was asthma and/or allergies to the (eurgh!) oilseed rape. Presumably he was labouring under the belief that thin people never get ill or have any allergies whatsoever.

I was then presented with a shiny plastic device, light blue with a navy tip, which I knew from the other children at school was called an inhaler.

---

*Pronounced 'Ugly' and most famous for having an 'Ugley Women's Institute'.

I was beside myself with delight. I'm not at all sure why, but back then asthma seemed like an exotic, desirable thing to be afflicted with and the inhaler like a Bond-style gadget, ripe for whipping out and showing off in the playground. Yes, I was chuffed to bits with my inhaler, self-importantly pressing it to my lips at every given opportunity and for no genuine medical reason.

So no one could have been more surprised than me when, a few weeks later, I found myself struggling to breathe again. This time I was indoors, nowhere near anything naturally occurring that could cause respiratory issues. It was decided that I must have reacted adversely to the Mr Sheen polish with which my mum liberally and bi-daily smothered our furniture (an assumption I used to gleefully swerve household chores from then until . . . ever, if I'm honest).

It was only twenty years later, when I finally received a diagnosis of an anxiety disorder, that it dawned on me what was happening back then was a series of panic attacks. Whilst my GP concerned himself with my weight, blood pressure and asked whether we had a history of hayfever in our family, he had neglected to ask me anything that might have given him an understanding of what was happening for me emotionally at that time.

My cousin Chloë, who was a year younger than me, lived a few miles away and was as close to me as a sister, had (suddenly, it seemed) moved to Norfolk. Shortly afterwards, she developed an aggressive type of stomach tumour. I didn't understand what a 'tumour' was, really, but I knew it was a bad word and that whenever it was mentioned it made people cry.

I spent hours of my life vomiting in the back of cars (from, I now understand, anxiety rather than the assumed carsickness) as I was ferried to and from Addenbrookes Hospital in Cambridge, where I was never sure what state I'd find Chloë in. Once she was skidding up and down the ward in her black velvet slippers, laughing; another time she was strapped to a terrifying, bleeping machine in intensive care with her eyes closed, barely moving; yet another time she was in a wheelchair, crying because she was sore and exhausted from where people kept sticking needles into her.

I didn't know what the rules were. At first, Chloë and I used to talk about the usual sorts of things – Michael Jackson's latest 'totally wick' music video, or why Um Bongo was superior to all other drinks in the universe – but after a while it started to feel wrong to be joyful or even normal.

Chloë hung around on this spiritual plane just long enough to meet my brother, Joe, who was born a couple of months before she died, aged nine, of a virus. It was only several years later that it struck me how ridiculous and unjust it was that Chloë had battled the cancer into submission but the chemotherapy treatment had left her immune system so battered that she essentially died of a cold.

When it happened, I felt curiously numb. Chloë had a 'real' sister, Cyan, who was five at the time and was studiously channelling her grief into learning martial arts and kicking the shit out of everyone. I swallowed my anger and my hurt, because if a girl half my age could be that brave then, I reasoned, it was ridiculous for me to fall apart. I didn't feel entitled to make a fuss.

Besides, I had plenty of distraction. Joe had been born four months premature, just ten months after my other brother Ethan, weighing a teeny-tiny two pounds. I remember the first time Ethan and I went to SCBU (Special Care Baby Unit) at Addenbrookes (again) to meet our new sibling, and looking into his incubator thinking 'That is not a baby. That is the Crazy Frog (except it's 1990 so we don't technically have that frame of reference yet)'.

Joe required a lot of care when he came home. He woke up every two hours during the night and, unlike me, had genuine and severe asthma which meant he couldn't be left alone to cry. In an effort to help my poor, sleep-deprived mother, I took on a lot of the responsibility of caring for Ethan, feeding and changing him, playing with him and tidying away his toys after I got home from school. My teachers and family friends began remarking how 'responsible' and 'mature' I had become and what a good girl I was. I began to define myself in these terms, measuring my worth as a person by the degree to which I was useful to the people around me.

Joe's birth and Chloë's death marked the abrupt end of my childhood. That sounds terribly dramatic. Perhaps it has given you a false impression, conjured images of ten-year-old me sitting in a threadbare dressing gown morosely listening to Morrissey records, smoking and drinking whisky from a heavy-bottomed tumbler. It wasn't anything like that, of course. I don't remember being particularly unhappy or neglected during this time. I simply lost the ability to be spontaneously or healthily emotional.

I understand now that feelings, like all energy, can never be truly destroyed. They can be expressed and let out into the ether. They can be converted into a different type of energy through creativity or physical activity, but they cannot ever be simply dismissed and forgotten about. In swallowing all my emotions – my indignation, my sadness, my fury and my confusion – during this time I had not made them disappear.

Instead, I had created Nigel . . .

is for . . .

## ANXIETY

# INTRODUCING NIGEL

**'Nigel' is the name I have given to the lump that lives in my throat. He appears when I am at my most distressed and, prior to giving him a personality and moniker, I'd built him up in my mind as a malevolent force with total control over my mood and actions. The appearance of Nigel almost always precedes a panic attack and, as anyone who has ever had a panic attack will tell you, they feel like holy death on a stick.**

A therapist advised me that, in an effort to make the prospect of my throat lump less terrifying, I should try to anthropomorphize it, i.e. give it human characteristics.

'What you want is someone you consider to be evil, but who is also a figure of fun. Someone you can laugh at. A ridiculous person. No one with genuine power,' she cautioned.

That was how I came to name the most tangible attribute of my enduring anxiety disorder after the former leader of the UKIP party, Nigel Farage. And, reader, the further you take this analogy the more beautifully it works: my anxiety disorder thrives on irrational scaremongery and paranoia, it often demands booze (but should not be given alcohol because it only makes it worse) and just when you think you have got rid of it for good, it pops up again. It is an irritating fantasist, drunkenly shouting ridiculous, half-baked notions into the ether.

Nigel has been a presence in my life since I was ten years old, cycling about the countryside with reckless abandon and weeing in bushes. As children have a tendency to do, I assumed I was normal and that everyone had a Nigel. This presumption was only solidified by the fact that my mum has a Nigel (they can be hereditary, although whether through nature or nurture I am not sure) and would often talk about how she couldn't swallow or eat when she was distressed. Annoyingly, I developed the opposite inclination and would overeat when Nigel made an appearance, in a futile attempt to 'squash him down'. This would lead me ultimately to spending eight years of my life with my head in a toilet, in the clutches of bulimia nervosa. But more on that anon.

It was only much later, when I was in my early twenties and my first long-term romantic partner remarked on how strange it was that he had never heard me raise my voice (in fact I found it impossible to muster even a whispered sentence during a conflict) that I considered myself to be in any way peculiar. Things that 'should', according to the laws of more common human behaviour, scare me simply don't. I have been speaking in front of audiences of more than a thousand people since I was in Year Seven at school. Appearing on live television doesn't freak me out in the slightest. I've stood up in the Houses of Parliament and told politicians off without so much as a single heart palpitation. Yet put me in an intimate confrontation, or a situation where I have to voice an emotional need, and I'll flounder like a guppy out of water.

My theory is that it is all this swallowed energy and unarticulated pain that Nigel feeds on. But I've only come to this conclusion after a concentrated period of therapy and self-indulgent navel-gazing. Throughout my life, I've been so unaware, so cut off from my inner musings on a day-to-day basis, that it seemed as though Nigel made his appearances almost randomly and certainly without sufficient warning.

People often ask me if it feels as though I'm being strangled by invisible hands, but it's more like I'm choking on a great, spiky lump of tangible toxicity. It's as enjoyable as you would imagine from my description.

I didn't go to the doctor about Nigel until I was thirty-frickin-one. By that stage, I was spending three out of every seven days unable to function, seized by profuse sweating, wild, sporadic fluttering of my heartbeat and episodes of hyperventilating that could strike even as I was laying in bed. I was drinking heavily in a misguided attempt to self-medicate and was beginning to self-harm in more traditional ways. In fact, it was an episode during which I spontaneously took a breadknife out of the block on my kitchen counter and used it to carve up the skin around my hipbone that finally gave me the impetus I needed to seek professional help. It seems even I am not immune to the ridiculous and all-pervading notion that mental illnesses are only worthy of attention when they cause you some sort of visual, physical harm.

Since then, I've been trying to get the balance in my life right. I have restricted my alcohol intake. I try very hard only to eat when I am genuinely, physically hungry. I exercise regularly – running and boxing – after realizing the sum total of my physical exertions during my twenties had been confined to sexual activity and sporadic, Beyoncé-inspired booty-shaking. I got myself a counsellor. I sampled a variety of anti-anxiety medication, with varying degrees of success, until I found a type and dosage that allowed me to keep a lid on my panic attacks without either numbing my feelings or preventing me from being my (if I do say so) rather gloriously eccentric self.

Recovery is not an exact science. It requires monitoring and regular updating. Yet I cannot adequately convey how fantastic it feels to be able to say that my anxiety disorder is now simply a facet of who I am, just as it would be if I had a physical ailment, rather than an all-encompassing vortex pulling me closer and closer to the abyss.

## ANXIETY: THE EMOTION

According to the font of all knowledge and truth the Mail Online, the average human spends approximately six-and-a-half years of their life worrying. That's 3,416,400 minutes contemplating the past or the future and therefore not being fully immersed in the moment.

Other animals do not do this, firstly because they don't have our brain capacity and secondly because if they did they'd probably be smart enough to realize it was completely pointless.

Anxiety is, in many ways, a gift from our unusually gigantic human brains. If you read the works of reproductive biologist Dr David Bainbridge you will learn that the development of our cognitive abilities was fundamental to our survival and evolution as a species. Human beings are, physically at least, a bit shit. We aren't strong or fast when compared with other mammals. So we needed to find more creative ways to ensure we weren't hunted to death and mauled into extinction.

Bainbridge's theory goes that, at some point in our history, a change in climate or natural disaster forced human beings out from the comfort and shelter provided by the forests where we had been dwelling and onto the open plains. Without the safety provided by tree cover, the most important commodity a person could possess became intelligence or 'having your wits about you'. Cleverness literally became the season's must-have and that changed everything that was to come.

The necessity of prioritizing intelligence over other attributes marked the stage at which we began to find cleverness attractive in potential mates. (It's also interesting to note here that humour is an indicator of intelligence, which explains why pretty much all my adolescent, and indeed current, crushes are stand-up comedians.)

I know it's difficult to believe whilst reading comment threads on YouTube, but humans have since evolved so that the most stupid of us were weeded out. Today, our brains are approximately three times larger than they technically need to be.

In many respects, our superior intelligence is marvellous. Our gigantic human noggins have in turn given us society as we know it: science, art, culture, architecture, engineering, transport, sanitation, space travel and Pez dispensers. On the other hand, it is our extra, not-strictly-necessary cognitive capabilities that cause us to spend so much time worrying, fretting, working ourselves into a lather and generally sweating the small stuff. All that additional brain-space has to do something.

Next time you are watching a nature documentary, observe the way a herd of zebras go about their day. They graze away happily, until one of them does that twisty thing with their ear flap because they have detected an approaching lioness. They signal to the herd, who instinctually start pegging it in the opposite direction. They run as a group, swift and elegant and inexplicably hardly ever careering into one another, until the lioness manages to pick one of them off. The lioness drags her dinner to a convenient spot where she and her cubs can devour it and the zebras . . . just carry on grazing like nothing has happened.

You don't see the zebras reassembling for a debrief afterwards, wringing their hooves together and saying, 'I can't believe she got Julie. The last words I ever whinnied to her were in anger. It could be me next time!' Zebras, as far as we know, exist entirely in the present and don't expend unnecessary time and energy considering anything which has or might occur outside of it.

During the episode with the lioness, the zebras have gone into what is usually referred to as 'fight-or-flight response'. It should actually be 'fight, flight or freeze response' but no one can be arsed to say that in real life. All animals including humans possess this ability, which transforms our bodies into faster and stronger machines.

When our mind considers us to be in danger, it puts us on autopilot, which is the realm of the unconscious. This harks back to a time when we were cave people and regularly encountered predators during our daily meanderings. When faced with a hungry bear, roaring and salivating, any hesitation would almost certainly result in instant death. Our only chance of living to tell the tale was to act swiftly and instinctually, without overthinking it.

The fight-or-flight response happens when a primitive part of our brain known as the amygdala (see *B: Brain*) goes 'AAAAARGH!' causing our body to have two responses. The first is to shut down conscious thought, as described above. The second is to flood our system with a chemical called adrenaline. Adrenaline circulates around our bodies with impressive rapidity, feeding and enlarging our muscles. In fight-or-flight mode, we have the best possible chance of successfully running away from or (much less likely) fighting the hungry bear. Alternatively, we might 'freeze', keeping perfectly still so that the bear isn't alerted to our presence, which is where not thinking consciously comes in handy. Conscious thinking often leads to verbal proclamations, unnecessary movement and general dithering, all of which aren't going to serve you particularly well in this situation.

The physical act of running away from or fighting our predator uses up the adrenaline our amygdala has released, meaning that once the encounter is over we are back to where we began. It's a perfect little system. If you're a caveperson.

Living as I do in twenty-first-century London, it's highly unlikely I'm going to bump into a sabre-toothed tiger on a leafy corner in Ealing Broadway. The problem is, the amygdala can't distinguish between generalized anxiety and danger. So, if I'm sitting on the number 73 bus on my way to a meeting (top deck at the front, pretending to drive it, like the cool kids do) and start to think 'Oh, God. I'm dreading this meeting. What if . . .', that thought process might very well trigger a fight-or-flight reponse.

In this instance, I am now left with a body that is flooded with adrenaline, but no tangible outlet to release the chemical into the ether and get me back to a place where my conscious brain is fully functional. After all, I can't punch the bus driver and run away. That sort of behaviour is generally frowned upon.

If you cast your mind back to a time when you did something out of character, or behaved in a way you're not particularly proud of, or your body didn't seem to be obeying the commands of your mind, the chances are you were in fight-or-flight mode. There are a hundred things which could prod you towards fight-or-flight on any given day. Remember, you are part sophisticated, spiritual being and part shaven chimp in metallic brogues.

We aren't meant to be in fight-or-flight mode all the time, but overcrowding, excessive noise, relentless pace, never-ending to-do lists, stressful meetings, tricky social situations, exams, pressure to be 'perfect', a barbed comment on social media can all provoke a fight-or-flight response. In the short term, adrenaline can cause us to shake, feel sick, faint or dizzy, have an uncontrollable urge to go for multiple excretions, hyperventilate or experience other uncomfortable changes in breathing (hello, Nigel), render us mute or unusually aggressive. In the long term, it can cause the body to over-produce a tricksy little chemical called cortisol, an excess of which is one cause of depression.

There's another undesirable long-term effect, too. When in the throes of fight-or-flight, we might develop above-average strength and agility, but this comes at a price. In order to garner and focus all the energy necessary, our body shuts down any physical or mental processes it doesn't consider to be essential in that moment. This includes hunger (which is why highly stressed people either don't eat or comfort eat in response to emotional rather than physical cues) and the immune system. Anxiety can both increase your vulnerability to viruses, stop cuts and bruises from healing and affect your skin, nails and hair, all for that very reason.

## ANXIETY: THE ILLNESS

Given the plethora of anxiety-inducing stimuli in the modern world, is it any wonder that in 2016 the *Guardian* reported that anxiety disorders were the fastest-growing illness in young people? Or that the most recent version of the Diagnostic and Statistical Manual of Mental Disorders (DSM), which is considered to be the 'bible of psychological disorders' by those in the profession, identified no less than twelve different types of anxiety disorder?

I should point out, at this stage, that there is a great deal of difference between common-or-garden human stresses and worries (which, whilst annoying, aren't generally debilitating), a period of extreme anxiety in response to a stressful event (which is a healthy psychological response) and an anxiety disorder.

It was only about a century ago that anxiety started to be thought of as problematic. Before that, philosophers saw it as a welcome and inevitable side effect of the knowledge that we are mortal, the universe is infinite and death is inevitable (which, in fairness, are pretty terrifying concepts if you allow yourself to dwell on them and don't distract yourself with Twitter). To experience the emotion of anxiety was even thought of as enhancing for the human spirit; a consequence of genuine psychological freedom.

Try telling that to Claire Eastham, founder of ridiculously popular blog 'We're All Mad Here', author of a book of the same name and experiencer of an acute anxiety disorder. Claire suffers from social anxiety, which she experiences as an obsessive paranoia and fear concerning the way she is perceived by others as well as panic induced by social gatherings, meetings and public speaking. This is one of the commonest forms of anxiety disorder. Others include:

## Generalized Anxiety Disorder (GAD)

This is defined by the NHS Choices website as 'a long-term condition that causes you to feel anxious about a wide range of situations and issues, rather than one specific event'. It is used to describe the phenomenon of feelings of distress which don't anchor themselves to a specific fear, but can strike at any time. Essentially, if you have GAD you're spending large quantities of your life responding as though a sabre-toothed tiger is in the room.

## Obsessive Compulsive Disorder (OCD)

This is categorically not, despite the way the term is often used colloquially, 'liking things to be neat and tidy'. It drives me to distraction whenever I hear someone say, 'I'm a bit OCD. Everything on my desk is perpendicular. Mwah hahahahaha' and I have to quell the urge to grab them by the collar and screech, 'DO YOU BELIEVE THAT IF EVERYTHING ON YOUR DESK ISN'T PERPENDICULAR YOUR FAMILY WILL DIE?'

The 'O' in OCD relates to thought patterns that are relentlessly repetitive in nature, for example 'there are germs everywhere' (which there are, but most of us don't give it much thought). The 'C' describes something one feels compelled to do in order to stop the obsessive thoughts – like washing hands. 'Disorder' signals something which is happening long term. In this example, thoughts about germs return even after the person in question has washed their hands, so they wash them again, sometimes several times. If left unchecked, the person could develop other compulsive behaviours like not touching certain objects for fear of germs, until they reach the stage where they can't leave the sanctity of their disinfected house.

Another common manifestation of OCD is convincing yourself that something terrible will happen to those you love. People experiencing OCD may develop a set of rituals in an effort to express and calm these kinds of distressing thoughts, like switching the lights on and off exactly twenty-five times before they go to sleep.

## Post-Traumatic Stress Disorder (PTSD)

Another charming side effect of fight, flight or freeze is that our mind places anything it isn't able to deal with in the present moment – because it would distract us too much from the task in hand or is simply too overwhelming to contemplate – into a box labelled 'things to deal with later'. Memories of events that have often been shielded from the conscious mind and 'forgotten' will come hurtling back towards people with PTSD at unexpected, seemingly random moments.

PTSD is most often associated with the armed forces, since we now know that huge numbers of people who have served in combat have been left traumatized and therefore afflicted with the condition. However, it is also possible to develop PTSD in response to a wide range of events, not least of all sexual assault.

In fact, the reason that it is important to acknowledge 'freeze' when discussing the fight-or-flight response is that it answers the question thatused to be asked routinely by judges to rape victims: 'Why didn't you fight back or struggle?' The implication used to be that unless you fought back against your attacker you couldn't have been sexually assaulted, which led to hundreds of victims never receiving justice.

Now we understand not only that can we freeze in response to danger, but that our minds can produce a simultaneous 'flight' response. Essentially, if you're physically unable to remove your body from a dangerous situation, your mind will shoot off anyway. That's why we so often go blank when we are nervous. It also explains some of the mechanisms involved in trauma.

A psychologist once told me if you want to understand what it's like to be traumatized, think of a time when you have drunk alcohol to excess. If you have ever woken up with a hazy-to-non-existent recollection of the night before, trying to piece together what happened from the fragments of memory, that is a very similar sensation to the effect of trauma.

Trauma is often more subjective than we give it credit for. It is not for us to define what induces trauma in others. Bullying can cause trauma, whether it's emotional, physical, sexual, psychological or all of the above. Trauma can induce painful and unexpected jolts as memories resurface, often as fresh as though the person were experiencing the incident anew. When this happens regularly it is the defining characteristic of PTSD.

### Panic Attacks

Ah, the bane of my otherwise enjoyable life: the panic attack. Ask a professional and they'll tell you a panic attack is merely a concentrated, dramatic and fleeting manifestation of the fight-or-flight response, characterized by a heightened awareness of sound and colour, increased heart rate, feelings of dizziness and nausea and difficulty breathing normally. Ask a person who has had one and they'll say something like, 'The world went in and out of focus like I'd taken something hallucinogenic, I couldn't breathe, I thought I was dying briefly and then I cried for half an hour and had the overwhelming urge to eat a packet of Hobnobs' (although the biscuit thing could just be me).

## A BEGINNER'S GUIDE TO BEING ANXIOUS

To say 'I feel anxious' is not automatically to perform an act of self-diagnosis. 'Anxiety' is a perfectly common-or-garden type word, derived from the Greek 'angh' meaning 'to press tight or strangle'.

As a person who has, on most days, got to grips with panic disorder through a combination of medicine, sport, music and practising the Buddhist art of observing my emotions from afar and impassively thinking, 'Oh, look at that. I'm feeling anxious' (or, as my husband describes it, 'telling my brain to fuck off'), I make it my mission to explain to people the differences between my disorder and the more usual transitory feelings of worry, apprehension and dread.

The first question to ask yourself is this: is my anxiety in response to something specific and/or tangible? If the answer is 'yes' then ask yourself 'is this something most people would get at the very least a little nervous about?' If you're vomming at the very thought of your impending driving test but are perfectly content the rest of the time then that, whilst of course deeply unpleasant, is probably not a medical issue. It's an understandable response to what is generally acknowledged to be a stressful life event.

If, however, the prospect of doing things that are usually considered to be easy or pleasurable, like meeting friends for dinner or having a conversation with the person at the supermarket checkout leaves you quivering and sweaty, then you are meandering into 'disorder' territory and should probably chat with your doctor. (Please note the importance of not self-diagnosing. Make sure you seek advice from a medical professional.)

The first step in combating panic is almost always to try and regulate breathing. Traditional wisdom tells us to breathe into a paper bag to combat shallow breathing associated with anxiety. Even now, some doctors swear by this, but it's worth noting that the latest thinking doesn't recommend the paper-bag technique, firstly because there is a chance of sucking up a receipt or other sundry item and choking, and secondly because the benefits of the bag are in part psychosomatic (it gives you something to focus on when you're panicking) and of course you might not always have one to hand.

A useful technique I learned is to tense every single muscle in my body for a count of five and then release for a count of ten whilst exhaling. Either that or to bring my shoulders right up to my ears and then slowly lower to a count of seven, again whilst exhaling. Both these techniques make you seem slightly odd during a business meeting, but then again so does hyperventilating, shouting at people for no reason, becoming inexplicably mute, puking into a wastepaper basket or overheating and having the sudden urge to rip all your clothes off.

The next step is to think like a caveperson and identify an outlet for the adrenaline coursing around your system. Exercise is a great one, even if it's just going for a brief, brisk walk, doing a few star jumps or whacking on Queen's greatest hits and boogying around the room whilst hoovering, Freddie style. If the situation allows, there are some great apps available which have five- or ten-minute guided meditation or mindfulness exercises on them (see *S: Self-Care*).

Experts differ on whether it's better to 'ride the wave' of your anxiety or tell yourself to calm down. I tend to dwell with the former camp because I find the term 'calm down', even when I'm saying it to myself, incendiary. I'm quite contrary like that – I don't like even telling myself what to do. In fact, I find it effective to go in completely the opposite direction and say to my anxiety, 'Come on then! Let's 'ave you!' When in this confrontational, channelling-Danny-Dyer-type state it's virtually impossible for me to feel anxious. Of course, medication might be necessary (see *D: Drugs*).

Ultimately, life is gloriously, sometimes terrifyingly random and you are a unique being trying to navigate it. Ignore anyone who tells you they have the definitive solution to anxiety, and concentrate on finding the combination of techniques that works for you.

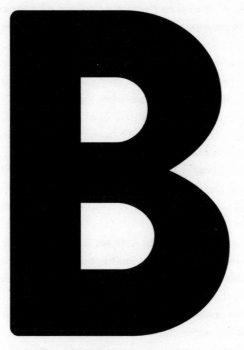

is for . . .

**BRAIN**

**An adult brain weighs around one and a half kilograms, which is slightly less than two average-sized bags of sugar. It contains 150 billion nerve cells, each of which are capable of making thousands of connections. That means there are trillions of connections between nerve cells happening in your brain at this very moment.**

The first part of your brain to spring into life after birth is the amygdala. As we saw in the previous chapter, the amygdala can be a right little bastard. Its job is, technically, to keep you alive, but since it evolved for when humans were living a radically different type of existence, it does this by initiating strong responses either to perceived danger or to the opportunity for some kind of instant gratification.

So, how do we manage to override the amygdala's response and behave rationally, in line with social protocols and our own moral compass? The brain has some in-built structures to help us with that, including the septal nuclei.

We have two septal nuclei, one for each hemisphere in the brain and their job is to inhibit the amygdala if it considers that to act on its impulses would be more destructive than constructive. So, for example, 'I like that guy's boots. But if I wrestle him to the floor and steal them off him I'll probably go to prison.' We develop septal nuclei at around eight months old, a time when most children become mobile and need to be able to assess degrees of danger in a more sophisticated manner.

It's not until we're about two or three years old that the most complex part of our brain, the one that contains our morals and more sophisticated elements of our personality, begins to form. We are given two hippocampi (named after a mythical creature because of their resemblance to seahorses), which allow us to relate what is happening to an emotional narrative and to learn from past errors in judgment.

Our brain continues to grow and develop until we are approximately twenty-two years old, but most psychologists believe the first five years of our life are the most crucial in terms of our emotional development. This is because we keep referring back to our first experiences of the world in order to affirm our understanding of what reality is. As cognitive neuroscientist Anil Seth points out in his TED talk, it is not your brain that sees things, it is your eyes. Ditto ears and hearing, the nerve endings in your fingertips and touching, etc. The brain's job is to interpret all of these signals in an attempt to build some kind of understanding of the environment in which the body finds itself.

The experiencing part of our brain feeds signals from the body to a narrating part, which selects and uses information to create stories about our identity and the world in which we inhabit. As we get older, the narrating part of the brain, which has built up a significant bank of beliefs and stories, enjoys increasing dominance.

This brings me to probably the most staggering and important thing I have ever learned: our brain hallucinates our reality. As an adult, the brain gives itself more information than it receives from the outside world. Most of what we experience is therefore a manifestation of what we were expecting.

The example that is often given by pediatricians is if you tell a child 'most cars are red', they will start to pay more attention to red cars than any other colour. The belief you have planted will therefore become a self-fulfilling prophecy because their brain has been primed to notice red cars disproportionately. This is a good example to understand the principle, but it doesn't fully convey the enormity of it. Most of what we experience is a hallucination of our expectations. If we could climb into the brain of another person the world might very well look, sound and feel entirely different.

Richard Merryn Hare, who was a Professor of Moral Philosophy at Oxford University from 1966 to 1983, described each person as having a 'blik'. The word probably derives from the German 'blick' which literally translated means 'view' or 'way of seeing' (Hare's work was influenced by German philosopher Ludwig Wittgenstein). Hare envisioned the blik as a pair of goggles worn by each person, so that they see the world through the prism of their beliefs, morals, values and experiences. Crucially, these goggles are not removable (although they are, in my opinion, fluid in their nature – you can't change that your blik exists but you can change the nature of it).

Neuroscientists have only really just begun to see the importance of Hare's theory in the past quarter of a century, but it has huge implications for every aspect of life, particularly for mental illness. If reality is just a group of people having the same hallucination and agreeing upon it, then it doesn't necessarily follow that people who see the world differently have anything 'wrong' with them. It simply means they are experiencing something most other people do not. (I'll discuss this more in *P: Psychosis*).

Our entire existence, therefore, could be described as an exercise in what's known as confirmation bias. We take on a basic set of ideas and beliefs in early life and then select and process the information we receive from the outside world to confirm what we already think.

The average human receives around two million pieces of information every single second they are awake. However, the conscious mind only registers between five and seven of those pieces of information. The brain filters out anything it considers to be irrelevant according to what's most crucial for your survival in that moment, as well as through a metaphysical colander comprising of your essential values, beliefs and expectations. That means a staggering 1,999,993 pieces of information are invisible to our conscious brains and essentially 'lost' every second. We are all experiencing tiny corners of the total available reality.

A quick note here on autism: my experience working with people with autism is very limited. However, an educational psychologist once told me that the conscious minds of people with autism experience more than the standard five to seven stimuli per second. Hence there is the phenomenon of 'sensory overload', where a person with autism becomes unable to cope with everything they are hearing, seeing or feeling.

So, in light of the importance of our first few years on this planet and everything that follows being shaped by them, why is it possible for us to change our mind? I can't speak about this from a scientific perspective, but I believe the simple answer is: humility.

In some ways, I envy people who never deviate from the narrative they established in early life. The sort of people who relish the notion of 'telling it like it is' and scoff at the opinions and experiences of anyone they don't consider to be as clever as they are. It must be wonderful to have that kind of self-belief.

Yet I also think there's a perverse sort of comfort in the notion that there is no such thing as objective reality and everyone's brains are colluding in an agreed mass hallucination. For, in the words of Johann Wolfgang von Goethe, 'there are none so hopelessly enslaved as those who falsely believe they are free'.

## A BEGINNER'S GUIDE TO YOUR BRAIN

In my experience, knowing the mechanics of what is happening in your brain during times of turmoil is a useful component of living successfully with mental illness. I have been known to have conversations with my amygdala (which gets me 'looks', but I consider being thought of as slightly odd by strangers preferable to having a panic attack). I thank my amygdala for trying to alert me to danger by sending in Nigel, but inform it in no

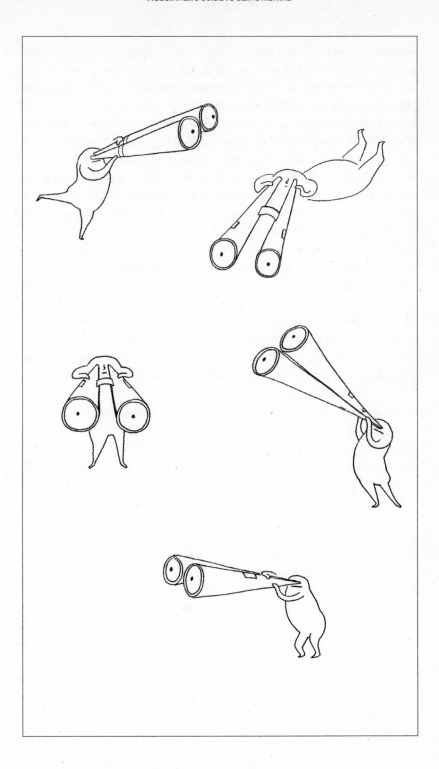

uncertain terms that we're going to do the scary thing anyway. We're told so often to 'trust our instincts', which is generally good advice, but it can be difficult to differentiate what is genuinely an instinct from your brain experiencing a temporary temper tantrum.

When I was young, if I told my mum I was feeling poorly she would say, 'In your body or in your mind?' Whilst I hadn't yet received a diagnosis of anxiety, my mum knew me well enough to have ascertained that sometimes my inability to function had a psychological as opposed to a physical cause and therefore required a different sort of care. This was a useful way of attempting to distinguish exactly where the discomfort was coming from. It took practice for me to be able to differentiate, since the body and the brain don't exist in silos (to this day I am occasionally plagued by mysterious '24-hour flus' that turn out to be anxiety-related), but it was a useful habit to get into.

Now I take this practice further and ask, 'Is this in my brain or in my mind?' Your brain is just a (brilliant, incredibly complex) organ, doing its best according to the chemical circumstance it finds itself in and the external signals its receives. But your mind – your brain's metaphysical counterpart – that is the essence of you. It's yours and yours alone, to change and shape according to your will and that, really, is the point of being alive.

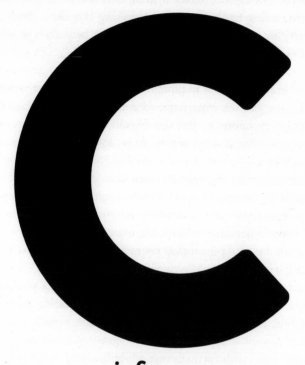

is for . . .

# CAPITALISM

**What we call our 'conscious mind' – the part we are aware and in control of – accounts for approximately nine per cent of our total capacity for thought. There's a little dispute amongst experts on this figure, owing to the fact that thinking is quite a difficult thing to quantify in percentage terms, but most broadly agree that the unconscious is much larger and more powerful.**

The unconscious really only responds to one influence: repetition. Anything you do, say, see, hear or experience repeatedly becomes unconscious and thereby not only automatic, but also invisible to the conscious – which is why people who live in very untidy houses lose the ability to notice their own mess.

Historically, this has proven very handy in allowing humans to acquire skills. If we perform an act often enough, what was once an activity we had to concentrate on consciously is absorbed into the realm of the unconscious and becomes a habit. Thus, we can enact inane, day-to-day tasks on autopilot whilst freeing up the conscious mind to solve any unique problems that might be thrown our way.

The best example of this is driving a car. Normally, you spend your first couple of driving lessons frantically contemplating how on earth anyone can be expected to operate signals, mirrors, hazards, gears, steering and clutch control simultaneously. I remember wondering how drivers achieved all of this with apparent ease whilst listening to the radio, chatting to their passenger or smoking (because I was having these thoughts in the 1990s, when having a fag whilst driving was practically mandatory).

After someone has been driving for a while, however, they are likely to find that not only has the mechanical process of operating a car become automatic, but so have specific journeys. Most regular drivers find themselves realising that at times they don't remember getting from home to work, for example.

For non-drivers, the best way to highlight the difference between conscious and unconscious thought processes is to recall a time when you forgot how to walk. This usually happens in response to seeing a person of whom one, to put it in a fashion which is as romantic as it is delicate, fancies the absolute pants off. Upon glimpsing this fabulous human, the conscious mind will begin to ask itself questions it has no hope of responding to – things like 'Is this a good-slash-sexy walk?'

For most of us, walking is an unconscious act, something we do without the need for focus or concentration. The conscious brain's response to being asked questions about walking will therefore be 'I don't know, that's not my department', at which point the questioner will, for a brief moment, quite literally forget how to do it. More often than not, this results in the oft-witnessed spectacle of a person attempting nonchalance and falling arse-over-tit in front of the object of their affection.

Any thought that you're aware of has come from your conscious while things you can do without difficulty on autopilot are unconscious. The disadvantage of the brain being designed in this way is that it means we can take on ideas and beliefs not because they are true, or indeed because they are what we would choose to believe if given free reign, but simply because they have been repeated to us. This is what a stereotype is – a notion that has been repeated to us so often that it has become unconscious and is thereafter subject to the powerful machinations behind our mind's power of confirmation bias.

This renders our environment incredibly important, since it is responsible for the concepts we are exposed to repetitiously and will, therefore, unconsciously absorb. It would be lovely if the increasingly popular libertarian movement had it right and we each had unbridled intellectual freedom and selected a bespoke belief system by thoughtfully and consciously choosing from the almost-infinite available options. Unfortunately, our enormous propensity for the adoption of unconscious ideas means that we are all, to a greater or lesser extent, a product of our culture. In fact, the most advanced neuroscience is rapidly reaching the conclusion that there is no such thing as free will, at all.

If further evidence of the above-stated opinions is what you want, all you have to do is observe the way prevailing notions of morality, beauty, sexuality, gender, success and happiness differ from country to country or from generation to generation. As uncomfortable as the notion might be, much of what we consider to be 'obvious' and innate has in fact been learned from our environment. In a climate in which instances of depression, anxiety, eating disorders and self-harm have, by any empirical measure, increased dramatically, it's safe to assume that the cause is likely to be less individual and more social than we might imagine. In that spirit I don't believe it is a coincidence that we have begun to suffer more psychologically since Thatcher and Reagan effectively gave permission for capitalism to switch to turbo-charge mode in the 1980s.

The relationship between prevailing cultural ideals and individual wellbeing is incredibly tricky to navigate in the context of consumerist capitalism. In the West, the entire fabric of our financial and social system depends on citizens parting with money in exchange for products and services. It is therefore incumbent on our culture to persuade us that we need material objects to achieve success and happiness. The problem is of course that a genuinely contented person wants for nothing, so increasing amounts of energy, money and creativity must be poured into ensuring that we are never satisfied with what we have.

The moment individuals collectively cease to want, society as we know it will cease to function.

The most visually obvious example of capitalism's impact on cultural norms is how it dictates beauty ideals. Notions of what is 'attractive' have become ever-narrower and more difficult to attain to keep us in a state of shame and apology over the state of our physical forms and, therefore, spending in attempt to rectify this. That's why the paradigm has shifted from the relatively attainable Marilyn Monroe to the improbably sculpted Kim Kardashian.

The moment we look in the mirror, or at our wardrobe, or house, or car, or life and think *Yes, I am satisfied with this,* we lose our value as a consumer. Thus, capitalism conspires to keep us in a perpetual state of fear, anxiety, jealousy and perceived need.

We can see from history that communism isn't necessarily the answer, but neither do I believe that means not having any restrictions on the so-called 'free market' whatsoever. Cambridge Professor Ha-Joon Chang points out in his brilliant book *23 Things They Don't Tell You About Capitalism* that those who say rules such as increasing the minimum wage or banning zero-hours contracts restrict the free market do so on the false premise that we operate within a market place that is otherwise completely unimpeded.

Hard-won human rights such as not allowing children to work in factories were disputed when they were first proposed on the basis that they would damage the free market, but are now considered so essential that we have forgotten to notice them. We can place rules within capitalist structures if we consider the thing that unbridled capitalism is harming to be more important than the acquisition of wealth.

At present, the wellbeing, self-esteem and mental equilibrium of the population is ranked lower than the pursuit of profit in society's list of priorities. From infancy, we are indoctrinated into a belief system that tells us we are inadequate, that we should feel shame and embarrassment at our natural state and that we must part with money in order to rectify this. The messages are often contradictory in their nature with, for example, a bulimic culture fostered and maintained through the daft fetishization of food on one hand and the commodification of the 'body beautiful' on the other.

As Russell Brand points out in this book *Recovery*, if you seek to escape feelings of distress through heroin use you are diagnosed as having addiction 'issues', but if you do it with shoes, or cars, or a legal recreational drug, you are a more valuable cog in the capitalist machine and you're mostly left alone or even encouraged in your pursuits.

Capitalism is, at least in theory, morally neutral – It has no agenda other than the pursuit of cash. The only time corporations have been overtly induced to change their behaviour is when the net cost to the country is, on balance, greater. Thus in the UK, tobacco companies have had their rights to advertise significantly curtailed because of the strain that smoking-related illness places on our state-funded health service. Discussions regarding refined sugar continue for similar reasons.

Capitalist messages are everywhere – on every billboard, bus stop, shop window, magazine, newspaper, TV and radio show and are never designed with our wellbeing in mind. This is particularly pronounced on social media (see *I: Internet*), where the wages of the employees of huge corporate organizations like Instagram (which has over 800 million active users, 500 million of them using the site daily), are paid through advertising revenue. Social-media advertising is not only often blink-and-you'll-miss-it subtle, it's also tailored to our interests based on cookies, which track our activity per device or server, across several websites.

The net result of this is that social-media advertising is often rendered invisible to the conscious brain, but that doesn't mean its messages aren't being absorbed unconsciously. Every time we go online, creatively and expensively designed messages, made specifically to magnify and exacerbate our insecurities, are being beamed into the part of our mind that accounts for an estimated 91 per cent of our total cognitive capacity. Is it any wonder that, since the invention of social media, mental-health issues such as body dysmorphia, anxiety and eating disorders have sky-rocketed?

I don't want to suggest that social media's problems are restricted to advertising, or that the rotten core of modern capitalist culture is restricted to social media, merely that this represents a handily relatable crystallization of the problem. There is a balance to be struck, clearly, between being a functioning member of a social structure that relies on regular financial transactions and safeguarding our own self-esteem. In order for this to happen effectively we individual citizens must compromise, but so must the powers behind media, advertising and commerce. For, in the words of Jiddu Krishnamurti, 'It is no measure of health to be well adjusted to a profoundly sick society.'

## A BEGINNER'S GUIDE TO PROTECTING YOUR MENTAL
## HEALTH IN A CAPITALIST WORLD

As Dr Jean Kilbourne says in her seminal documentary *Killing Us Softly*, 'the first step is to become aware'. As a lover of experimental fashion, former glossy-magazine columnist and regular-ish gym-goer, I'm the last one to suggest we eschew any sort of costly self-expression and spend our remaining days living in a mud hut, wearing a hessian sack. Rather, the trick is to train the unconscious to automatically scan our environment for capitalist agenda and to question its value in our lives.

My favourite way to improve mind-fitness in this way is to analyse visual advertising, if only because it's hilarious. In my school classes we play games centred around spotting legal disclaimers ('the model is wearing hair extensions', 'only effective if used alongside a calorie-controlled diet', 'scene not featured in actual video game') as well as questioning the stereotypes by which the messages of capitalism are propagated.

The most effective advertising messages rely on tapping into mythical and powerful notions of gender (see *X: X Chromosome*), race and sexuality, and what is desirable or normal, which, because they are so all-pervasive, grease the wheels of our mind's inherent propensity for confirming its own prejudices. If we practise changing our own internal narrative, we begin to notice every time women are portrayed as stupid, or men as incompetent, or heterosexuality as assumed, or beauty ideals as dangerously narrow, and that awareness prevents us from mindlessly absorbing the damaging rhetoric.

The second thing to do is to change our environment. I used to believe this was largely impossible, being as we are so relatively powerless compared with multi-billion-pound corporate giants. However, it should be noted that those corporate giants rely on our continued engagement with and investment in them and, as such, they dedicate a lot of time and energy into anticipating, as well as dictating, trends. In this regard, social media, for all its myriad faults, has given us some of our power back. Where once we had celebrities, we now have 'influencers' who, whilst not generally part of traditional or mainstream media, have built up a sufficient online following to elevate them to the status of taste-creators.

Do you think the fashion industry would have chosen, of its own volition, to accept size-26 model Tess Holliday into its bony clutches were it not for the huge army of adoring fans she has amassed online? I can tell you with some authority that they would not. During my brief and distant modelling career (which took place pre-social media and pretty much pre-widespread internet use), a casting (audition for models) involved taking your place in a procession of identikit skeletons wrapped in what might as well have been cling film, to be perfunctorily and sneeringly assessed by a man behind a desk and, nine times out of ten, casually dismissed. The campaign creators had a definite idea of who they were looking for and would sift through hundreds of hopefuls sent from various agencies until they found her.

Now, the models who get the bookings tend to be the ones with the biggest social-media following. From a financial point of view, it makes sense to display a product on a person with a ready-made and substantial audience. Who we follow, therefore, matters. By opting to engage with a person online you are effectively 'voting' for that person. You are telling the internet and, by proxy, the corporate machinery behind it 'I'd like to see more of this'. Just as Tess Holliday and her ilk have changed the landscape of fashion and beauty, so this is achievable for almost every facet of consumerist capitalism, if we make smart choices.

Yet consumer power doesn't absolve business of any responsibility. At the moment, there are very specific laws that prevent false advertising, but they are incredibly easy to circumnavigate, judging by the lengths to which corporations will go to persuade us that their fragrance or sports drink or vacuum cleaner will make us more desirable, successful and happy. History tells us that big business will, unless tethered, do as little as it can get away with in terms of social or environmental responsibility. Therefore, laws need examining. Incidentally, I selected the party I voted for in the last election based almost exclusively on a manifesto pledge to ban fast-food advertising aimed at children, for this very reason.

However cosy or apparently well-meaning the message being conveyed to you by a company, their sole consideration is their bottom line. Use what industry has to offer as a means of expressing yourself but don't allow them to use you for their agenda and to sacrifice your wellbeing at the altar of capital gain in the process.

Question everything, spend wisely and use your social media to change the wallpaper of your world.

is for . . .

# DRUGS (PRESCRIPTION)

**In the Autumn of 2017, I had the privilege of being invited to Bournemouth University to watch an intimate Q&A with a sportsperson who is so well loved he has been elevated to the status of 'national treasure'. He has a diagnosis of bipolar disorder, which was famously and sensationally revealed in a series of media pieces when he was sectioned. It's testament to all the great work that has since been done by campaigners that a cursory glance at the press coverage of his illness reveals much less enlightened times.**

At one point, the interviewer tackled the thorny issue of medication. The sportsperson spoke about his strong belief that if he had continued on the strong drugs that left him 'dribbling in the corner' he wouldn't be here to share his story. At that moment I wondered whether, without the aid of my daily dose of anti-anxiety medication, I would have been there to hear it.

The sportsperson was quick to qualify his perspective by pointing out he can only speak from his perspective and that is everyone is different. That's what people who are fervently anti-mental-health prescription drugs so often fail to acknowledge and I felt grateful to him. He went on to say that too often medication is prescribed when it is talking therapy and community support that is needed, which I don't think any reasonable person would contest.

The reason I tell this story right out of the starting blocks of this chapter is because there are no absolute rights or wrongs in the arena of head meds. What there is, however, is still a helluva lot of stigma. Bizarrely, there is often more judgment associated with the taking of prescription medication than there is for having a mental illness in the first place. I've presented to audiences who have sat perfectly calmly whilst I've recounted details of the extent to which anxiety has previously rendered me unable to function, but let out a collective, horrified gasp when I have revealed that I take 100mg of Sertraline per day as part of my ongoing recovery.

As a direct consequence of stigma, you're likely to find more extensive and zealous diatribes written by people who are anti-medication than those who are pro. Having said that, the industry that produces mental health medication is rife with corruption and, particularly in countries where there is a financial incentive for them to do so, have a tendency to pathologize the human condition for their own gain.

I am grateful to live in a country where spuriously defined illnesses are not routinely advertised on the television in the way they are in the United State as an attempt to invent problems and sell cures. I'm equally grateful to be both geographically and historically in a place where my panic attacks have a pharmaceutical solution, as opposed to one centred around an assumption I am suffering from 'hysteria' and need either a vibrator or a lobotomy. But even with the benefit of a responsible and functioning care system, the fact remains that the pharmaceutical solutions are just as multifaceted as the mental illnesses they are designed to treat, and therefore conversations around them are equally as open to errors in judgment and understanding.

All of the above is my roundabout way of saying: it's complicated. I'm not a doctor and therefore not in a position to diagnose and prescribe in person, let alone from within the confines of this book. The information below is offered as a handy reference guide to drug treatments currently used for mental illness, and not in place of medical advice.

### SSRIS: WHAT ARE THEY?

By far the most commonly prescribed mental-health medication is the SSRI, which stands for 'selective serotonin reuptake inhibitor'. They are recommended to doctors as a suitable treatment for depression, generalized anxiety disorder, OCD, panic disorder, severe phobias, PTSD and bulimia nervosa. Increasingly, SSRIs are also being prescribed for premenstrual syndrome and to help combat the symptoms of menopause. There is some dispute as to whether they are necessary or effective in these instances.

Between 80 and 90 per cent of serotonin is produced in the gastrointestinal tract, with the remainder being found in blood platelets and the central nervous system. Serotonin has several absolutely crucial jobs. One of these is as a neurotransmitter, i.e. a chemical emissary that transports messages between nerve cells and the brain. It is thought that people experiencing low moods or persistent anxiety are probably producing enough serotonin, but that they reabsorb the chemical too quickly, before it has had a chance to reach the brain. Thus, SSRIs prevent the 'reuptake' of serotonin to keep levels within the brain at the optimum balance.

Whilst SSRIs are widely considered to be a good way to treat adult depression, the evidence on their efficacy in under-18s is sketchy. In 2015, the BBC conducted an investigation into teenagers being prescribed antidepressants as a substitute for poorly funded Child and Adolescent Mental Health Services (CAMHS) and was fairly damning in its conclusions.

There are various different strains of SSRIs, all with a unique set of side effects. Currently, there are seven different types prescribed in Britain, some of which have a couple of brand names. These are:

**Citalopram** (Cipramil)

**Dapoxetine** (Priligy)

**Escitalopram** (Cipralex)

**Fluoxetine** (Prozac or Oxactin)

**Fluvoxamine** (Faverin)

**Paroxetine** (Seroxat)

**Sertraline** (Lustral)

In theory, your doctor should prescribe you one of the above based on what is recommended not only for your symptoms and their severity, but also taking into account other considerations, like your age. You should take the first two weeks under supervision, regularly reporting to your doctor before they can assess the suitability and whether you're on the right dosage. In reality, however, it rarely works like this (see *G: GP*).

According to NHS England, side effects of SSRIs can include feeling agitated, shaky or anxious, feeling or being sick, dizziness, blurred vision, low sex drive, difficulty achieving orgasm and difficulty maintaining an erection. Since all of these are also symptoms present within the illness they purport to cure, you may be left wondering why anyone takes them.

The answer is that the above symptoms generally tend only to last for two to four weeks, after which, if you have been prescribed a type of SSRI which 'agrees' with you, you'll start to feel better. In the interim, however, it's important to be monitored, either professionally or by a friend, or ideally both. Some anti-SSRI articles state that they initially put the patient at a greater risk of suicide. Whilst they are written by experts in the field, they aren't peer-reviewed in the same way the NHS website is. Having said that, I believe them.

When I was strapped in to witness the spectacle of Panic Attacks III, The Revenge (This Time They're Angry) just over two years ago, my GP (who is, mercifully, quite clued up on mental health) initially put me on Citalopram and a six-month waiting list for cognitive behavioural therapy (CBT). I began on a low dose, which was incrementally increased as it became clear that the Citalopram wasn't simply not helping but was actively making me worse. My doctor advised me to stick with the medication and, owing chiefly to the fact that the CBT sessions were inevitably delayed, I did. A year later I spent an evening laying in a bath dreaming up ways to kill myself.

Everyone has the odd thought of 'It would be better if I wasn't around' or 'I just want everything to stop for a minute', but to have gone from that to considering methods told me, thanks to my training in the area, that I was moving along the suicide spectrum. The next stage would be to settle on when and where. The final stage would be an attempt on my own life.

I'll never know whether it was the Citalopram which pushed me further along the suicide spectrum. What I did know was that I was worse off than when I'd started taking it. I booked an emergency appointment with my doctor the next day and he suggested I try Sertraline.

If I had a pound for every time I heard a fellow person with an anxiety disorder screech 'OMG, I LOVE Sertraline' I'd probably have enough for the Kurt Geiger embellished ankle boots I currently have my eye on. Anecdotally, I've observed that there does appear to be something about this particular type of SSRI that makes it particularly suitable for the anxious.

Having said that, for the first two weeks your life on this drug will be defined to a large extent by crap – and I mean that in the literal sense. The list of side effects does warn you of 'stomach cramps', and a cursory glance at the chat rooms dedicated to discussing the relative merits of different types of SSRI will leave you in no doubt that sertraline is the one most associated with diarrhoea. By the time the first fortnight was up, my bum hole felt (and probably looked) like a chewed orange.

I was also extremely tired for the first month or so. Fortunately, I began taking Sertraline during the holidays, meaning I wasn't dashing around the country visiting schools. I'd wake up around 9am, go for a walk, do a couple of hours of work and then have to take a nap. What with all the sleeping and pooing, I was much like a giant baby during this time.

I've been taking Sertraline for over a year now and occasionally I wonder whether I ought to try and relinquish it and 'go it alone'. SSRIs aren't designed to be taken long term, although most doctors recommend not even thinking about trying to come off them for the first year. Ideally they should be a 'stop gap', enabling you to function whilst experimenting with lifestyle habits and seeking therapy. On the other hand, journalist and activist Bryony Gordon, who has a diagnosis of OCD and depression, speaks for many when she says that she envisions being on SSRIs for the rest of her life.

Ultimately, I don't know what the future holds for me, medication-wise. What I can tell you is that finding the right SSRI improved the quality of my life (though my arsehole might beg to disagree). It didn't do any of the things I'd heard tales of, like making me docile and my thinking fuzzy. If anything I felt sharper and more motivated, because I was finally able to channel my energy away from anxiety and towards living.

## ANTIPSYCHOTICS

Here, we enter trickier territory. Most of the horror stories you hear online involve antipsychotics, with users reporting severe insomnia as well as being 'jerky' and 'twitchy', sometimes long after they have stopped taking the medication.

However, it's important to note that, just like with SSRIs, it's difficult in a lot of cases to differentiate between the symptoms of bipolar disorder, psychosis and schizophrenia and the drugs that are designed to regulate them. Depression and anxiety, if they are sufficiently severe, can produce bipolar-like symptoms and, in that instance, antipsychotics may not be the most appropriate treatment. On the other hand, bipolar and schizophrenia are in many cases characterized by what's called knight's move thinking (where the person experiencing it jumps to conclusions based on a number of assumptions that have no foundation in evidence or reality) and paranoia. It can therefore be a precarious task to balance honouring a patient's wishes and doing the best thing, objectively, for their wellbeing.

The primary aim of antipsychotics is to stop distressing instances of psychosis, like voices instructing the person hearing them to harm themselves. The commonest forms of antipsychotic prescribed in the UK are:

**Olanzapine** (Zyprexa)

**Quetiapine** (Seroquel)

**Risperidone** (Risperdal)

**Aripiprazole** (Abilify)

**Ziprasidone** (Geordon)

**Clozapine** (Clozaril)

Additionally, people with a diagnosis of bipolar or schizophrenia are often prescribed lithium, which helps to regulate mood by reducing instances of mania (the opposite of depression – where unexplained, artificial elation and feelings of invincibility lead to dangerous, risk-taking behaviours). Scientists still aren't entirely sure why lithium works, but it is thought to strengthen the connection between nerve cells and the brain regions involved in controlling thought and behaviour.

Just like SSRIs, lithium and antipsychotics can take a number of weeks to enter the system and begin to take effect, and they are not intended for long-term use. They also have potential side effects including tremors, increased thirst, vomiting, weight gain, problems with memory and concentration, drowsiness, muscle weakness, hair loss, skin issues and decreased thyroid function, which can in turn lead to very low energy levels.

According to the NHS website, as well as testimonials from service users, early interventions for people with conditions involving hallucinations can reduce the need for medication and minimize enduring symptoms. Whilst it's more more costly in the short term, treating psychosis in this way means that the person affected is far more likely to be able to reintegrate into society and find a job, meaning the cost to the system is significantly less in the long run.

Early-intervention teams – which are increasingly rare since mental-health services were brutally slashed under austerity measures from 2010 onwards – work with people affected by psychosis over a period of years. They use a combination of talking therapy and outreach programmes so that the family and friends of the person affected are educated about the condition. The mother of one patient described how, prior to finding the early-intervention team, her son was merely given a 'bag of medication' and 'told to go home' with no instructions for aftercare.

The conclusion I came to whilst researching medication for psychosis is that in an ideal scenario a person wouldn't reach a stage where medication was necessary. Psychosis can be managed by lifestyle changes and therapeutic support.

However, for other symptoms of bipolar and cyclothemia (which is bipolar's little sister) it might be necessary to take mood-stabilizers. Where medication is necessary it should not be viewed as a solitary solution and should be taken under careful and compassionate medical supervision.

## THE ANTI-DRUG ARGUMENT

According to a report by the BBC in September 2017, £70 million is lost every year in Britain to unnecessary antidepressant prescriptions. One expert, speaking in the documentary *Billion Dollar Deals and How They Changed Your World* described them as essential for about 5 per cent of users and actively harmful for approximately 25 per cent.

The problem in the UK is one of resources and time. Ideally, all mental-health issues would be dealt with swiftly, using a combination of emotional support and lifestyle changes. However, therapy sessions, and family and community interventions are costly and time consuming, making them nonviable in areas without sufficient funding for services. It is far easier and cheaper to prescribe antidepressants.

In theory, antidepressants are designed for short-term use whilst other measures of support are put in place. In reality, it doesn't tend to work like that. People are left on medication indefinitely, hindered in no small measure by prohibitive waiting-list times for CBT or talking therapy (one service user tweeted me just yesterday to say he had been put on a 72-week waiting list). There are also some systemic problems within services themselves that make them difficult for users to engage in, some of which I will explore in chapter *T: Therapy*.

In Britain, pharmaceuticals represent the NHS's second-biggest spend (after staffing), but at least there is some regulation. The American situation is quite different. With privatized healthcare, there is an incentive for pharmaceutical companies to encourage hypochondria in order to sell their products. As a result, people who suffer from stress, misery, normal anxiety, bereavement and heartbreak are regularly offered a drug-based solution. American citizens are literally encouraged to medicate themselves in order to deal with being alive.

In his book *Crazy Like Us*, the *New York Times* journalist Ethan Watters describes how America has effectively exported its definitions of mental illness to the rest of the world, so that its pharmaceuticals could in turn expand their global market. Traditionally, different cultures have had different ways of discussing and dealing with mental-health issues. For example, in Japan 'depression' was historically only used to describe people who were actively suicidal and the treatment involved a stay in an institution. Watters describes how, in the year 2000, GlaxoSmithKline began a carefully researched and aggressive campaign to market SSRIs in Japan – a country that had no comprehension of depression the illness as defined by the West.

There are two ways of looking at this. On the one hand, you could argue that GlaxoSmithKline had identified the suffering of Japanese people who didn't believe they were sufficiently ill to be deserving of attention and provided a nifty solution. On the other, you could say that they marketed an illness as well as its solution and potentially persuaded millions of Japanese people they were clinically depressed when in fact they were having understandable, normal and human responses to the stresses of everyday life..

This brings me to the biggest argument against mental-health medication: that it justifies and allows social injustice. Blackpool has the largest amount of antidepressant use per capita in the UK. It also has the highest levels of social deprivation. Where a person is experiencing symptoms of depression because they are unemployed, on the poverty line, abused or discriminated against, critics argue that antidepressants merely numb them to the inevitable outcomes of their social circumstances.

I agree with this view to a large extent. However, I can also understand the perspective of many GPs who work in areas of high social deprivation and say that the impact of, for example, long-term unemployment on their patients is so severe that they need antidepressants if they are to have any chance of getting a job and thereby addressing the root of the issue.

Ultimately, the discrepancy lies in what medication can do for the individual versus the implications it has for the society we inhabit. These environmental and socio-economic elements to the debate must, I fervently believe, be addressed as urgently as possible. In the meantime, many of us may find we need medication in the short term to stop us from losing our minds entirely.

## A BEGINNER'S GUIDE TO PRESCRIPTION DRUGS

There is no shame in taking any kind of medication and no one should be allowed to judge you for the choices you make during your recovery process.

If you do decide to try prescription medication, here are the main things to bear in mind:

**1.** Your GP might be hasty when prescribing antidepressants and give you whatever brand their computer suggests. Be guided by them but don't take their choice as gospel.

**2.** All prescription meds for mental illness take a while to enter the system and become effective – usually between two and four weeks. Be patient.

**3.** In the interim period, your symptoms may become worse. It's important your friends, family and employer know that there will be an adjustment period during which you might need additional support.

**4.** If, after a fair trial period (from my experience, three to four months), you don't think the brand you are taking is working, ask to try a different one.

**5.** Keep a journal of how you're feeling and the symptoms, psychological and physical, you are experiencing day by day. That way, if you need to change medication, your doctor has information to help them give you the right type and dose.

**6.** Don't see medication as either a sole, or long-term solution. You will need to make lifestyle changes and address the root cause of your distress. The idea behind medication is that it gets you to a point of equilibrium where you can do this.

**7.** Most doctors recommend sticking with medication for at least a year before trying to wean yourself off it. Never just stop taking your meds, even if you feel entirely better. You'll need to have similar support in place during the 'coming-off' process as you did when you began. If you're pregnant you'll need increased medical supervision and should be offered counselling sessions whilst coming off your meds.

**8.** If your doctor suggests you take some medication but doesn't properly explain it, or you need additional information, try www.headmeds.org.uk.

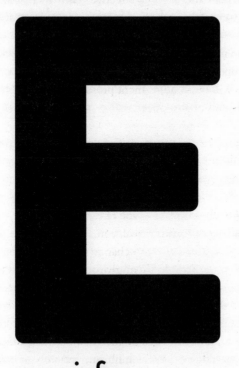

is for . . .

# ENDORPHINS

**Throughout my twenties, I had what could at the very best be described as a fractious relationship with exercise. I did a lot of walking, but that was principally because I was poor and needed to get from A to B. My lack of a formal exercise routine was born at least in part out of the arrogance of youth – I had simply assumed I would live forever and could abuse my body in whichever ways took my fancy without much consideration for the consequences. It was also, I have come to understand, a direct result of the alienation I felt from the world of sports and gym culture.**

Even back then, in the mists of the long-forgotten pre-Instagram era, when picture-based social media was less all-pervading than it is today, I had the general impression that recreational sport was not for people 'like me'. Whenever I felt a fleeting desire to investigate the exciting world of exercise I'd quickly become fairly exasperated by the perky, judgmental conceit of the people I encountered.

Now, of course, developments in technology have rendered the issue even more intolerable. The keyword-sensitive algorithms employed by, in particular, Instagram, which tailor sponsored posts to my perceived interests, seem to have assumed because I talk about body image I want to see endless pictures of abdominal muscles swathed in a measly 2 per cent body fat. These are always accompanied by captions clearly designed to motivate but that, in my case at least, succeed only to infuriate, like, 'The miracle way to lose 2 stone of pure fat, fast', 'No pain no gain' and, my personal bête noire, 'Nothing tastes as good as skinny feels'.

As a side note, whoever first uttered the phrase 'nothing tastes as good as skinny feels' had clearly never wrapped their chops around a full platter at Nandos. Or dry-roasted peanuts. Or Black Bomber cheese. Or salted-caramel flavoured Hagen-Dazs. Or Baileys-flavoured squirty cream licked from a makeshift serving platter of hot, naked flesh. All of which I can state with some confidence – having been at various junctures throughout my life very thin and very hungry – taste better than skinny feels.

If, like me, the sight of a status update reading 'Just done my morning 10k and about to drink a kale smoothie! *smiley face*' renders you apoplectic, then know this: exercise doesn't have to take over your life and your personality. It's perfectly possible to do it and not instantly be rendered a loathsome, intolerable twat. In my case, unfortunately, it took a near-death experience to alert me to this, but you can enjoy the benefit of my hard-earned wisdom entirely free of charge.

In 2014, I moved into a block of flats above a gym. I interpreted this as a portent. One day, I thought, 'I'll just have a little go on the treadmill, since fate has brought me here.' I promised myself if I hated it I'd stop. Which I did and I did. After about four minutes. Yet I noticed a peculiar sense of elation. I was renewed with an inexplicable extra vigour that seemed to have come from the ether. This, I now know, was the endorphin effect and it is exquisitely, almost horribly addictive.

Today, I run at least once a week, twice if my schedule allows, and supplement that with some light resistance training. No one was more surprised than me when running turned out to be 'my thing'. I don't mean that I have a particular talent for it. I'm neither fast nor particularly impressive with my distances. I simply mean that I have found it to be both enjoyable and life enhancing. Incidentally if you are like me a perfectionist, it's a gift to your psychological wellbeing for you to partake in an activity at which you, for want of a better word, suck. Perfectionists avoid things they aren't convinced they'll excel at and miss out on a lot of creativity, fun and relaxation in the process. I return from a run with my endorphin tank newly topped up which, I now understand, is as beneficial to my mindset as it is to my physical fitness.

Endorphins are most commonly referred to in their capacity as pleasure-giving chemicals. They are released to signal enjoyment during activities that have a demonstrable, positive impact on wellbeing, such as exercise, laughter, sex with an appropriate partner and other creative endeavours. They are also released during more potentially self-destructive behaviours like eating vast quantities of sugar, having sex with an inappropriate partner or more classic forms of self-harm, like cutting (see *J: Just Attention Seeking*).

Endorphins are produced both in the central nervous system (brain, spinal cord, etc) and in the pituitary gland. Their name is a result of the smooshing of two words: 'endogenous', which means it has an internal original, and 'morphine'. That's right, the high you get after physical activity is not dissimilar in its nature to that experienced by users of heroin, which is why exercise addiction exists.

As well as inducing a giddy, euphoric, incredibly pleasant sensation, endorphins' other principal function is to inhibit pain (which is often referred to as their 'analgesic effect'). This, incidentally, is why humans enjoy eating spicy foods. Chillies burn the highly sensitive taste buds on our tongues, which should induce pain, but because endorphins come to the rescue in an attempt to mediate our discomfort, we have the overall impression that, for example, curry is yum. (Now there's an insight you're unlikely to find on the menu at your local Indian restaurant.)

Endorphins also have a role to play in reducing stress and feelings of depression, which is why they are so prevalent in discussions around mental health. It seems they can take the edge off psychological distress, too; not least because if you are indulging in a positive endorphin-generating activity, like laughter or creativity, you are also releasing the cortisol and adrenaline from your system (see *A: Anxiety*). According to the rather brilliant animated public information video 'I Had a Black Dog' made by the World Health Organization in 2012, exercise can be as effective in treating mild to moderate depression as medication or therapy.

I had the honour of interviewing then newly crowned Global Teacher of the Year (and recipient of a $1 million prize) Maggie MacDonnell in September 2017. Maggie was raised in Nova Scotia, where she developed an interest in the psychological impact of colonization. She spent time working in sub-Saharan Africa before moving to the northernmost tip of Canada, which is mainly inhabited by native Canadian Inuits.

Salluit, where Maggie took a job teaching sport, is fraught with social issues, which stem principally out of the brutality of the colonization process. There's an unusually high prevalence of recreational drug use amongst the young people as well as a terrifyingly high adolescent suicide rate, particularly amongst the young men. Owing to the climate, the place also has a high turnover of non-native visitors: the migrant average teacher lasts approximately six months in the role before they move on.

At the time of writing, Maggie has been teaching in Salluit for seven years. She has reduced incidences of suicide and dependency on drugs, as well as persuading more local young women to turn up to school – essentially all through the power of physical activity. She has started running and kayaking clubs, as well as a centre where the students can meet to play games like basketball. She has created a mutually supportive community through sport, acknowledging that not everyone expresses themselves via words. Or, if they do want to talk, they might appreciate the distraction and intimacy that doing team exercise at the same time can provide.

A few years ago, I had just finished a sixth-form lecture and a young man approached me and told me, quite bluntly, that he intended to kill himself. Having done mental-health first-aid training, I followed the appropriate safeguarding procedure, ascertaining that he hadn't planned how he was going to do it and thereby satisfying myself that he was not in the immediate 'danger zone'.

We talked about why he was feeling that way. It turned out to be because his rugby club had been closed. When local authorities close sports clubs or sell off school playing fields often they do not consider the profound and far-reaching impact it can have. For this young man, his rugby club was where he found his sense of belonging, a place where he felt supported and understood and, perhaps most crucially, on the pitch he could express his anger in a controlled way at some of the other things happening in his life.

I am duty-bound to report at-risk students to a member of staff and when I did the deputy head and school nurse immediately set about creating a care plan for him, which included finding him a new rugby club slightly further away and offering to drive him there and back every week.

I think we can all agree that both Maggie's work in northern Canada, and the effect that losing his rugby club had on this young man are testaments to the enormous power of exercise (and great teachers) in combating severe, as well as mild, mental-health issues.

I have a theory that one of the reasons why sport, art, music and other creative activities are so effective, both in establishing a baseline of good mental health and in terms of their therapeutic value for mental illness. It is that they are a way of connecting human beings with the life they were designed to live. Early humans spent an average of seven hours a day hunting and gathering, which involved a great deal of physical exertion, and then would return to their tribes where they'd make music, tell each other stories and, if TV archaeology programmes are to be believed, draw rudimentary pictures of yaks.

As I've already described in *A: Anxiety*, the average modern lifestyle is eons away from the way we were supposed to live. This might explain why Netflix documentary *Happy*, which I discuss more in *H: Happiness*, found a tribe in Namibia, who lived a lifestyle broadly akin to the one detailed above and were entirely untouched by so-called 'civilizing' influences, to be amongst the happiest people in the world.

## A BEGINNER'S GUIDE TO CREATING ENDORPHINS

No matter where you dwell on the mental-health spectrum, whether you have a desire to maintain good mental health, are looking for potential solutions for stress, or designing your recovery plan for mental illness, endorphins are essential.

Now, if you have ever had the misfortune to find yourself staring into the bleak, unforgiving abyss that is depression, I can guess your reaction to some of the sentiments I have expressed above. You are thinking, 'When you are depressed you can't even bring yourself to get out of bed in the morning, let alone don top-to-toe lycra and indulge in a bit of yoga in the park, you patronizing bastard.' This is a reaction I sympathize with entirely.

Depression and anxiety live side by side on the psychological spectrum and I understand only too well the sensation of not being capable of achieving the most basic, simple things. At those times, the most effective method I have found for achieving a state of something approaching functioning is to break down the task in hand into smaller, more achievable components. I bargain with myself first to put my feet on the floor. Then to stand up. Then to make a cup of tea, because there is nothing that a cup of tea can't make seem at least marginally, even if only 1 per cent, better. Ditto hot showers. (Incidentally, after having befallen a wide and exotic variety of fairly severe physical and mental ailments in my lifetime, it's my conclusion that everything seems more surmountable if you have clean hair.)

Sometimes, I only manage a short walk, rather than anything that could reasonably be described as a run. When my anxiety has been at its most acute I have made it a hundred yards along the pavement before finding myself unable to cope with the glare of sunlight, noise and bustle and have had to turn on my heel and retreat to the sanctuary of my flat. But at least when I return I am cleaner and more dressed than I was when I woke. However briefly, I did get out into the open air and, as a wise therapist once told me, 'All affirmative actions, however small, are a victory.'

I'd also like to make a case here for the therapeutic power of endorphin-producing laughter. If physical activity is genuinely not a feasible option, then groping for some sense of the daftness of it all might be your first step to salvation. I am convinced that the ability to laugh at yourself and/or the inherent ridiculousness of life can be a valuable catalyst in the recovery process. There a hefty dollop of evidence-based truth is the old saying 'laughter is the best medicine'.

Furthermore, to find a way to laugh at your mental illness shows you have established some distance between it and the precious vestiges of your true personality. It demonstrates that a small chink of light has penetrated the darkness. In the aftermath of the times when I have been most poorly, whether that has been physically or mentally, the first time I have laughed has always seemed hugely significant to me. It has signalled that I am still somehow connected to myself.

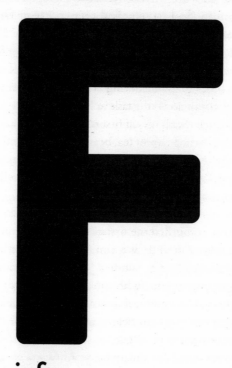

is for . . .

**FOOD**

**This is a chapter of two halves. Nutrition has been shown to have a powerful impact on a person's mental health. Although some of the studies on this are in their infancy, they are producing some impressive results. So I have called on experts in the field to share their tips on the best things to eat for wellbeing of the mind.**

I also want to talk about eating disorders, both in the classic, clinical sense and the myriad other ways humans find to have a dysfunctional relationship with what they consume. I'm going to do this first, because I want you to leave this chapter feeling positive and empowered, and some proactive nutritional advice is more likely to inspire that response.

As I mentioned earlier, I have extensive personal experience of eating disorders. Whilst I'm comfortable discussing the underlying anxiety that was the catalyst for my enduring issues around food, I find my various historical eating disorders difficult to discuss. This is partly because I am less clear on what compelled me towards those behaviours, partly because I am concerned about meandering into the realms of unhelpful cliché and, I am ashamed to admit, partly because I remain embarrassed about it. I'm an educated person who somehow managed to spend seven years with her head in a toilet. That's a significant chunk of my life spent in proximity to vomit, shit and bile, and an almighty waste of potential.

I'm going to try very hard not to write anything that might be considered 'instructional' in this section. Anorexia in particular can be a perversely competitive illness and I don't want to induce any kind of imitational behaviours. Also, eating disorders are mental illnesses and the tendency to dwell on the details of how they manifest themselves physically often means people forget that fact.

Before I begin: I do not claim to speak for everyone who is currently wrangling with or has experienced an eating disorder. There are a thousand ways a person can have a fucked-up relationship with food, exercise and their perception of their own body and a million unique reasons that may have informed those behaviours. But I thought it useful to give you a glimpse into the mind of one person in the grips of first anorexia, then compulsive eating disorder, then bulimia nervosa. Here goes.

## MY DYSFUNCTIONAL RELATIONSHIP WITH FOOD:
### A BRIEF HISTORY

I am fourteen years old. My maths teacher, a lovely old lady with a kind, round face called Mrs Woolley, is telling me that I am moving up to the top set. My maths has dramatically improved this term, she says. I register that she is pleased, yet I can't seem to take in what she is saying and connect it to my inner emotional landscape. It's as though there is an invisible wall between us. Nothing is in sharp focus. I don't feel as happy as I should. I don't feel anything at all (except cold).

There is a reason I've developed new mathematical prowess. I spend every second of every day doing mental arithmetic. I am constantly totting up calories, calculating the physical activity required to burn off what I have consumed, or how much I will have to restrict myself tomorrow to make up for today's 'splurge'. I don't trust myself to settle on the correct conclusions and it's very important to me that these sums are 100 per cent accurate. So, once I have finished estimating my daily calorific input and output, I begin the entire process again. I do this all day, every day. It is indescribably boring, yet I can't seem to stop. My mind is like a tumble dryer, spinning these numbers around again and again, until I'm too exhausted to continue. Then, I lie on my bed for hours, listening to the rumblings of my protesting stomach, too tired to think but too hungry to sleep.

Whilst this has been a bonus for my performance in maths, all my other subjects have gone to shit. I can't concentrate. I am moody and make sarcastic remarks in class. My head of year is aghast. She pulls me in for a meeting and asks why I am behaving in this way, which is so 'out of character'. I tell her it's because I've started my period and am full of hormones. This is a lie. All the other girls in my year have 'come on' but my own ascent into womanhood alludes me.

I can't seem to grasp and lock down my ideas. It's as though my head is full of cotton wool. I'm just trying to get through each day – existing rather than living. Every night, once I do eventually fall into a fitful approximation of sleep, I dream about food. In the realm of my subconscious I feast on the forbidden things. I awake panicked and sweaty and then relief washes over me. I didn't succumb. I reach beneath the duvet and feel for the reassuring bones that tell me I am still in control.

One day, I am waiting in line for the pay phone in the entrance hall, grasping a ten-pence piece. Mrs Mackrill, our drama teacher, has told us rehearsals will go on late tonight and I need to let Mum know. We're doing *The King and I* for the school production this year. I don't have a big part. I am in the chorus, playing the part of a nameless 'Siamese girl'. People like me don't get lead roles. Actors command space. I occupy my head.

Lucy – a tall, confident girl in my form with a great mane of glossy curls, a smattering of freckles and an imposing presence – has just finished on the phone. She turns and walks back along the queue, as though inspecting us. We're all a little bit in awe of her and I shrink back a little. Without warning, she points a finger at me imperiously and shouts, 'Put some weight on, Natasha, okay?' It isn't said kindly. I can tell she thinks I am 'attention seeking'. Internally, I shout *FUCK YOU.*

One day, though, a few months later, I do eat. I'm with my parents at a barbeque – it's some sort of party in aid of something (by this point I don't have the mental capacity for those kinds of details). The daughter of one of my mum's friends is there. She's a year younger than me and with a gang of her mates from a different school. She has always looked as though she's been Photoshopped. Her physical beauty is the stuff of local legend.

Our mums push us together and command us to play with each other, like we're five. She gives me what I call the 'Essex once-over', a look that sweeps from the tip of the head to the soles of the feet, sizing you up. Without speaking, she turns on her heel and goes to join her friends from school. They are immediately rapt and it's clear she is the alpha of this particular gang. She turns and looks in my direction. They are talking about me. I slink off to find some grown-ups.

A group of my parents' business acquaintances are talking about Mum's friend's daughter in language I don't fully understand but know isn't appropriate. They're in their forties. She's barely fourteen. They are obviously drunk, clutching sweating bottles of beer to their protruding bellies. As they speak, they practically salivate. Alerted to my presence, the ringleader turns to me, a smile plastered across his pale, quivering jowls. His mouth is smiling but his eyes are saying something entirely different. He too gives me the Essex once-over. Somewhere inside me a distant bell is ringing. I know what that look means. I run to the buffet table and start shovelling food in my mouth. I don't stop for two years.

I am seventeen years old. My best friend Caz is round at mine. It's the last time we'll see each other before we're each off to university in far-flung corners of Britain – me to Aberystwyth, her to Edinburgh. We're sitting on my bedroom floor, laughing hysterically for no reason. This is the activity that characterizes and epitomizes our friendship.

I get the feeling that I know means I won't be able to concentrate on anything until I eat something. I am now assaulted by this sensation approximately every half an hour. I ask her if she wants to go and get some fish and chips. The chip shop is a twenty-minute walk away and I struggle in the summer heat. My thick, black, boot-cut trousers aren't appropriate. I'm sweating. I have to keep asking Caz to slow down.

I eat fast and mindlessly, forking grease-sodden potatoes and batter into my mouth with a glazed expression. I can't concentrate on what Caz is saying, but I make what I think are the right sorts of noises at the appropriate junctures. When we're done and I'm back within the cool sanctuary of my bedroom with the curtains drawn, I go to the bathroom.

There, I perform the same ritual I've been doing several times daily for as long as I can remember. I lift up my top and stand on tiptoes to stare at my belly in the mirror. What is my tummy doing today? I can't determine what mood I'm in until I know how flat or protruding it has decided to be. My life essentially revolves around the whims of my tummy. I imagine that I can see the meal I've just eaten, resting in my gut. I feel the sudden urge to get it out, somehow. It's making me feel sullied, heavy and unclean. I bend over the toilet bowl.

I'm twenty-two and waiting for the results of my degree to come in the post. I've been doing a bit of modelling in between studies. I finally approximate the beauty standard everyone apparently aspires to. Women stop me in the street and ask me how I achieved my figure. I can't tell them the truth, so I have started saying 'yoga'. I notice a few of them recoil slightly at my breath when I speak. I am rotting from the inside.

I'm dating a famous musician. He picks me up in his Audi TT and takes me clubbing in London at the weekends. There, I'm expected to dangle on his arm and look pretty. I don't speak, I just drink the glasses of champagne that are thrust in my direction. At some point, he usually deposits me in a cheap hotel and goes off to an afterparty. If I'm 'lucky' he returns in the wee small hours for sex. Often, I wake up alone and have to figure out where I am and how I'm going to get home.

None of this feels how it was meant to. By the standards carved into my core by Essex, I have achieved everything I was meant to. I look 'right'. My life appears, to the outsider, vaguely glamorous. Yet I'm entirely hollow – I can't remember the last time I experienced a genuine emotion.

Some of my parents' friends from the village are in our kitchen. I have been waiting by the front door for the postman to deliver the mail. After what seems like an eternity, I hear footsteps coming along the front path, our letterbox swings open and my results, with their official-looking University of Wales stamp, land on the doormat. I am trembling. My university's grading system works on a sliding scale, so the marks you get at the end of your third year count for more than those achieved at the beginning of your first year. This is supposed to be a system that rewards progress, yet in my case it may mean that I have been able to salvage three years of puking and inebriation with a couple of nights of cramming in the run-up to exams.

I rip open the envelope. I have passed. Not only that, it's a good pass. I give silent thanks for my ability to remember facts under timed conditions whilst knowing, deep down, that this isn't the same as intelligence. I go into the kitchen to break the good news. My parent's friend turns to me and says, 'Oh Natasha, you must be so proud! You're STICK THIN!'

I hate her. I hate the world we inhabit. Most of all, I hate myself.

Back to the present day. I am thirty-six years old. I have found feminism and use it to remind myself daily that my worth is not tied up in how I look or how sexually viable I am. I have to do this regularly, since everywhere I turn I seem to be bombarded with imagery and messaging designed to convince me otherwise. Physically, I've ended up right back where I started as a child – unusually tall, substantially built and with a propensity for weight gain round the middle. It's just how I'm designed. I try to eat well, but am occasionally confused by all the huge abundance of conflicting information I encounter. Sometimes I find myself reaching for my collarbone or hip bone when I need reassurance. I know that's wrong. I feel guilty when I eat food designed for pleasure as opposed to pure function. I know that's wrong as well.

I have been a victim of sexual assault. I still find that difficult to say out loud. I now recognize the ways in which what happened have interfered with my ability to enjoy and celebrate my body. Some days I own my physical self and on those days I think I look fucking fantastic. On others I'm distracted by every shop window I pass as I furiously scan myself for 'flaws'. If I can make it through an entire day without having a fleeting internal conflict about food or how I look, I consider this an almighty triumph. What I know to be true and what I feel are regularly at odds.

There is a lot about the above that isn't natural, yet I still describe myself as having recovered from my eating disorder. The reason for this is that, as unpalatable as it might be, experience has taught me that I am now 'normal' by twenty-first-century standards. Everything – from the guilt and shame tied up with certain foods, to the flashes of hatred towards my physical form, and even the sexual assault – is an entirely ordinary part of being a woman in 2018. This is something I have become determined to help to change.

## EATING DISORDERS

I don't propose to list the various diagnostic criteria that categorize clinical eating disorders. This information is widely available and if you're looking for a reliable breakdown I can recommend Lynn Crilly's *Hope with Eating Disorders*, which contains an extensive and well-researched list. What I would like to address are the still widely believed myths that exist around the illnesses.

It should be obvious from reading my testimonial above that in my case (and indeed the vast majority of instances) the problem didn't actually have anything to do with food, or indeed the objective state of my body. It's more accurate to say I was using starvation, bingeing and purging to express my distress, in a way that had a lot in common with self-harm (see *J: Just Attention Seeking*).

And despite what I said about being a 'normal' twenty-first-century woman, eating disorders are not something only experienced by women (see *X: X Chromosome*). The statistics tell us that it's more common in females, but up until very recently the average GP's checklist for eating-disordered behaviours was written with women in mind. For example, it used to be impossible to get a diagnosis of anorexia unless your period had stopped, making it technically impossible for men to have the illness. You'll also find that men are given a far less compassionate response when they do speak out, which probably makes them more reticent to do so and more likely to suffer in silence.

When I'm training adults and ask them to define what anorexia is, I often hear, 'It's someone who is very underweight but looks in the mirror and sees a fat person.' This is wrong on both counts. Anorexia is an illness characterized by strict, unbending control around food and exercise in response to mental or emotional triggers.

It doesn't necessarily follow that the person experiencing the illness will be thin, although for obvious reasons it's likely to cause rapid weight loss. It's a far more reliable barometer, in my experience, to look at how much weight a person has lost and over what time period than to dwell on how slender they are in the present moment. It's also important to be aware that there will always be anomalies – some people are naturally very thin and are perfectly healthy in their mind and habits. Others have a sluggish metabolism and are in huge amounts of mental distress, restricting their food intake to dangerously low levels, but appear outwardly 'healthy'.

It's also erroneous to assume that someone with anorexia thinks they are 'fat'. A lot of the people I've encountered when visiting rehabilitation

facilities know precisely how thin they are, they simply don't consider it to be thin enough. There is also a fear that if they 'lose control' and eat something outside of their strict, self-imposed regime they won't be able to stop, so that they will become fat. This is not wholly unfounded because long periods of starvation do induce an obsession with food and a desire to binge – the body's way of compensating for the lack of calories consumed. There's a lot of truth in what a colleague of mine who mentors young people with learning difficulties says: 'When someone with anorexia claims they can't eat because they'll "get fat", our response shouldn't be "no you won't", but rather "so what?" Being fat isn't the worst fate that can befall a person.'

I dislike the way anorexia and bulimia are often said in the same breath. Having had experience of them both, I can say with some confidence that they are entirely different in their nature – although it is quite typical for people to move from one to the other. Anorexia is most like OCD (see *A: Anxiety*) in that it revolves around obsessive thoughts and compensatory behaviours. Bulimia is much more like drug or alcohol addiction (see *W: Weed*). Bulimia nervosa is an illness that begins with low self-esteem, giving rise to a need for distraction, self-medication and over-indulgence, leading to guilt and shame, which then feeds back into low self-esteem and begins the entire, hideous, ever-spiralling cycle over again.

It's highly likely that a person with bulimia won't be underweight. The illness tends to cause initial weight loss, but this is mostly due to dehydration. Our bodies are adept at responding to the situations they find themselves in and the innards of a person with bulimia quickly become able to hold on to as many calories as possible after they are consumed, knowing that a purge is on the horizon. According to Beat, the UK's largest eating-disorder charity, the majority of people with bulimia have either a 'normal' BMI or are slightly overweight. This has been historically problematic, since a GP's first response to the suspicion of an eating disorder of any kind was often to weigh the patient.

I become hopping mad every time obesity is either talked about as though it is automatically an eating disorder, or disregarded completely from the discussion. For reasons it would probably be unwise to pursue (because it would tell us something unpalatable about human nature), the visual spectacle of a very underweight person provokes sympathy, whereas a very overweight person inspires the opposite sentiment. There is an inability to grasp, in some quarters, that stuffing one's unwilling gullet with industrial quantities of food without pleasure or purpose isn't logical behaviour and therefore, in all likelihood, is motivated by some kind of emotional discomfort. We tend to assume greed and lack of so-called willpower are the only motivating factors.

I get this a lot with the teenagers I work with, who have somehow arrived at the conclusion that it's 'dangerous' to love their body no matter how it might look, because to do so would inevitably result in them sitting on their sofa consuming huge quantities of lard. I have to explain that people who love themselves are more likely to look after their bodies, in just the same way that people who love their car ensure it's given the right sort of fuel.

I understand now that my being significantly overweight in the past was a defence mechanism. I wanted to smother myself in a protective layer of fat so the 'real' me could hide away. Today, my status as a slightly overweight person is a combination of my genetic make-up and the devastating impact several years of yoyoing has had on my metabolism (in the words of Eddie Izzard, 'I just look at a piece of lettuce' and I blow up).

Of course, I'm not suggesting that all overweight people have an eating disorder. That would be daft. Human beings, and in particular the female of the species, come in a broad spectrum of shapes and sizes, all of which can be totally healthy. After all, health is a lifestyle, not a look.

Having said that, there's a school of thought that holds that everyone in the modern age has an eating disorder, or at least engages in some form of disordered eating. A couple of years ago, I was listening to Susie Orbach, author of the seminal *Fat is a Feminist Issue* (and in my opinion a bona fide hero-without-a-cape), speaking in Parliament. She said that when she began practising as a psychotherapist thirty years previously, if someone had come into her office and said they were cutting out entire food groups she would have declared that they had a serious eating disorder and referred them for treatment. Now this is a weight-loss technique advocated by countless 'clean-eating' YouTube and Instagram gurus (who, incidentally, don't have a nutritional qualification between them).

This has given rise to the phenomenon of 'orthorexia' – an obsession with 'healthy' eating, that is closely linked to anorexia. It used to be that people with anorexia would suddenly discover vegetarianism, not out of a genuine political or moral stance, but as an excuse to avoid certain foods. The modern social acceptability of the 'clean eating' and 'gluten-free'*

---

*Unless you are a genuine celiac and thereby severely intolerant to gluten, in which case crack on.

brigades has also made it much easier for a person in the early stages of anorexia to normalize and hide their food-restricting behaviours.

## A BEGINNER'S GUIDE TO EATING RIGHT

This brings me to the central conclusion to which I have arrived at after more than a decade of struggle and an equal amount of study: the belief that any kind of food is 'the enemy' isn't healthy. Everything's fine in moderation. It would be far more beneficial, both to individuals and to society more generally, if we focused on the benefits food can bring, rather than eschewing anything with fat, sugar, carbs, 'toxins', or indeed flavour. The aim should be to nourish and nurture, rather than to punish ourselves. It's a subtle switch in attitude; one dedicated to celebrating, rather than demonizing food.

In that spirit, I shan't use this section to tell you to avoid sugar, or caffeine or alcohol. Chances are, if you have a mental-health issue, you've probably been told that approximately 246 squillion times. Although I will take the opportunity to quickly espouse the virtues of avoiding foods you might have minor allergies to.

Dr Rachel Abrams, who specializes in using food to promote healing, talks about the negative impact of 'inflammatories' on the mindset. In short, they can make you irritable and anxious, since they're quite literally irritating you from the inside out. I can testify to this, having discovered I was slightly lactose-intolerant by noting the 'scratchy feeling' I got (and the subsequent desire to tell everyone to just sod off and leave me alone) after drinking a grande latte. I switched to soya- and oat-based alternatives – although doing so flexibly (if you offer me some cheese I will bite your hand off).

Here are some nutrients that the latest research tells us are helpful for mental wellbeing:

### Vitamin B12

Found in fish, poultry, eggs, milk, fortified breakfast cereals (if you are vegan many health professionals recommend you take B12 supplements, which are widely available). Physically, vitamin B12's main functions relate to the immune system. It assists with healthy red blood cell formation, promotes circulation and good digestion. This is beneficial to mental health in that feeling 'under the weather' or constipated has a knock-on effect on mood.

When it comes to the more specific ways vitamin B12 helps with psychological wellbeing, the evidence is at present a little more sketchy.

Scientists don't yet know precisely why it assists, just that it does. One theory is that it helps with the formation of neurotransmitters, which in turn ensure that emotional information is properly 'communicated' throughout the body.

### Omega-3s

Found in vegetable oils, walnuts, kale, spinach, fatty fish (e.g. mackerel and salmon). There is research suggesting that omega-3s can be beneficial in stabilizing mood, making it a good choice for people experiencing depression (particularly postnatal) or even bipolar.

### Turmeric

In its natural form, turmeric looks like what would happen if a piece of ginger had sex with a sweet potato, but it's most often sold ground up into a vivid orange powder, which you can sprinkle on pretty much anything. Turmeric has been linked to 'mental clarity' and there are numerous testimonials online that espouse its benefits in lessening depression.

### Soluble fibre

Found in apples, nuts, seeds, lentils and beans. Again, soluble fibre is said to be good for 'clarity', with some studies suggesting it can be beneficial in warding off dementia and can help lessen mood swings for people going through the menopause.

It should be noted, of course, that none of the above are a substitute for medication where it's needed and they won't 'cure' mental illness on their own. Yet, since we know recovery from mental illness and maintenance of mental health are rarely attributable to one thing alone, it's worth adding these to your repertoire.

Being physically healthy means ensuring we eat all the requisite food groups, including plenty of fresh and, if possible, locally sourced produce. Being mentally healthy means not allowing these sorts of considerations to dominate your day. Maintaining a vice-like control over self-imposed food 'rules' is unlikely to lead to psychological wellbeing. Having a happy relationship with food includes the ability to treat yourself sometimes. To enjoy and savour the food you consume. To understand that sometimes the most ideally healthy option simply isn't available.

After all, as the old adage goes, we should eat to live, not live to eat.

is for . . .
**GP**

**Warning: This chapter contains graphic medical descriptions some readers might find upsetting, plus a detail about my eating disorder that is potentially triggering. If you don't want to see these, skip the section entitled 'Me and My GPs'.**

## WHAT IS A GP?

In the UK, general practitioners (GPs) are the first people we are encouraged to seek advice from for any kind of medical complaint. GPs can be in community doctors' surgeries (for registered patients who live within a close geographical radius), walk-in centres (for anyone who happens to be in the vicinity) or the accident and emergency departments of hospitals. Their job is to assess the symptoms of the patient, prescribe medication if it falls within their remit (that being, as far as I can tell, 'mild to moderate illness') or refer them to a specialist if the problem is severe or they aren't sure what it is. They are the gateway to all other forms of medical care.

By definition, GPs are *general* practitioners. That means that whilst they have been through extensive medical training, they don't specialize in any one particular area of medicine. They know a little information about a range of conditions, whereas a specialist is an expert on either one part of the body or one set of related conditions. Having said that, GPs have some flexibility over what they study and can choose to gain more in-depth knowledge in a particular area of interest.

At present, mental health is a tiny component of compulsory GP training, despite an estimated one in three GP visits being for a mental-health issue and many physical ailments having a knock-on psychological impact. (It's been shown that long-term physical illness can increase your chances of developing depression, for example.)

Ultimately, any visit to a GP for a mental illness is, at present, a game of Russian roulette.

## ME AND MY GPS

I want to preface what I'm about to say with a couple of disclaimers. The first is that I am indescribably glad and grateful that in the UK we are able to access an appointment with a GP free at the point of use. I cannot imagine a better utilization of tax revenues. Secondly, I know the vast majority of GPs to be hard working and dedicated and the public are, quite a lot of the time, massive hypochondriacs.

If you read Adam Kay's excellent book *This Is Going to Hurt*, you'll get an idea of some of the ludicrous reasons why medical attention is sought. I can only imagine that this has been exacerbated by 'Dr Google'. It must be incredibly frustrating to have to deal with patients who have wrongly convinced themselves they have a deadly disease from searching their symptoms online and who refuse to be convinced otherwise by a medical professional.

What I'm clumsily attempting to convey is that I know GPs are doing their best. However, within the context of my daft life I've had some really bad experiences and (probably) a disproportionate amount of bad luck with doctors.

When I was born, I had a condition called pyloric stenosis. This means I had an enlarged pylorus muscle, which is the gateway between the stomach and the small intestine. In layman's terms, I was essentially a bulimic baby – I projectile vomited everything I ate. This is fairly common in infants and not too serious if treated quickly, but it requires an immediate operation, without which the baby will die because they cannot digest food properly.

When my mum took me to our GP, she was told that I probably had a 'little ear infection' that 'all babies are a bit sick' and to calm down and stop being dramatic. Later, Mum saw that the doctor had written 'anxious first-time mother' in her notes.

By the time I was four weeks old, Mum was forced to feed me every half an hour in the hope I was retaining at least a tiny bit of milk. She decided that this was definitely not normal and, in an act of desperation, fed me in front of our GP so she could see the *Exorcist*-style spewing that ensued first hand. I was sent immediately to the hospital just in the nick of time. A couple more days and I would have starved or dehydrated to death.

Three decades later, when my spleen spontaneously ruptured (for no reason – I am the worst sort of medical miracle), the GP at the accident and emergency department told me my abdominal pains were indigestion. When I refused to go home on the grounds that I was spasming into a full body lock of excruciating pain every twenty seconds, which had spread to my shoulders and chest and wasn't like any indigestion I'd ever had, he said I was a 'big girl' and probably ate too much spicy food (in fairness, I am partial to a Nandos) and that maybe it was a stomach ulcer. He reluctantly agreed to give me a scan and see.

Scans of my appendix, gall bladder – all the usual suspects that would cause abdominal pains – came back fine and still I refused to leave. They kept telling me to go home, made me feel like a massive wuss, a waste of NHS funds and a bed blocker. Were it not for the combination of my brief training in clinical negligence when I worked as a legal secretary in my twenties and my friend Bee (who is one of the scariest people on the planet when she's on a mission) coming to the hospital, pretending to be my sister and refusing to leave my bedside until I was seen, I think I probably would have been booted out.

It was me who insisted on having an exploratory op to see what exactly was going on with my pesky innards. Doctors advised me not to, as there was a chance of bowel perforation. When I signed a consent form and told them to do it anyway they found a litre and a half of internal bleeding (which is why I looked fatter than usual and the first GP thought it was wind). If I'd have taken their advice and waited, the likelihood is I would have slowly bled to death.

So that's twice I have nearly died because of different GPs thinking their patients are exaggerating. But I forgive entirely all of the people involved in these incidents. In both cases the conditions were rare (pyloric stenosis is not often seen in female babies). For every one of me there's possibly a hundred patients who are exaggerating. Perhaps most importantly, once the problem was recognized the NHS acted swiftly to save my life. So really what I should be saying is thank you, NHS, you absolute bunch of hugely underpaid and under-appreciated legends.

However, what I cannot forgive is the way my GP at university responded when I went to him asking for help for bulimia nervosa. The first time I approached a medical professional was in my third year of university, which was 2002. By that point, I was bingeing and making myself sick about eight times per day. I was plagued by exhaustion, constant cold and flu-like symptoms, an inability to concentrate, stomach cramps and crumbling teeth. They were different, less enlightened times, but it still didn't take a genius to work out what was wrong with me.

If people with physical health problems have, on average, a tendency for exaggeration and overreaction, people with mental-health issues are the opposite. It takes a momentous amount of courage, in a climate still rife with stigma and misunderstanding, at a time when you can't think coherently and everything makes you anxious, to get yourself to a doctor's appointment.

A part of you believes that this is self-inflicted and that you're wasting the doctor's time. Therefore, the last thing you need is to be treated as though your problems are self-inflicted and that you're wasting the doctor's time. The first thing my GP did when I managed to choke out the words, 'I think . . . I have problems . . . with food and my weight and stuff,' was to look at me dispassionately, tell me that I didn't look visibly underweight to him and instruct me to step on the scales. When the machine confirmed that I had a 'healthy' BMI he shrugged and told me there wasn't anything he could do for me.

In that moment I couldn't have felt more ashamed. I left the surgery with my head down, battling the Welsh winds, reflecting on all the pictures I'd seen of emaciated people in their underwear on the pages of weekly women's gossip magazines. 'They are the ones with the real eating disorders', I thought. 'They are the ones who really need help'. I was making a fuss about nothing.

I didn't try to get better again until 2006.

## GPS AND MENTAL HEALTH

On average, a GP is allocated six minutes per appointment. That means they have 360 seconds to try to ascertain what the hell is wrong with you and prescribe the appropriate remedy. If what is wrong with you is that your finger is broken, or you have a chest infection, or a bit of lego stuck up your nose, that's achievable. If what is wrong with you is a complex combination of psychological factors that may incorporate deeply buried past traumas, often involve unhelpful coping mechanisms and aren't visible to either the naked eye or to an otoscope, six minutes ain't going to cut it.

As well as difficulties around diagnoses, people with mental illnesses are often also reticent about – or ambivalent towards, or just too scared and dysfunctional to engage with – treatment. In chapter *N: Number 10 Downing Street*, I explore the epic deficits in funding that lead to ever-spiralling waiting lists for people to be seen for therapeutic care. In chapter *T: Therapy*, I'll touch on how mental-health services are often fairly grim and uninviting places, which don't feel nurturing or welcoming for those in psychological distress.

A GP will often use a strengths and difficulties questionnaire (which asks questions such as 'how many times in the past week have you had little enjoyment in things you usually enjoy?') to ascertain whether the patient has symptoms of anxiety or depression. If affirmative, they usually give them a prescription for antidepressants and put them on a waiting list that can be anything up to two years. During the interim period, the medicine will either help or it won't and the patient will deteriorate, in which case by the time they have their first appointment for therapy they're not in a fit state to engage with the treatment being offered. This is, under any analysis, a systematic fuck-up of epic proportions.

Recently, there has been a lot of talk about 'treating the whole patient' and I've personally seen evidence of that. During my last appointment to renew my prescription for anti-anxiety medication I was asked about my job and my home life, made eye contact with and generally made to feel like a person as opposed to an inconvenient slab of meat. But then, who can say whether that's because I'm in a good place now and was therefore smiling back, answering questions comprehensively and generally not being a pain in the arse? Under this analysis, it's not outside the realms of possibility that the people who are the most well will receive the most compassionate medical care.

That's the thing we often forget: people who are ill are often, through no fault of their own, not particularly pleasant or sociable or articulate. It's clear that when it comes to treating patients with mental-health concerns, in addition to more funding and training, a different tack is needed.

## DOCTOR MENTAL HEALTH

It would be remiss of me to talk about doctors and mental health without acknowledging that the increasing demands of a stretched and under-funded healthcare system is having a devastating impact on the psychological wellbeing of its employees.

In 2015, junior doctors (which just means anyone who isn't a consultant; there is actually nothing 'junior' about them) went on strike to protest changes that would effectively see them working longer hours for less pay. The response from the Department of Health and their friends in the mainstream media was to paint junior doctors as lazy, greedy and grasping. Doctors responded that the changes threatened their number-one priority: patient safety.

At around the same time, I was in the Sky News studio doing a newspaper review when Secretary of State for Health Jeremy Hunt was patched over from a different studio for a live interview. The presenter, Eamonn Holmes, said I could ask him a question if I wanted, so I decided to give him the benefit of the doubt and invite him to explain precisely how his proposed changes were going to benefit the nation. You can still find online the hilarious screenshot as sent in by one viewer of me looking bemused and frustrated during the ensuing explanation. It was, as far as I could tell, utter bollocks. It was an attempt to save money wrapped up in a PR campaign about 'efficiency' and junior doctors being 'selfish'.

As a direct result of this attempt to cast aspersions on his colleagues, former doctor Adam Kay, who is mentioned above, decided to publish some of his diaries from his time working in an NHS hospital, in an effort to portray the realities and to provide some balance to the media spin. Adam was forced to leave a profession he loved because the demands on his time and the extent to which his motivation to save human lives was exploited and destroyed his mental health.

I contacted Adam and he told me, 'At no point in the application process for medical school do they check you're psychologically fit for the job . . . They put everyone from astronauts to *Big Brother* contestants through psychological tests, but medics are somehow exempt.'

He described to me how, at medical school, he was trained in breaking bad news to emotionally fragile patients, but that no one ever considered that dealing with this kind of thing on a daily basis might affect him. He told me about a process of conditioning, whereby he could witness any number of objectively traumatic and upsetting events but then come home and tell his partner that his day had been 'fine'.

One particularly bad day, following months of lack of sleep and increasing workload, led Adam to leave the profession. He said, 'I strongly suspect that if I'd just been given a couple of weeks off work to recover I might still be working as a doctor today. But this is the NHS. There is no slack in the system to allow for this and certainly no cash to pay for counselling.'

## A BEGINNER'S GUIDE TO GPS AND YOUR MENTAL HEALTH

Below are some handy things to bear in mind when seeking help from a GP:

- Increasingly, doctors' surgeries are required to have at least one in-house GP who specializes in mental health. When booking an appointment, ask who that person is and ask to see them.

- You can request for a friend or family member to come with you into your GP appointment if you don't think that you'll be able to get the words out.

- Don't take your GP's word as gospel. You can be guided by them, but if you don't get a satisfactory response don't hesitate to ask to see someone different for a second opinion.

° Remember that whilst the situation with GPs can
be incredibly frustrating, your doctor is very likely to be
overworked and stressed, too. Doctors are victims of a system
at breaking point as much as their patients are.

° Finally, follow charities such as Young Minds and MP
Luciana Berger, former Shadow Minister for Mental Health,
to learn about how you can support campaigns calling for
more GP training and funding for mental health.

is for . . .

**HAPPINESS**

**In 2016, the UK came twenty-third in the United Nations World Happiness Report. This was despite the fact that at the time we had the fifth-largest economy in the world. It appears, then, that old adage 'money can't buy happiness' holds true. In this chapter I want to explore what does.**

In a TEDx talk which has now been watched almost 10 million times on YouTube, thirteen-year-old Logan LaPlante says: 'If you ask a little kid [what they want to be when they're older] sometimes you get the best answer. Something so simple and so obvious and really profound: when I grow up I want to be happy.'

Similarly, if you ask most parents what they want for their children they'll usually say, 'I just want them to be happy.' The problem is no one is quite sure what happiness actually is.

There are lots of transitory pleasures that are easily mistaken for happiness. The brief high you get after spotting something you've been hankering for in your size at half-price in the January sale. The feeling of anticipation when a delicious-looking plate of food is placed in front of you in a restaurant. The giddy euphoria associated with the first throes of romantic attachment. None of these are happiness, in the true sense.

In 2011 a group of researchers made the brilliant Netflix documentary *Happy*. In it, they examine how various communities across the globe live, from the swamps of Louisiana to the slums of Kolkata, in order to distil the components of genuine happiness. Crunching huge amounts of data involving thousands of participants, they defined happiness as ongoing contentment rather than how most of us experience it – brief moments of artificial euphoria stitched together by a constant low hum of dissatisfaction.

Happiness is more of a low-key sensation than most of us give it credit for. It is, in essence, the diametric opposite to the feeling most of us carry around all day – that niggling sense that something isn't 'quite right'. Happiness is probably most accurately defined as an absence rather than a presence of feeling.

Once, when I was in my mid-twenties, one of my fellow bartenders and I decided to throw caution to the wind and go out dancing in our beer- and muck-splattered work clothes after our shift. We found a club that was open late and danced frantically and unselfconsciously to a megamix of truly awful RnB until about 3am. When I got back to my flat, ears still ringing from the strains of R Kelly during his infamous 'cornrow era', I sat on the sofa and thought 'now what?' I was aware of something I'd rarely felt. I wasn't thirsty. I wasn't hungry. I didn't want to call out for a kebab or pizza. I didn't want to watch TV or listen to music, or text anyone. I had no urge to distract myself in any way. I just wanted to sit there and . . . well, *be*.

That feeling of being content to merely exist is, I believe, the essence of happiness. It's a sense of being complete and feeling connected. It is, as we discovered in chapter *C: Capitalism*, something that our environment continuously and aggressively conspires to rob us of.

That isn't to say that happy people are satisfied with total inaction and never get anything done. Purpose and achievement are key components of a rounded, happy lifestyle. Yet again, however, social conventions have defined what it means to have purpose and dictated which achievements are rewarded in a way that isn't particularly conducive to most people's ongoing happiness.

As I type, it's early December, which means that we're in the third month of what is now the Festival of Consumerism known as Christmas. Christmas generally has a bad rep in the mental-health community, with good reason. If you have social anxiety, the expectation you'll attend endless parties is panic-inducing. If you have an eating disorder the requirement to consume in front of others can be overwhelming. Many people have fraught or difficult relationships with their families – unresolved conflicts or buried traumas that are magnified by being forced to spend time in close proximity to them.

I take all of that on board, but I want to take an opportunity to mount a defence of Christmas. Bearing in mind we all have a mental health, I think there's a lot about the season which can and does nourish the mind. It's all a question of which parts are most pronounced.

Christmas is ostensibly the day we celebrate the birth of Jesus. However, most historians agree that we don't really know when the historical Jesus was born and those who have tried to date his actual birthday tend to place it in mid summer. So why 25 December?

The answer is that the Christian festivals of Easter and Christmas were merged with pre-existing, already established pagan festivals to oil the wheels of religious transition. A commonly accepted theory is that pre-Christian pagans in the northern hemisphere deemed it necessary to break up the long winter months with a festival of light, warmth and hope. Essentially, Christmas began as a primitive solution to seasonal affective disorder. It was a way to combat low mood and generate happiness during a time when everyone was feeling the wellbeing-reducing effects of the season. In some ways, it still is. How many times have you heard someone say, 'I'm okay with winter until the bit after Christmas. That's when I really start to struggle'?

If we take away all the plastic, consumerist crap associated with Christmas and boil it down to some of its more substantive components, there are revealed some important ingredients for happiness all year round.

## COMMUNITY

Christmas is traditionally associated with a sense of relaxation and merriment, which in turn means you see people on the street smiling and making eye contact with one another in a way that is rare in the age of the smartphone. Saying 'Merry Christmas' provides important social lubricant to crack the rigidity of the British stiff upper lip. There is a sense of everyone experiencing the same thing at the same time, which in turn makes us feel connected to one another – an essential component for happiness.

## CHARITY AND GIVING

The documentary *Happy* concluded that one of the four essential factors in attaining fulfilment is helping others. Christmas is a time when we are encouraged to be generous. Charitable donations go up. People living on the streets report a rise in both the cash and the non-monetary acts of kindness they receive. The time and energy we expend in being kind pays multiple dividends in terms of our own wellbeing.

## MUSIC

Music is, literally, ancient. Yet, unlike most ancient rituals, there isn't an obvious reason why we evolved to make it. It doesn't aid our survival in an obvious way. That is, of course, unless you are astute enough to realize that happiness is essential to our survival. Without happiness we'd give up, fester and die. Music is not only a way to express and therefore exorcise difficult emotions, but a traditional Christmas sing-a-long can cheer you right up. In fact, neuroscientists have shown that when we sing, particularly in groups, it fires up the right temporal lobe of our brain, releasing endorphins (see *E: Endorphins*).

## TIME OFF WORK

Recreation is essential for happiness. Doing things for their own sake as opposed to financial reward – like going for a walk in the (possibly) snowy park, or cooking a gigantic turkey dinner from scratch, or playing *Game of Thrones* Monopoly with your brother who gets you EVERY SINGLE YEAR because he has the foresight to buy up the brown side of the board in the early stages – are proven to make us happier.

A work-life balance is increasingly difficult to sustain given the reported strain on the world economy and, by proxy, on individual families and citizens. In fact, many people don't get time off at Christmas, and long gone are the days when everything shut for a week. But for those of us who are fortunate enough to get a holiday, Christmas represents an opportunity to redress some of the time lost to overworking throughout the rest of the year.

## FAMILY

As acknowledged above, not everyone has a good relationship with their families. Yet for those of us that do, even the rows could only happen within the context of a group of people who know us so well they can wind us up in three seconds flat. Belonging is a key psychological need. If you've ever had a conversation where you complain about a parent or sibling to a friend but then feel inexplicably incandescent with indignation when they join in, you know how it feels to have a tribe. They are your people. Even when they're getting right on your tits.

There's a lesson to be learned here, in that the parts of Christmas we think we love most – presents, pigs-in-blankets, the excuse to imbibe alcohol with breakfast – might simply be tangible accoutrements we associate with a sensation of contentment that is in fact being provided by other elements of the festival.

Unless you're five, you're probably more excited about giving gifts than receiving them. It's an opportunity to show appreciation and kindness to the people we love. All the eating is really symbolic of being free from the shackles of fairly arbitrary and constraining dietary regimes and associated feelings of body shame the rest of the year. Drinking in the morning means not having to adhere to our usual routines, letting go of our inhibitions and having an 'excuse' to be spontaneously loving. In that sense, I'm with Noddy Holder when he wished it could be Christmas every day.

A 2017 commissioned 'masculinity report' conducted by shaving brand Harrys in partnership with University of Central London revealed that the classic portrayal of the 'perfect' man – mute, gym-sculpted and uber-wealthy – is bullshit and British men know it.

The report showed that what most British men aspire to, whilst broadly traditional in terms of values, is far from the archetype of the alpha male. It revealed the majority of respondents thought that their mental health was more important than their physique, that the quality they most wanted to emulate was trustworthiness, and that men in a stable, loving, long-term relationship were happier than their single counterparts.*

The so-called cult of the individual has indoctrinated us into the belief that we can never have 'too much'. However, a study conducted in America in the early 2000s (and updated in 2017) showed that whilst the difference in happiness between those who earned under $10,000 and those who earned between $10,000 and $50,000 was significant, the difference in levels of happiness between the second category and those who earned over $50,000 was negligible.

There is a simple reason for this: it isn't possible to provide for your basic needs on a budget of under $10,000 in the USA. A wage of $50,000 is, however, usually enough for a decent standard of living (allowing for variations such as whether you live in a city, or how many children you have). If you have a roof over your head, enough money for food and clothes, can comfortably support any dependants and perhaps afford a holiday each year, you're as happy as wealth can ever make you. Unfortunately, that isn't a cornerstone upon which consumerist capitalism can afford to build itself.

## A BEGINNER'S GUIDE TO BEING HAPPY

Happiness is, to a large extent, understanding what truly motivates you. Sometimes, I do an exercise with school pupils where I ask them to name something they couldn't live without. It's a reflection of the age in which we live that the most popular answer is 'my phone'. Then I ask them to think about why their phone is so important and what it represents. It might be a portal to boundless seas of knowledge and information, in which case the motivation is learning. It might be the security that comes from knowing there is a way to Google or communicate one's way out of potentially tricky or dangerous situations, in which case the motivation is being safe. More often than not, though, it's about connection. People love WhatsApp groups because it makes them feel plugged in to a community of like-minded people and that's a need human beings have had since before the invention of . . . well, anything.

---

*Just a quick reminder here of the difference between causation and correlation – it could be that happier men attract partners more easily, as opposed to the simple fact of a relationship making them happier.

As well as being mindful of the universal components for happiness – helping others, having some time for recreation and having a sense of purpose – it is also important to honour our individual values. If you work slavishly in the same office every day with ever-spiralling working hours and your core value is freedom, for example, you'll never be happy, no matter how many zeros are on the end of your salary.

A therapist once taught me an easy way to work out what your core value is, if you aren't sure. Think of a time when you were inexplicably outraged. One of those times when you knew, deep down, that the amount of anger you were feeling was disproportionate to the event, but you couldn't seem to help yourself. The likelihood is that whatever had happened had violated your core value. When that occurs, the objective importance of the event in question is immaterial because a psychological 'button' has been pushed.

As I've already mentioned, fairness is undoubtedly my core value. I'm not particularly wealthy, I'm not fantastically beautiful, I don't have many of the things that society tells me I'm supposed to aspire to but – thanks to the benevolent fate that has allowed me to do a job I believe helps to make things a little bit fairer –I am, on most days at least, happy.

is for . . .

# INTERNET

**In 1920s and '30s, ordinary households began investing in their own radio, sparking concern amongst self-appointed experts whose research convinced them that the resulting 'overstimulation', particularly of young people, might impede brain development. Thirty years later, there was a widely held belief that televisions 'rotted children's minds'. Today, these same types of arguments are made about the internet, smartphone technology and, in particular, social media.**

There has been understandable backlash against this. Young people's worries span everything from the destruction of the planet, student debt, prospective unemployment, academic anxiety, the impossibility of being able to get on the housing ladder and the culture of mud-slinging and hatred that has been created post-Brexit. In this context, it seems a little reductionist to blame rising levels of anxiety in under-21s on the iPhone.

The internet should never be used as a convenient excuse to ignore all the other things that are wrong with the world and yet politicians do it often. When Secretary of State for Health Jeremy Hunt was asked by then Shadow Minister for Mental Health Luciana Berger in 2015 why he thought so many young people were experiencing poor mental health, he gave one answer and one only: social media. This response caused understandable ire, since it conveniently absolved his government of any responsibility to address some of the other potential contributors. My 2016 TEDx talk 'Is Society Breaking Children's Brains?' explored this and was in many ways a direct result of my fury at Jeremy Hunt.

Having said that, it's equally dangerous to ignore the impact of technological advancement altogether. It could reasonably be argued that smartphones are fundamentally different from either radio or television, in that they are not confined to a corner of the sitting room and have, in many cases, effectively become a fifth limb. However, the similarity in all three examples lies in the fact that hardly anyone is likely to surrender exciting, shiny new technology voluntarily.

As I am a pragmatist, I prefer to conduct my work from the basis of a shared understanding that people do and will regularly access social media, pornographic imagery and misinformation and it is better to help them to deal with the world as it is than to waste energy lamenting the passing of a less complicated, more innocent era. Furthermore, anyone who tells you definitively that they know of the neurological and psychological impact the internet is having on humanity is lying. Technology develops with such terrifying rapidity that it has invariably evolved before scientists can reliably measure the mental-health implications of its previous incarnation.

Most scientific theory in this area is either based on conjecture or has been rendered largely irrelevant by the time it is released. Take, for example, the incredibly comprehensive research paper, published in 2016, which examined the link between Facebook use and poor body image/low self-esteem in adolescents. When the study was begun some years earlier, Facebook was the social networking site of choice for teenagers. By the time the necessary funding had been acquired, research associates hired and the study's subjects reliably and extensively examined, the demographic under scrutiny had moved on to Instagram and Snapchat.

However, there are a few things that have been unearthed by experts and are applicable across various internet platforms. For example, when we receive a notification on our smartphones, we have what's called a Pavlovian response.* No matter how anodyne the alert – a friend inviting you to play Candy Crush, Apple asking if you'd like an update, your partner asking if you can pick up some dishwasher tablets on the way home – phone activity produces a dopamine spike.

Dopamine is a feel-good chemical whose job it is to bring our nerve cells to a level of excitement where they are ready to fire. In the context of technology, it is responsible for the compulsion we feel to jump on our phones straight away when we receive a notification. Phone use is highly addictive for that reason, and the dopamine effect it induces has obvious potential to interfere with concentration. In 2015, I was involved in a local news report for the BBC which found that more than half of twelve- to fourteen-year-olds feel actively guilty if they don't respond to WhatsApp or other social-media messages immediately. With multiple users in WhatsApp groups it's easy to see, then, how many of them end up texting under their duvets long into the wee small hours, thus interfering with their sleep (see *S: Self-Care*).

Perhaps more worryingly, there is concrete evidence to show that 'prolific' smartphone use (generally defined as more than four hours of total screen time per day) can interfere with what is considered to be the

---

*Pavlov was a Russian scientist who discovered that if he rang a bell before giving a dog food, eventually the dog would salivate with anticipation upon hearing a bell, regardless of if there was any food present. Which, I'll admit, does look a bit mean when written down but taught us something important about the way our minds associate apparently unrelated sensory information with memory.

normal development pathway of an infant or adolescent brain. The part of our frontal lobe responsible for our understanding of where we fit within our perceived social hierarchy usually begins to develop at around seven or eight years old (which is why children of this age tend to begin to have friendship issues at school). Studies have shown that, for the prolific social-media user, the pre-frontal cortex is larger than in their peers. Some experts go on to hypothesize that social-media use compels us on a neurological level to obsessively compare ourselves to other people, which in turn damages self-esteem.

In her University of Sussex professorial lecture 'Digital Childhoods', Dr Rachel Thomson suggests that today's young people see school and family time as 'pauses' in their online social existences, which are more 'real' to them than the three-dimensional world. As such, they are essentially competing in what seems like a very real way within a terrifying global hierarchy, consisting of millions of people showcasing their 'highlights reel' and Photoshopping their entire existence.

There is also a good deal of concern about what technology means in terms of a human being's capacity to connect accurately and meaningfully with our own memories. Some of this comes from 'I've-been-paid-to-have-a-five-hundred-word-rant-for-a-tabloid-and-I'm-on-a-deadline' style bluster, centred around the 'yoof' eschewing traditional, leather-bound encyclopaedias in favour of Wikipedia and thereby becoming intellectually stunted (and usually ending with a call to bring back national service). Other worries have a more legitimate, evidence-led foundation. Integrative psychotherapist Dr Aaron Balick, for example, has found that our propensity for taking photographs of or filming life events as opposed to simply experiencing them has interfered with our ability to remember them accurately. It's also probably a barrier to achieving a state of mindfulness (see *S: Self-Care*).

What the 'children today don't know they're born – we had to learn everything from a dusty textbook' brigade fail to acknowledge is the pure volume of available information the modern person is subjected to. A psychology teacher once told me that we take in more information in one day than our grandparents would have received in a year of their lives. It's therefore entirely possible that, volume-wise, we retain just as much, but it represents a much smaller overall proportion of the total amount of stimulus to which we've been exposed.

Overstimulation is probably the most urgent psychological issue resulting from technology. The barrage of information to which we are subjected often seems actively aggressive, as well as being highly addictive. As someone with a propensity for anxiety, having a small handheld device that gives me instantaneous access to, well, everything doesn't do anything for my overriding sense of guilt and unease when I'm supposed to be 'relaxing'. The cumulative impact of all the right-v-left, feminist-v-menanist, Brexiteer-v-Remainer arguing online also regularly makes me feel like an infant crouching in the corner of the kitchen with her hands over her ears whilst her parents have a loud, drunken ding-dong.

Ultimately, however, I know enough about human nature to realize that none of these phenomena, or the knowledge that they are doing us harm, will be sufficient to make us surrender our smartphones or eschew the instant gratifications provided to us by the technological age. (Unless you are my friend Geary, who refuses to upgrade his Nokia from 1997 and does appear to be, in fairness, one of the most genuinely contented people I know.)

In that spirit, here is some information I have found handy to have in arm's reach of my consciousness and can provide a self-esteem boost during those times when it seems like the world is run by our screens.

## MISINFORMATION

The best thing about the internet is that it gives everyone a voice. The worst thing about the internet is that is gives everyone a voice. This has, in turn, blurred the lines between fact and opinion and provided a platform where all viewpoints are considered somehow equal, regardless of how little objective evidence there is for them.

The web has also polarized everything. The people with the most extreme views have always shouted the loudest, but historically they did so largely in a vacuum, or on the opinion pages of the *Daily Mail*. The internet has magnified their voices and given a false overall impression that most issues are simple and binary, when in fact they tend to be complicated and nuanced. It doesn't help, of course, that micro-blogging compels one to convey one's point of view in 280-character chunks. No opinion worth having can ever be adequately conveyed in 280 characters. (Apart from that one.)

When I was at university, we had one token conspiracy theorist in halls, who, after nights out as we munched cheese on toast, would hold forth with his marijuana-fuelled theories about how the moon landings weren't real and the world was really run by lizards. Now that conspiracy theorist is the internet, and far from being an odd-but-harmless beardy guy with an acoustic guitar who thinks he has been abducted by aliens, it's an all-pervasive force with real political influence. It's what allows Trump to screech 'fake news' in the direction of credible outlets who have observed the usual journalistic codes (you know – research, investigation, reliable citations, balance of opinions) and instead compel his supporters to believe outrageous fabrications on everything from former President Obama's country of birth to the national crime statistics of Sweden.

The traditional view is that all news has an agenda, but the extremes of the political fringe have inverted this for their own ends, whilst making it look as though they are exposing 'truth'. This isn't just confusing, it's having a measurable impact on the mental health of social-media users, particularly the young. In 2016, Childline reported an 82 per cent increase in calls, which happened to coincide with the vote to leave the EU. Whilst the likely removal of Britain from the world's largest single market is, according to most economists, a scary prospect, it's likely that the callers were more troubled by the general mud-flinging, xenophobia and shouty catchphrases flying around the cultural landscape at the time. Fear generates anxiety and, as we know, sustained anxiety can lead to depression.

The internet has also lent a megaphone to all the harebrained, half-baked, entirely evidenceless theories around the subject of health. I'm not for one second suggesting that Western medicine is the only way to cure or ease the symptoms of illness, but there are a lot of 'testimonials' out there that are either created with the intention of selling a specific product or service or have confused correlation with causation and attributed the results to a placebo.

My friend and founder of charity Coppafeel!, Kris Hallenga, was once approached by a self-proclaimed 'expert' via the internet who told her that in order to cure her brain tumour she should stop having chemotherapy immediately and instead eat three peaches a day. This is quite obviously ludicrous, dangerous nonsense. However, when it comes to mental health, the shysters are harder to spot. This is partly because mental illness is invisible, partly because our scientific understanding of the brain is in relative infancy and partly because 'mental health' covers such a broad range of conditions, all happening within the context of unique people with different personalities.

As you will discover in chapter *R: Recovery*, the solution to gaining and maintaining good mental health is rarely simple or one-stranded. You'll probably find it takes a combination of changes – be they medicinal, habitual, physical or spiritual – to achieve whatever optimum balance looks like for you. It's important to recognize where a person's expertise lies and what you can take from it.

I, for example, am often criticized for calling myself an 'expert' on mental health because I'm not a doctor. Whilst this is often upsetting because it's usually in the context of a comment aimed at tearing down my broader career, life and the general point of my existence in the world (see 'Trolls' below), I think it's a valid consideration. No one is an all-encompassing expert on mental health, just as no one can accurately describe themselves in this way in relation to physical health. The subject is just too vast.

What I have learned is to discern what a person's expertise is, whether professional or personal, give some consideration to their viewpoint (or 'blik') and extract the useful information from what they have to say. I harvest these nuggets of wisdom with a view to disseminating them. My particular expertise therefore comes from a combination of first-hand experience of mental illness, the fact that my job has afforded me the privilege of talking to thousands of other people who have first-hand experience and the further honour of having access to some of the world's leading scientific and sociological thinkers on the topic. That's the level of expertise I have to offer – nothing more, nothing less – and anything I say should be taken in this context.

For this reason, I hate it with the heat of a thousand burning, furious suns when newspaper articles describe me as a 'guru'. This word suggests I believe I have the ultimate answer and that's a notion as damaging to the reader as it is to my reputation. There is no simple solution that will allow you easily to navigate life in all its infinite complexity. Such a thing does not exist and anyone who tells you it does is selling you snake oil. All anyone can offer you is the benefit of their perspective.

## PRO-ANOREXIA/SELF-HARM WEBSITES

There exist on the internet places where people gather to share tips on how to conduct eating-disordered behaviours and how to self-harm. For the sake of brevity, I'm going to refer to them as 'pro self-harm websites' in this section, since eating disorders are, at least partially, a form of self-harm (see *F: Food*).

Self-harming behaviours are known to have a perverse, competitive element to them. They are also characterized by a feeling of not quite 'fitting in' with the world, of being abnormal, alien and misunderstood. What pro self-harm websites therefore offer to a vulnerable person is a community of like-minded people, a justification to carry on practising a behaviour that's become an emotional crutch and a way to gain information on extending, for want of a better word, their repertoire.

Pro self-harm websites have rightly been decried by the media, with politicians calling for internet providers to do more to locate and shut down this type of forum. What often remains unacknowledged, however, is that most online forums of this nature began as a support group.

The path is well worn: a person who is in recovery from self-harm thinks, 'Well, that was dreadful. I'd like ideally to reach out to and help other people with similar experiences.' They set up an online space and invite people in varying levels of psychological distress to communicate with one another. Because the creator of the forum is usually someone with other demands on their time, they cannot constantly monitor content.

Before long, users are sharing 'triggering' content (such as images of themselves when severely underweight or self-harm methodologies) or 'buddying up' – a name given to the phenomenon of creating a co-dependent relationship with a person going through similar issues. There is a reason why, for example, the twelve-step programme used by Alcoholics Anonymous advises that a mentor should be a person who has completed the process. Put two people together who are both unwell and using damaging behaviours to both exhibit and take the edge off their anguish and they will almost always make each other worse.

I have no idea how internet providers could be expected to legislate for such phenomena without curtailing freedom of speech to unacceptable levels. In the absence of a better idea, I usually advise that if people do want to share their experiences online, they should do so in monitored forums.

Beat, for example, the UK's largest eating-disorder charity, hosts regular web chats but there is around a two-second delay between typing your entry and it appearing in the chatroom. This is because a person at headquarters checks entry for any content that might be damaging to other users.

Recovery from my own eating disorder meant turning my back on friends who were engaging in similar behaviours. This was tough and I felt like a bitch, but ultimately it was an act of self-preservation. If the process had taken place during an era as dominated by social media as it is today, I would have had to block people who were in the same emotional hole as me, especially if they showed no signs of wanting to get better. This doesn't have to be a forever-tactic. Now I am recovered, I can safely surround myself with people who are very poorly and I can still maintain a safe psychological distance.

## SELFIES

Hello, people older than thirty! Do you remember a time when, if it was discovered you had taken a photograph of yourself, you were relentlessly ridiculed? The remnants of this attitude have remained with me and whilst I'm certainly not immune to taking selfies, I feel a huge sense of embarrassment if anyone catches me.

People younger than me apparently have no such qualms. To label it narcissism, certainly in the way the word is typically used today (i.e. interchangeable with 'vanity') is, I believe, over-simplistic. It is much more about an obsessive desire to document the minutiae of our daily routines, almost as though if we don't have pictorial evidence of something, it didn't happen. This is such a new phenomenon I'm not even sure what we should call it.

What do we think will happen if we engage in an activity and then fail to immediately upload evidence of it? I can only assume that it's a sophisticated, modern version of 'keeping up with the Joneses' in that if our social-media contact can run 10k, make granola from scratch, spot a celebrity on the Tube platform and buy a new pair of ethically sourced socks before 10am, we feel some sort of unspecified social pressure to generate an equivalent amount of activity.

In the absence of a better theory, I'm basing the above on the peculiar piece of cognitive dissonance. Most groups of teenagers I work with tell me that, all things considered, they wish social media didn't exist at all but, since it does, they feel obligated to partake in it because of FOMO (fear of missing out).

Selfies not only allow us to create the impression of momentum, they also tend to garner 'likes'. Girls (in particular, but not exclusively) are taught from an early age that the most benign and useful function they can fulfil is to please other people. We prime them to seek external validation and therefore to outsource their self-esteem.

The gaining of 'likes' is not only addictive, the chances of it happening are hugely improved by the use of filters and Photoshop apps. What many people don't realize is that smartphone technology is now so sophisticated that their phones probably have filters built in. I know for a fact that, without my intervention or permission, my phone camera makes me look thinner and my eyes look bigger. Now, when I look in the mirror, I not only have the perceived weight of an endless stream of preened and perfected images of others bearing down on my consciousness, I'm also essentially competing against an idealized version of myself.

The average person now takes twenty-two selfies before selecting the one they post online. This renders Instagram a series of highlights reels, against which we unfavourably compare our seemingly mundane and imperfect realities. There is, in my experience, a comfort in simply bearing this in mind.

There is a running joke in my friendship group that centres around a mutual acquaintance who insists on getting dressed up in what is essentially a ballgown every Friday night and posing in her sitting room with a champagne flute, with a caption reading 'prosecco time'. As far as we know, she doesn't go anywhere afterwards in her ballgown. In fact, she probably takes it off and swaps it for pyjamas as soon as the selfie has been taken. Why does she engage in this ridiculous ritual? A cursory glance at the comments underneath these pictures gives a definitive answer: 'Wow stunning.' 'Classy lady.' 'Gorgeous!'

Social media has a really fucked-up sense of priorities. When I posted a Facebook status saying I'd been awarded an MBE for services to young people, it garnered a third as many likes as when I posted a picture of myself in my kitchen all dolled up and ready to go to a glamorous award ceremony (not to receive an award, just to sit behind Rebel Wilson and get shamefully scuttered). If I was a different sort of person I could quite see how I'd end up donning a ballgown every Friday night and taking selfies in my living room. (What I actually did was delete my Facebook account.)

## PORN

According to research conducted by Cambridge University for the Channel 4 documentary *Porn on the Brain*, pornography appeals not to the part of our brain that concerns itself with sexuality, but to the part that is responsible for addiction. Scanning the brain of a person who consumes online pornography to excess (i.e. several times per day) reveals identical neurological patterns as you'd see in a drug addict or alcoholic.

The presenter of *Porn on the Brain*, Martin Daubney, now tours schools and universities, delivering presentations of the same name. His aim is to remove the conversation from the realm of judgments about sexual preference and instead to focus on the psychological aspects. He describes how algorithms, similar to those used to generate social-media advertising, track the 'preferences' of the porn user based on keywords linked to the videos they select, for example 'blonde', 'black', 'BDSM', 'anal'. The technology will then suggest a video that is slightly more hardcore in its content than the one the viewer has seen previously. Over time, the viewer will find that the kinds of content they were originally watching are no longer sufficient to garner the required level of sexual excitement – it's the same principle as a drug addict needing larger and larger quantities of whatever substance they're using to achieve an equivalent high.

The aim of these algorithms is to get the consumer to a point where the free content being offered is no longer getting them off, thereby encouraging them to graduate to pay-per-view porn. Around 10 per cent of porn users pay to access the more hardcore videos hidden behind a paywall. In 1 per cent of cases, no visual material is enough and they will click on the various ads offering the services of escorts that pop up on the periphery of the videos. That is where the serious money is made. Like all internet content, 'free' pornography comes at a price. Not only do the addictive and destructive habits of a small proportion of users fund the entire industry, but the prevalence of porn has shaped a generation's attitude to sex and body image.

Research shows that 52 per cent of twelve-year-olds have seen pornographic online content. By the time they reach the age of sixteen this becomes 97 per cent. The same arguments about unconscious expectations created by the fashion, fitness and beauty industries apply here, except this time it's not just girls thinking they must be entirely hairless or boys believing a twelve-inch penis is 'normal' – it's also confusing attitudes towards consent.

Some of the most popular porn videos depict women pretending to be coerced into sex. There is no disclaimer, no indication (other than the invariably quite bad acting) that the scenarios aren't real. The narrative perpetuated by porn is that all women can be worn down to a point where they will eventually enjoy sex – that we are all secretly 'gagging for it'.

I'm not suggesting that any decent man would consciously argue this. But if the imagery utilized by the fashion and fitness industries has been enough to inspire an epidemic of self-hatred then it's not so ludicrous to expect that pornography can both create and justify misogyny.

Pornography isn't inherently bad. Done right (as seen, for example, on Cindy Gallop's website makelovenotporn.tv, or in other feminist reimaginings), where both the bodies and the orgasms are real, it's a useful way to explore, learn and get your rocks off. What the more mainstream sites have done, however, is create cultural norms that are damaging to the mental health of anyone who engages with them.

## TROLLS

According to a production company I worked with just after I was given the role of the government's first ever Mental Health Champion (see *N: Number 10 Downing Street*), I became 'one of the most prolifically trolled women in Britain'. I was, mercifully, completely unaware of this, since I'd judiciously used Twitter's mute button and had made my Instagram account private. As for below-the-line comments on newspaper articles by or about me, I'd been advised by an editor not to read them, as to do so would be 'akin to self-harm'.

However, in January of the following year I was approached by a documentary maker and asked if I'd like to participate in a programme where trolls and their victims are brought together. After quite a bit of deliberation, I eventually said yes, mostly because I'm often asked what motivates cyber bullies and I didn't have a response that was as far-ranging as I would have ideally liked. I relished the prospect of getting under the skin of the people who had targeted me, understanding them, maybe even helping them, since I reasoned that no one who is happy would ever behave in such a way.

As it happened, I never got the opportunity to confront my trolls because – and here's the first thing you need to know – they are chicken.

Online, behind their anonymous avatars and pseudonyms, they're all 'if I ever meet you I'll fucking kill you, bitch', but when given the opportunity they'd rather stay at home (probably) wanking. I'm not saying that online threats never lead to actual violence (the case of murdered MP Jo Cox proves otherwise), or that this should in any way be construed as a reason not to take them seriously, merely that there's solace in knowing that most of the time they're all mouth (or, I suppose, finger) and no action.

But I'm getting ahead of myself. Before I knew that none of my trolls would have the bottle to face me, I was handed a thick wodge of documentation by the producers of the show, in which they had handily compiled all the worst things said about me across various platforms on the internet. I was delighted to discover I'd made it onto the weekly list of 'Feminists We'd Like to Punch' on an alt-right online magazine, as well as being mentioned at a frankly desperate rate by publications like Brietbart and Spiked, whose readership had concluded that my ingratiation into the establishment basically heralded the end of civilization.

Most of the comments related to my appearance, gender and ethnicity. 'Fat' and 'ugly' were the most commonly used words ('mind-bendingly ugly' in one instance). Depending on the political proclivities of the audience, I was either Jewish and therefore automatically part of a global conspiracy, 'part black' and therefore intellectually inferior, or just plain 'foreign' with therefore no right to be interfering in British state business.

This is the second thing I learned about trolls. Their comments are almost always targeted at perceived 'weaknesses'. I am a little bit chubby, after years of eating disorders playing havoc with my metabolism. I am a complicated ethnic mix that encompasses both some Jewish and some African elements and, whilst I'm both proud of my mixed heritage and also secure in my status as a British citizen, they weren't to know that.

The third thing I learned about trolls is that what they don't know they'll assume, based on some stereotypical blueprint they have acquired. As a feminist, it was deemed that I must be gay and/or single, and therefore sexually frustrated, so my opinions on gender equality were nothing that 'a bit of cock' wouldn't 'sort out'.

Trolls tend to target people who threaten them by wielding some form of genuine power. The average woman has a built-in body-image 'shame trigger' and so any woman who reaches beyond an ambition to be forever in servitude to patriarchal values will be targeted on this basis. Men, with their shame triggers around strength, will more likely be called 'cuck' ('cuckold' – an old-fashioned word that used to be given to men whose wives were rumoured to be cheating on them – that is the level of maturity with which we are dealing).

Of course, trolling is just one aspect of cyberbullying, but it's also the one with the least clear solution. If you research cyberbullying online, you will find downloadable documents containing sensible, if slightly futile advice compiled by various charities as well as the Department for Education. All recommend ensuring your parental controls block offensive language and certain websites, as well as stressing the necessity of open communication with your child around the potential dangers that lurk in cyberspace. All of them make the fundamental error of assuming that cyberbullying only ever happens to children.

Advice on trolling, conversely, is mostly often written by and for business owners, and assumes that the troll doesn't pose any meaningful threat, other than damaging the reputation of a particular brand. Social-media users are advised to screenshot evidence, block or mute trolls and then report the incident to the internet service provider. But when it comes to cyberbullying amongst adults, the general consensus appears to be that it's like farting in a lift – not technically a criminal act but something polite people wouldn't do.

Much of the problem rests with the highly subjective definition of bullying and the extent to which it depends on the (largely unseen) motivation of the perpetrator and the feelings induced in the victim. I was accused of cyberbullying when I called the government's Behaviour Tsar a 'bellend' on Twitter in 2015. I didn't tag him in the tweet or mention his name, I simply attached a statement from him containing what I perceived to be a number of rather bellend-y sentiments and wrote, 'This guy seems like a bit of a bellend'.

It was deemed by a jury of my Twitter peers that I had transgressed, so I swiftly deleted the tweet and apologized to the man in question, even though I had never in my wildest fantasies imagined that he would see it. I realized I had caused distress and that it is this, crucially, which is the defining factor in any act of bullying.

Confusingly, a few months later, a Twitter user threatened to 'send the boys round' to 'lean on me' after disagreeing with something I wrote in one of my columns. I was quite frightened by that, especially as it happened in the same week that Jo Cox was murdered and the reality of just how volatile and violent people can be was especially fresh in my mind. When I took the above advice and reported the incident, I was told that it didn't violate the user guidelines. Furthermore, the consensus amongst the Twitterati this time was that he was 'clearly joking', 'never intended any harm' and I needed to 'get a sense of humour'.

In a world where calling someone a bellend is deemed unacceptable but directly sending someone a threat is not, I don't consider it surprising that no one understands what the rules are.

The law can't help on this, for two reasons. Firstly, because making any kind of amendment to legal procedure takes fucking forever and technology develops so fast. For example, laws that, quite rightly for their era, proclaimed it illegal to be in receipt of photographs of child abuse (sometimes referred to as 'child pornography', although that seems to me to be a contradiction in terms) were for some years being used to discipline fifteen-year-old boys who were sexted by their thirteen-year-old girlfriends. Which, I think we can all agree, is daft.

Even when legal change occurs, there are so many considerations and exceptions to take into account that applying blanket laws is notoriously tricky. For example, one suggestion that was tabled and subsequently dismissed was that it should not be possible to set up anonymous social-media accounts; that everyone should need a 'blue tick'. Whilst this would solve issues around the difficulty in tracing persistent trolls, it also disadvantages people who use social media to seek advice or share information and are in difficult circumstances – victims of domestic abuse, members of the LGBT+ community who aren't 'out' or whistle-blowers who work in the public sector.

The second problem the law faces is that of resources. I spoke to an officer who works for the Metropolitan Police about trolling. I asked him if a lack of funding for the police service meant that victims of online abuse aren't getting clear advice or expedient action. He told me (anonymously):

> The police have a long way to go with that sort of thing.
> More training is definitely required to prepare frontline
> officers to recognize warning signals [in the event that the troll
> might act upon their threats]. Lack of funding definitely has an
> impact. Having said that, even though the technology to track
> trolls is available, I can't see it ever being used for lower-level
> crimes. Even with more staff, I think the pure volume would
> be insurmountable.

That really only leaves the internet service providers themselves with any power to address this issue. I am one of those people who does believe that social media has a duty of care to its users. There are those who dismiss the idea that the Great and Powerful Ones at Twitter should have any say in our output, based on notions of 'free speech'. What they fail to recognize is that free speech doesn't actually exist. If I donned a giant sandwich board that said 'KILL THE MEXICANS' and stomped down the street with a megaphone shouting racist slurs I would, quite rightly, be arrested and detained. Society has rules about what is and isn't considered acceptable.

But, perhaps more pertinently, social media and society aren't actually the same thing. Providers are perfectly within their rights to set whatever rules they see fit. If a golf club can insist you wear a blazer before stepping over the threshold then Twitter can stamp down on trolling. We could conceivably live in a world where we all operate on the basis that, if we want to partake of everything this service has to offer, them's the non-negotiable rules.

## A BEGINNER'S GUIDE TO SURVIVING ONLINE
Try having one screen-free day per week. You will, in all probability, absolutely hate it at first. However, if the evidence I see in schools who adopt this principle is anything to go by, eventually it'll become your favourite

day. Screen-free periods provide much-needed respite and perspective and allow us to reconnect with the imperfect, visceral, fleshy world of three dimensions that exists all around us. A genuine sense of connection is a vital cornerstone of mental wellbeing.

Remember that someone's social-media feed represents the closest you'll ever come to observing them in a vacuum. Friends who exist purely online don't generally know you intimately, they can't see your facial expressions or read your body language. They don't properly understand the circumstances that led you to post whatever you did. Their reaction is a reflection of their own internal navigation system and your content is being viewed through the kaleidoscope of their blik. By all means consider their perspective, but don't let it pollute the purity of your online voice, or derail a mission you have to pursue something you believe is right. Never, ever allow yourself to be silenced by trolls.

Be mindful of sources when it comes to seeking information and always ask yourself what the agenda is. Even the most benign-seeming endeavours, like charities, technically have an agenda – they must justify and perpetuate their own existence.

Remember that, whilst the friendships you create online are valuable, they are different in nature from the relationships you have IRL. The version of yourself you present for the delectation and consideration of internet users will be airbrushed and therefore easier to become superficially infatuated with. The real you is flawed – and so is everyone else.

A person who can embrace you in your entirety - who still loves you when you're hungover and smelly and your hair is pointing in twenty-seven different directions, or visits you in hospital when you're sick, or comes round with a tub of Ben & Jerry's after a break-up, or with a jump lead when your car won't start, or lends you a great book – this is someone who will inconvenience themselves beyond the simple click of a button in order to make your life a little bit better. It's these interactions that are worth a million 'likes'.

is for . . .

# JUST ATTENTION SEEKING

**Satveer Nijjar has worked with the Institute of Chartered Psychology and is an incredibly passionate educator and advocate around self-harm. She has personal experience of cutting and controversially called her self-harm awareness-training business Attention Seekers. I asked her, if she could change one thing about the world, what it would be.**

'I'd get rid of the word "just",' she replied, without hesitation. 'JUST attention seeking. JUST a cry for help. It diminishes the distress a person is trying to communicate to you when they self-harm. And, despite what people think, it is always a symptom of some kind of distress.'

Experience has taught me that the majority of people associate self-harm with cutting. Yet the act can broadly be defined as anything a person does that they know harms them but makes them feel temporarily better. In this context, I'd defy you to find a human alive who hasn't done it at some point.

Think of the last time you had a challenging day. Perhaps a work colleague was grating on your last nerve. Maybe there was some sort of dispute in your friendship group. Perhaps you had a disagreement with someone you love. Maybe something you'd been hoping would happen didn't come off. These are all ordinary forms of stress, the type it would be impossible (and unhealthy) to try and insulate yourself from. Now, think about what you did at the end of that day when, full to the brim of frustrated, unarticulated rage, you finally snatched a moment to yourself.

If you imbibed some form of alcohol, ate something full of sugar or fat with little nutritional value or smoked because you'd had a 'tough day' and 'deserved it', you were self-harming. If, conversely, you denied yourself food (or something else you associate with pleasure) because you'd had a terrible day and didn't feel as though you were 'entitled' to it, you were still self-harming. If you needed an outlet for all your toxic energy and started an argument with someone at home for the sake of needing to shout, or indeed if you isolated yourself from the people you live with because you knew you were feeling narky and didn't want to cause any upset, you were self-harming. In fact, if you did anything other than acknowledge your feelings of discomfort and let yourself ride them out, perhaps with the aid of a healthy coping mechanism like going for a walk, you were, in the technical sense, self-harming.

There are myriad, almost-infinite ways a person can self-harm: staying in an abusive relationship; not eating, exercising or maintaining personal hygiene; even, motivation dependent, getting multiple tattoos and piercings. Like most things that are problematic, it all tends to begin with a lack of self-esteem.

We constantly encounter situations and consequent feelings we find difficult to process, and it is human nature to want to 'take the edge off' somehow. Self-harming behaviours provide the distraction and sense of release we crave. Like anything, it depends on the context; they're not always inherently 'bad'. However, they are always communicating something about our emotional state at the time and, as such, are ignored at our peril.

Of course, some forms of self-harm are more physically dangerous than others. Of those who need hospitalization for self-harming behaviours, 63 per cent are female and indeed it is an act considered to be somehow inherently 'feminine' in its nature. Like all the statistics relating to gender and mental health, I am a little sceptical (see *X: X Chromosome*). There is, for example, a largely unreported and unacknowledged phenomenon of men and boys provoking physical fights they know they can't win for no other reason than that they want to feel pain. If they're beaten to the extent that they need medical care, the hospital is unlikely to log it as an incident of self-harm, despite that being precisely what it is.

Until recently, it used to be referred to as 'deliberate self-harm'. The first word was ultimately dispensed with because it was considered to be judgmental in its nature and to encourage a less empathetic response. It suggests that the person could stop if they really wanted to, which isn't the case any more than it is of an alcoholic or drug addict.

However, it is necessary to apply some sort of distinction between common and usually only minimally harmful behaviours – a typical 'bad day at the office' response – and other types in which the person is more consciously aware that they are self-harming. I think that the defining factor here is the desire to punish oneself. Self-harm of this kind is not defined by the medical community as a mental illness in its own right, but as a symptom that can be a result of depression, anxiety, borderline personality disorder or psychosis.

There's a prevailing belief that self-harm is a way of attention seeking, or that it is somehow 'trendy' – a form of fairly harmless rebellion that has more in common with rock'n'roll than mental illness. And yet we know that it is still mainly done in secret and ensconced in guilt and shame, which undermines these damaging views.

Nor is self-harm exclusively the remit of teenagers, and the phenomenon existed long before the internet (the first recorded incident of self-harm in the way we understand it today was in 1909). Having said that, concerns about there being an element of 'contagion' aren't entirely without merit.

According to an investigation undertaken by the *Sunday Times*, hospitalizations in the UK for eating disorders and self-harm in under-21s doubled between 2013 and 2016. Many pointed the finger of blame squarely at social media. I have been to schools where they have experienced a self-harm 'epidemic' and I can only conclude that, if you are experiencing a difficult time emotionally (as teenagers often do) and are alerted to the possibility of self-harm, that increases the likelihood of you doing it. If, however, you never learned that self-harm was an option, you'd inevitably find another outlet.

Satveer has some interesting views about self-harm – particularly in relation to her own experiences – that a lot of people find contentious. She explains that in her case, it was 'about staying alive. It was the only way I could manage my feelings. A coping mechanism.' She does not believe self-harm should be universally condemned and maintains that it is 'the only reason I am here today'. Growing up against a backdrop of domestic abuse, self-harm was what allowed Satveer to cope. The worst thing anyone could have done, she says, was to take away her coping mechanism without addressing the reasons behind it.

As difficult as many people find this to accept, research supports Satveer's point of view. If a person stops self-harming but isn't given any assistance in managing and processing their mental anguish, it significantly increases their risk of suicide. To put it simply, they are still full to the brim of distress, but in the absence of an alternative strategy, there is nowhere for it to go.

We must also take into account the unpalatable reality that if someone is determined to self-harm, they will use whatever means they have at their disposal. Some boarding schools I have visited banned razor blades in a bid to stop their pupils self-harming, but later realized their students found other, more dangerous and less hygienic ways of cutting, risking infection and, in one instance, sustaining a severed artery.

This isn't to suggest that we should encourage self-harm. We shouldn't justify cutting as no different fundamentally from the people who smoke or drink recreationally – as just a way of blowing off steam. Rather we should concern ourselves with identifying the root cause.

## WHY DO PEOPLE SELF-HARM?

Once, after a workshop, a Year Nine pupil approached me with one of the strangest questions I've been asked: 'Can you help me because I don't know if I self-harm or not?' Somewhat perplexed, I responded with the three magic words best used in such situations: 'Tell me more.'

It transpired that the young woman in question was enduring regular migraines. She knew what they were since her mum suffered from them, too. She knew that the only way to cure her migraine was to lay down in a completely dark and silent place and hope she fell asleep. Nothing else worked. Her migraines induced blurred vision and sickness – not even water would stay down, so she couldn't take painkillers.

Her school nurse, however, thought differently, and told her to take some paracetamol and lie down in the brightly lit sick bay for 20 minutes until they kicked in. The pupil would try and plead with her, knowing it wouldn't work, but to no avail.

She told me, 'I'm so frustrated that no one is acknowledging what I am going through. Plus, I'm in so much pain. So when I'm in the sick bay I've started to bang my head against the wall. I'm worried, because it feels good . . . Creating pain on the outside distracts me from pain on the inside.'

This isn't, of course, self-harm the way we classically understand it, but it is an absolutely perfect allegory for it. People who self-harm are often frustrated by their inability to communicate what ails them, either because they lack the emotional vocabulary or because no one is listening to them. To hurt oneself, in this context, is to give oneself three gifts: distraction, self-expression (in the words of Satveer, a way to say 'look! This is how much it hurts!') and endorphins (see *E: Endorphins*).

Whilst self-harm is initially a conscious response to emotional triggers, over a surprisingly short amount of time it can become habitual (See *S: Self-Care* to read more about coping strategies and how habits are formed). When this happens, self-harm can be an instinctual, unconscious response to neutral triggers, like a particular environment or a time of day. It is at that point it begins to feel like an inexplicable compulsion.

## A BEGINNER'S GUIDE TO DEALING WITH SELF-HARM

Bearing in mind the dangers of stopping self-harm without addressing the underlying causes and the difficulty a person who self-harms might have in articulating their distress, the solution, I have concluded, is to help them find a healthier way to achieve the same distraction, self-expression and endorphin production.

Exercise is an obvious example. Art, creative writing, listening to or making music, dance, drama and meditation are also good alternatives. These activities can also provide a way of becoming part of a new community. One of the biggest risk factors for people who self-harm (and indeed people with eating disorders) is that they begin to mix only with other people who have the same issues, thus normalizing toxic behaviours and also inducing the desire to cling on to them for the sake of preserving friendships.

The National Self-Harm Network, as well as several other charities and experts, recommend using 'safe' forms of inducing physical discomfort, like holding ice cubes or twanging a rubber band against the skin. I'm not generally in favour of this, because I think it has a lot in common with prescribing methadone for heroin addicts – it's never going to 'take the edge off' in the same way and therefore increases the likelihood the person will relapse. Having said that, I'm at pains to recognize that everyone is different and so if it works, do it.

When it comes to discussing self-harm, my advice has always been to focus on 'whys' rather than 'hows'. This is partly because of the danger of the 'contagion' effect touched on above and partly because it's a more effective way of addressing the problem.

After all, as Satveer told me, 'It is a symptom of distress. Taking away the symptom doesn't address the underlying issue. You are, therefore, not doing anything if you focus simply on stopping self-harm.'

is for . . .

# KNOWING ME, KNOWING YOU

**I once sat at the back of a school assembly conducted by a poor, obviously unwilling worker at the local council, who had drawn some sort of short straw back at the office and had been drafted in to do a presentation about radicalization. This was part of the government's 'PREVENT' scheme, which (depending on who you ask) is either a brilliant endeavour designed to take early action when individuals are at risk of radicalization (and therefore terrorist activity) or a vaguely racist ideology which encourages communities to turn on one another based only on the most spurious of suspicions.**

The council worker had opted for the widely used and universally disastrous 'down with the kids' presenting technique and spent the first ten minutes trying to persuade her teenage audience she was one of them by using phrases like 'totes amaze' and 'lol'. (As an aside, I feel compelled to say the following: if you are an adult and find yourself in a situation where you need to present to a group of adolescents, please bear in mind that they, as a demographic, have the most finely tuned bullshit detector known to humankind. A group of teenagers will immediately seize upon any signs of inauthenticity and are unlikely to have any qualms about showing their disdain. Your best bet, therefore, is just to be yourself. And please also reconcile yourself to the indisputable fact that you do not understand the colloquialisms they use in peer-to-peer situations.)

As part of her presentation, she showed a slide listing signs that could indicate your 'buddy' (eurgh!) is vulnerable to radicalization. These included:

- A sudden change in appearance or style of clothing

- Being moody and withdrawn

- Acting aggressively

- Developing unusual beliefs that are at odds with social norms

- Spending a lot of time online

- Spending a lot of time in their room

- Rapidly changing friendship groups

- Having strong political opinions

- Suddenly losing interest in things they have previously enjoyed

I looked at this list and thought to myself that, aside from the online thing (because when I came of age we were still in the era of dial-up) it pretty much described an average day for me when I was a teenager. When I think back to secondary school, my non-academic experiences are categorized by semi-rational anger at the unfairness of life, tumultuous friendship dramas, constant fashion experimentation and wanting to hump everything I saw. (There are people who would argue I haven't changed that much.)

Equally, there's a hefty portion of that list that could be applied to mental illness. This is the problem when it comes to checklists designed to categorize something as nuanced, complex and multi-faceted as the human experience. Whilst symptom-checkers can be used with great effectiveness for physical or visible illnesses, it's usually futile trying to standardize the emotional experiences of individuals when they are infinitely diverse.

GPs and other NHS professionals are encouraged to use the strengths and difficulties questionnaire in order to diagnose mental illness. You can find this document online at sdqinfo.org. You might assume this document is deferred to because it has been consistently proven to represent the most accurate way of determining whether patients are experiencing symptoms of depression and anxiety. In reality, it's used because it's free to download.

The SDQ was originally created in the US and represented an effort to introduce some standardization across diagnoses of depression and other mental illnesses. This is inarguably a sensible aim, but unfortunately it's far from failsafe.

In an earlier chapter I mentioned one of the questions on the SDQ: 'how many times in the past two weeks have you felt little enthusiasm for things you usually enjoy?' The options are never, rarely, sometimes and often. You will likely already have clocked how potentially fraught with problems this type of vague questioning is. 'Things you usually enjoy' is an ambiguous concept. What does it mean? Chocolate? Sex? Badminton?

Feelings of lethargy, mild ennui and generally not quite being arsed are well within the spectrum of 'normal' human emotion. Ultimately, the person completing the SDQ would need to have experience of clinical depression against which to measure their current emotional state in order to answer in a way that is useful for their doctor. And therein lies the rub.

# REALITY

THINGS FEEL SO
ROUGH RIGHT NOW

YEAH, I KNOW
THE FEELING

LIKE THE WORLD
IS JUST SLIGHTLY
TOO SAND-PAPERY
AND MY BRAIN
IS FULL OF ANGRY
BEES

OH WOW, THAT'S
EXACTLY IT...

...HEY, I HEAR
YOU

THANKS

## SIGNS AND SYMPTOMS

For all of these reasons, I tend to be cautious whenever I am asked what the signs and symptoms of mental illness are.

I understand completely the abject frustration felt by people in the orbit of loved ones experiencing mental-health difficulties. I understand, too, the need to give something a label in order to render it less terrifying. I understand the need we have to believe the suffering of the people we love not only has a tangible solution, but that it is also not our fault. I cannot, however, tell you in good conscience that performing an amateur diagnosis based on me listing various signs and symptoms on these pages will allow you to do any of these things effectively.

It would be relatively easy for me to dust off one of the many textbooks adorning my shelves and reproduce the various vulnerability factors that statistically render a person more likely to experience poor mental health, but I've found that there are so many exceptions to these sorts of rules as to render them basically obsolete.

There's also the unwelcome potential consequence of inflicting blame and guilt. One of the potential vulnerability criteria in children, for example, is coming from a one-parent household. Which leads me to ponder what, precisely, we are supposed to do about that? Very few parents are single through choice and most are doing the best they can with the options and resources available to them.

You might argue that being able to identify people who fit high-risk indexes for mental illness might make you better at your job if you're, say, a teacher, and there is some wisdom in that point of view. However, it's also interesting to note a recommendation that came out of the 2015 Youth Select Committee report on mental health, compiled in part by young people who had been affected by mental illness. When the committee presented their report at Parliament, they stated that if they could change one thing about the education system it would be that their teachers had in mind that any of their pupils could be susceptible to mental illness. This suggests to me that placing too much emphasis on vulnerability factors might actually stop us from recognizing poor mental health in people who don't fit them.

Statistically, for example, people from lower incomes are more at risk of poor mental health. This leads inexorably to a conversation I am forced to have with my cab driver each time I am invited into a wealthy, independent school, in which the driver opines that 'the kids here don't have anything to worry about'. Yet my experience is that mental ill health is equal opportunity when it comes to who it strikes. Yes, social inequality undoubtedly doesn't help, not least because it reduces your chances of being able to seek adequate and expedient care, but that doesn't mean those from affluent backgrounds are never affected. Distress manifests in different ways amongst different demographics but, at the end of the day, it's still distress.

The thing you hear from bereaved friends and family of suicide victims, particularly if they are male, is 'no one knew'. The efforts people will go to in order to hide a mental-health issue they feel ashamed of, or are in denial about, often means that their death feels sudden. Another thing you hear is 'they were the last person you would have expected' when, for instance, the suicide victim has overcompensated and become the life and soul of the party, perhaps in an attempt to hide their true feelings or maybe because they are self-medicating with alcohol and drugs and their seeming-joviality is chemical. In this context, looking for signs that they aren't enjoying themselves is about as useful as getting on your hands and knees and searching for pennies on the carpet. It's equally ludicrous to extrapolate that everyone having a great time at a party is at risk of suicidal behaviours.

Lee Loveless, one of the trainers who oversaw my qualification as a mental-health first-aid instructor, would always say 'you can only deal with the person in front of you', which is a wise starting point. If you're looking down at a spreadsheet of symptoms, chances are you aren't being 'present'. It increases the likelihood that you'll miss something. Whilst it's wise to understand the nature of mental-health difficulties as covered in some of the other chapters of this book, the best thing to then do is tuck that information behind your ear and properly engage with the people in your world.

## A BEGINNER'S GUIDE TO KNOWING ME, KNOWING YOU

As I mentioned in the opening chapter, we have a tendency to only consider mental health, whether it be that of ourselves or of others, when it goes wrong. Self-care techniques are used more readily to mend than to maintain. Similarly, only when we suspect that our friend, or partner, or colleague has an anxiety disorder, or depression, do we wonder what we might be able to do to help them.

A monk I once struck up a conversation with at a conference (as you do) told me that life is like skiing. It's the tiny, barely visible shifts in balance that determine our overall direction. In reality, there is rarely such a thing as a crossroads, where our choice is a binary A or B. It is the thousands of seemingly insignificant actions and decisions that determined our momentum and have brought us to wherever we are.

We know mental illness is more treatable the earlier it is caught. But to ask, 'Is it really mental illness or a hormonal menopause-inspired shit fit?' is a red herring. Focus on dealing with the person and the distress manifesting in front of you. If it was an early indication of mental illness you may have helped set them on the path to recovery. If it wasn't, you've improved their day. Both are equally valuable.

In today's culture, it's still common to be told to pull yourself together, to be called a 'snowflake' and informed that the world isn't going to change so you had better. The message emanating from some quarters is that life is unchangingly harsh and fast-paced, and fortune favours people who can deal; to stop moaning, because there are always people worse off than you.

But imagine if we saw psychological distress in individuals as the responsibility of their community. Imagine if we acknowledged that, in most instances, humans break because their environment is fucked. Imagine if we all had time to actually listen to one another and try to find creative solutions to mental-health difficulties instead of this endless labelling and prescribing and numbing and soldiering-on. What a world that would be.

Sometimes, when I am conducting corporate training, I am confronted with a delegate who has clearly been sent under duress and really resents being there. This person will ask questions such as 'But WHY are people suddenly getting mentally ill now? My dad was in the war and him and all his friends were fine.' Or they'll make comments like 'Children today don't know they're born' in response to the statistic telling us that British young people are consistently at the bottom of the Global Happiness Index. In these circumstances, I usually tell the Bosnian rabbit story . . .

A friend of mine was born in Bosnia and came to this country as a refugee during the civil war when she was eight years old. In order to escape, her dad had to sneak them out of the country and during their perilous journey she saw things no one, least of all a child, should have to – including, in her words, 'a man get his head blown off'.

She arrived in Britain understandably traumatized, and her family settled in the north of England. On her first day at school, there was a girl sobbing in the playground. My friend assumed that something terrible must have happened to her and went over to ask her what was wrong.

Eventually, the girl managed to choke out the reason for her distress – her pet rabbit had died that morning. My friend, incredulous that someone could react in such a way to the natural death of a small, furry thing replied, 'We eat rabbits in Bosnia,' and walked away, tutting.

It took another twenty years for my friend to realize that whatever is the worst thing that has happened to you so far is . . . well, the worst thing that has happened to you, so far. The amount of grief you will feel is that of a person who has never experienced sorrow like it. The worst thing that had happened to my friend at that point in her life was seeing a man get his head blown off. In that context, crying over a rabbit had seemed daft. Yet it's not outside the realms of possibility that the amount of upset each girl felt was exactly the same.

What is important is not the objective significance of the traumatic event, but how the person affected feels about it. Grief is grief. Distress is distress. Sorrow is sorrow. If our reasoning is that we are only allowed to feel when the worst conceivable event has occurred, then no one would ever feel anything. There is, after all, always someone worse off than you.

## SUPPORTING RECOVERY

If your friend or family member had a heart attack you wouldn't immediately bellow 'fetch me a scalpel!' and begin performing open heart surgery on the kitchen table. Similarly, just because someone in your life is experiencing a mental-health difficulty it doesn't mean you are qualified to solve it.

You could be the most singularly gifted psychologist the world has ever seen (in which case I'm very flattered that you're reading this book, ta) but that doesn't render you able to perform therapy on the people close to you. It's a conflict of interest. There is a reason why therapists maintain emotional distance (see *T: Therapy*) as a non-negotiable facet of their job.

That doesn't mean you, as a friend, colleague or family member, aren't able to provide valuable support. As a general rule, think about what you'd do if the illness in question was physical and try to follow the same instincts. Keep in touch. Send texts, but don't be offended if you don't receive a response. Be guided by what they want to talk about. When someone is having chemotherapy sometimes they want to tell you about how awful it is, sometimes they want to have a conversation comprised entirely of quotes from *Peep Show* to remind them that they're still a human being. In just the same way, you can provide a precious reminder of life outside the bleak confines of mental illness.

Use unjudgmental listening skills (see *U: Unjudgmental Listening*). Try not to take a person's less-than-sociable responses or behaviour personally if they're having mental-health difficulties and resist the urge to store up any offending incidents to address later – it's probably their illness speaking.

You can provide distraction, entertainment and love, which are all just as vital as medicine.

## DON'T GET IN THE HOLE

Imagine you are walking along a road and you hear someone shouting for help. You investigate and discover a person trapped in a deep hole. They are too far below the surface of the road for you to pull them out. What would you do?

Perhaps you would alert them to your presence, talk to them and reassure them that you'd do everything you could to get them out of the hole.

Perhaps you'd throw things down – some water, a chocolate biscuit, a rope.

Perhaps you'd call the emergency services.

All valid responses.

Now imagine the least helpful thing you could do in this scenario. A lot of people answer that the least helpful thing to do is nothing – to continue walking down the road. This is undoubtedly quite unhelpful but it's not technically the least helpful response.

The most unhelpful thing you can do in these circumstances is to jump down into the hole yourself. What you are left with then is double the amount of people trapped in a hole, needing help. Similarly, our own mental wellbeing must always be our first priority, even when the people around us are struggling. It's not selfish to carve out some time for self-care (see *S: Self-Care*), it's an essential component of being in a position to help. People who are in the hole themselves don't make good saviours.

I am told often that I naturally encourage people to open up about their mental-health problems by being genuinely interested. And that's what I am – I'm interested. I'm not making it about me. I'm not gnashing my teeth and pulling out my hair, thinking that if I emulate their distress it somehow makes me a better, more empathetic person. I understand that their pain is exactly that – theirs.

As I type the above, I realize it might sound cold. Yet in fact, it's the opposite. I remember a fundamental component of my overall distress when I was in the grips of mental illness was guilt at inflicting inconvenience on the people around me. This was compounded every time I saw evidence that my emotions or behaviour were taking their toll on my friends and family. The worst thing I could have heard was 'think of what this is doing to me'. At times, that was all I could think about, but with the best will in the world that consideration couldn't have compelled me to 'snap out of it'.

Yes, the environment we seek to create should be one characterized by empathy and compassion, but the fact is that people who aren't completely consumed by their own issues are better able to be empathic and compassionate.

Most importantly, these are qualities that we should all attempt to put into practice every day, not just when we suspect someone might be in a hole.

is for . . .

**LOW**

**As I write this, it's a Sunday. Sundays are always a struggle in our home. Because Sunday is traditionally a day of 'rest' and one in which I am left to explore the confines of my own anxious brain unimpeded and undistracted, I invariably have to spend the whole day staving off a panic attack. This coincides with my husband's almost-weekly dose of the 'blues'.**

It isn't the usual sort of 'end of weekend, back to work Monday' mild, pedestrian cheesed-off-ness. On Sundays, Marcus starts questioning the meaning of existence. Unless we step in swiftly to halt it in its tracks, it can be all-consuming. On a Sunday, Marcus has been known to take to his bed for the entire day, like an Austen heroine, to suffer excruciating migraines, to (completely uncharacteristically) refuse even the allure of a *Star Wars* film and a bag of pickled-onion Monster Munch decanted into his special Darth Vader bowl.

When we first began dating, one of the first things Marcus told me about himself was that he has a history of depression and that episodes of it have plagued him for as long as he can remember. There is, he was quick to assure me, no tangible 'reason' for this. He had a happy childhood. He was loved and cared for, and there is nothing he can put his finger on as being especially traumatic. He wanted to let me know that his bouts of mild depression are both regular and inevitable and that, if we were to be together, they were something I would have to live with, too.

I, like a total idiot, thought 'This is my field! I speak and write about mental health all day long! This'll be a breeze!' I hadn't yet learned that the closer a person is to you emotionally, and the more you love them, the more difficult it is to be objective about their mental illness.

Contrary to popular belief, depression doesn't make Marcus 'sad' in the classic sense. Mostly, he is just devoid of enthusiasm, optimism or energy and mildly misanthropic in his views. Everyone annoys him, but not enough for him to say anything. In the worst scenarios, Marcus snaps at me, which, if I am feeling particularly anxious or sensitive, plunges us both into a vortex of self-perpetuating despair – adding guilt to the already crushing weight of negative emotion Marcus is experiencing and leaving me hyperventilating in the corner.

Marcus is a musician and our 'couple personality' is characterized by a propensity for daft, borderline-philosophical conversations, telling rubbish jokes that only we find funny, doing accents and impressions, and a shared love of vintage rock'n'roll. Marcus and I seem to be known amongst our friends as good company and fun to hang out with. Like so many people, our struggles with our mental health happen behind closed doors. Mercifully, though, we don't have to hide them from each other.

Accepting the presence of depression in our relationship is a work in progress. We have talked about it, at length, when we are both in a good head space. I have come to understand that there are certain times when Marcus genuinely wants to be left alone and that no amount of me making cups of tea, or decanting savoury snacks into *Star Wars*-themed receptacles, or doing impromptu semi-naked daft dances in his eyeline is going to change that. It isn't personal. I could be a Nigella Lawson-Giselle Bundchen hybrid proffering gourmet creations whilst wearing nothing but a leather thong and it wouldn't change his mood.

We have created preventative routines that are sometimes enough to stave off the Sunday blues. We get up at a reasonable hour instead of lounging around in bed, because too much sleep is one of Marcus's triggers. We take a walk to the local park and try to imbibe some all-important vitamin D from what was, in this morning's case, a weak winter sunshine. We pick up a latte (decaf for him) and a muffin and watch all the local pet dogs walk by, fantasizing about a time when we'll have one of our own. Then we go to the butcher and I try not to barf while Marcus salivates over all the various cuts of raw meat and discusses roasting techniques with the ever-so-friendly bloke behind the counter. It's a simple ritual, but it ensures we get out, do some exercise, breathe in some fresh air (or the closest available London equivalent) and focus on hopeful, pleasure-giving things like pet dogs and roast chicken. On around every other Sunday it's enough to lift both of our moods to a place that might be described as 'normal'.

Marcus's depression isn't predictable enough to strike only on a Sunday – three or four times a year it will descend for a few days at a time, usually in winter. Whilst it is fairly disruptive, it's what a doctor would call 'mild to moderate' and we have enough experience to realize it will, eventually, pass. I've never asked Marcus 'why?' but I've heard him tell other people that it's 'just part of who he is'. Whilst occasionally the depression/anxiety vortex has resulted in spilled tears (me) and recriminations (him), I don't hold either of us responsible, in the same way I wouldn't if Marcus were a diabetic and I had a bad back. Yes, those things are inconvenient, but you can't deny their existence, wish them away or blame the person experiencing them.

Whilst mixed anxiety with depression is a common diagnosis, the two conditions are radically different in their nature. Persistent anxiety can lead to feelings of depression because of the way adrenaline and cortisol batter our mental and chemical defences (see *A:Anxiety*) but I don't believe I have experienced anything directly equivalent to Marcus's depression.

I have been diagnosed with 'low mood', which has lasted for a brief, transient period, and I have on more than one occasion been suicidal, but it has always been more of an active feeling of frustration and anger (coupled with weariness at the constant burden of that frustration and anger) that has brought me to that place. Marcus's illness is in the realms of 'ennui' – he is deflated, negative and generally Eeyore-like, as though his depression is a fire blanket that has extinguished his joie de vivre. When my mental health has been at its worst I have actively vibrated with a dark vigour, something that my therapist once described as surplus nervous energy turned inwards so that it erodes and destroys the self.

Depression is a term that encompasses a vast number of conditions, all with different characteristics and triggers, and, like all mental illness, it exists on a spectrum, the farthest reach of which is suicidal ideation or behaviour. Whilst it is by no means certain that depression will lead to a person taking their own life, an estimated 90 per cent of deaths recorded as suicides happen as a result of untreated depression or substance abuse, so it's important to address this.

## DEPRESSION V SADNESS

The word 'depression' has entered the common vernacular as a way of melodramatically conveying sadness. Case in point: in *Bridget Jones: The Edge of Reason* the lead character's mum asks why she hasn't turned up for a shopping expedition following a break up and she responds, 'I'm suicidally depressed.'

There is a clear understanding between the characters that the words are being used for dramatic effect and not to be taken literally. This understanding extends to the audience because, lest we forget, *Bridget Jones* is a romantic comedy. If anyone involved suspected Bridget Jones meant the words literally, an ambulance would have been called and it would have been a very different sort of film.

Now, I'm not for one minute suggesting we should ban this kind of hyperbolic language, or that I've never been guilty of it myself. However, it does rather leave a person who is genuinely 'suicidally depressed' with limited options to convey their situation when the words they might have used have been hijacked by Renee Zellweger to describe the sensation of no longer being shagged by Colin Firth in a light-hearted rom-com.

There was some (completely justified) consternation when 'grief' was added to the Diagnostic and Statistical Manual of Mental Disorders (DSM). Grief isn't a mental illness in its own right. It can certainly be a contributing factor or a catalyst. But if someone you were fond of has shuffled from this mortal coil it's normal, even healthy, to feel incredibly sad about that.

Depression, conversely, happens regardless of context. That isn't to say that objectively awful things won't have happened to the person experiencing depression, more that their emotional state doesn't peak and trough in direct response to outside stimulus.

I've heard many people describe depression as a numbness – a total absence of any sort of feeling at all. People in the grips of depression often actively long to cry, because in order to cry you have to feel something, and that would be welcome respite. It is the absence of emotion that becomes, over time, unbearable.

You're far more likely to hear a depressed person say that they aren't good at anything, or there is 'no point', than to deliver great poetic monologues of gnashing despair. People with depression often describe a sense of disconnection and isolation, as if there is an invisible barrier between them and the world. The partner of a depressed friend of mine told me he felt as though she was behind a thick pane of glass and he could not reach her.

Medically, depression can be diagnosed if a patient has experienced 'low mood' for a period of more than two weeks, although very rarely exceptions are made if the symptoms are considered to be severe and have a 'rapid onset'. In the UK, one in four women and one in ten men have had at least one episode of depression for which they have sought treatment. (See chapter *X: X Chromosome* for my theory on why there is a gender discrepancy in these statistics.)

Whilst depression doesn't generally have a 'reason', it does affect around one in ten new mothers. There are a number of theories as to why it happens, including hormone fluctuations, the trauma associated with giving birth and/or the general life disruption the arrival of a new baby brings. Postnatal depression lasts for weeks, sometimes months and is usually accompanied by feelings of anxiety around not being emotionally connected to the baby and thoughts or worries about harming them. This, understandably, often leads to guilt and shame. So-called 'baby blues' are a different thing entirely to postnatal depression and even more common. I would have thought, after carrying around another human for nine months and then pushing it out of your vagina, it would be a little strange if you weren't very tired and a bit tearful.

The other common form of responsive depression is seasonal affective disorder. Much like OCD, it's one of those things that everyone thinks they have 'a bit' but, unlike with OCD, they probably do. Countries that are colder and receive less sunlight have much higher levels of depression and suicide. Lack of vitamin D can have a profound effect, causing amongst other things extreme lethargy, which is in turn a symptom of depression. Again, SAD has had a relatively recent inclusion in the DSM and this caused controversy.

Anecdotally, I'd say that a person with an in-built tendency towards depression can be triggered towards an episode, or feel an episode more acutely, during the darker, colder winter months. Doctors tend to make a diagnosis of SAD if a person has had episodes spanning over a period of more than three years. It is described by charity MIND as 'a form of depression that people experience at a particular time of year or during a particular season'.

Experts argue endlessly about what characterizes depression. Despite it being the most commonly diagnosed mental illness, I have found there to be the least concrete information about what, exactly, it is. The general consensus seems to be 'if you had it, you'd know'. I usually tell people that the line between mental illness and mental health is about an ability to function. Yet plenty of people with depression get up, go to work and appear, for all intents and purposes, 'normal'. Huge amounts of time and energy are invested by depressed people into emulating sociable or cheerful behaviours that utterly belie how they feel inside.

In summary, we can see that there are a few points of tentative consensus. Depression isn't usually an understandable and timely response to a traumatic or tragic event. Depression is characterized by an absence of rather than a presence of feeling. Depression lasts for a period longer than two weeks. But even as I type, I know I will get letters from people whose experiences fall outside of even these vague parameters.

## A BEGINNER'S GUIDE TO FEELING LOW

I've heard depression described as an inevitable side effect of knowledge and intelligence. I can see the logic of this argument. In the context of a world where we're increasingly secular in our beliefs and science is 'proving' that life on earth is a cosmic accident in a vast, unfathomable universe, depression when defined as a sense of pointlessness is kind of inevitable.

That doesn't, however, mean that it is something we should have to endure. Just as the definition of depression is frustratingly imprecise, so the advice on how to counteract it seems a little futile. Whilst exercise has been shown to be as effective in treating mild to moderate depression as medication (see *E: Endorphins*), it's realistically best used as a preventative or maintenance-style measure. Seeing friends, getting fresh air and going for a run are all great ideas in theory, but for most people in the grips of severe depression, telling them to go for a walk is like asking them to fly.

My friend, journalist Rosie Mullender, wrote a column for me when I guest-edited a special issue of the *Eastern Daily Press* dedicated to mental health. Rather than focusing on the most shocking or extreme aspects of mental illness (how low people's weights became, how severely they self-harmed), I wanted instead to ask contributors to talk about what helped. This, I reasoned, would be much more useful to the reader.

Rosie chose to focus on the myths surrounding antidepressants, how when she realized she was depressed she feared going her GP because, she thought, 'even if medication works, you're not yourself any more'. When she did eventually try medication, she described it as feeling 'like the corner of a heavy dust sheet had been lifted up. And there I still was, hiding underneath.'

That's the thing about depression – like all mental illness it consumes the self until you're not sure who you are any more.

Depression is the most common mental illness, but it's also the one that attracts the least sympathy and most judgment. In Britain, in particular, we pride ourselves on having a 'keep calm and carry on', stiff upper lip-type mentality and seem to be labouring under the illusion that maintaining this throughout the horrors of the First and Second World Wars meant 'no one ever used to have mental-health problems'. I don't have enough words available to me in this book to convey the extent to which people irrefutably DID have mental-health problems during the wars.

Depression is often mistaken for 'feeling sorry for yourself' and is most likely to illicit the response 'pull yourself together'. In fact, Marcus tells me that when he is feeling depressed, there is a tiny version of him orbiting himself, shouting those very words.

If people with depression could 'pull themselves together' they would. Keeping calm and carrying on might have been a tactic that worked in the distant past – I couldn't tell you because I wasn't alive – but the world is very different now and so too is our understanding of it and the challenges we all face. We now understand that depression is more treatable the earlier it is identified and the better we understand our own triggers.

The biggest enemy of them all is denial.

## SUICIDE

Suicide happens when pain exceeds resources for coping with pain. Considering the vast amounts of energy required to function on even a basic level when dealing with depression, it's little wonder so many deaths by suicide happen as a result.

The first thing to know is that fleeting thoughts of 'Wouldn't it be lovely if I could just go to sleep and never wake up?' whilst an indicator of depression, don't necessarily lead to suicide. So-called 'suicidal ideation' is quite common and, according to the many psychologists I've spoken to, totally normal.

That's why it's crucial, if you suspect that someone you know could be suicidal, to follow a direct line of questioning. I've both attended and delivered extensive training around suicide prevention and there is always disagreement and resistance in the room about following this course of action. However, it's important to know that the UK's leading suicide-prevention charity, the Samaritans, following extensive research and consultation, recommend the following.

- Ask directly 'have you had thoughts of killing yourself?'

- Ask 'have you thought about how?'

- Ask 'have you thought about when and where?'

It is not possible to 'talk someone into' suicidal thoughts, if you stay within these parameters.

If the answer to all three of these questions is 'yes' then the person is at immediate risk, should not be left alone and an ambulance should be called. If the answer to the first, or the first and second is 'yes' then the person probably isn't in urgent danger but is moving along the suicide spectrum and likely to be depressed. That is where unjudgmental listening skills will serve you well (see *U: Unjudgmental Listening*).

is for . . .
# MEDIA

Warning: I am writing this chapter following a particularly stupid day. In summary, I've accidentally caused a media storm by *allegedly* (read: 'not') saying that the words 'boy' and 'girl' should be banned. Every tabloid has run the story and I've been personally lambasted by Piers Morgan during a five-minute rant on *Good Morning Britain*. I accepted an invitation from *This Morning* to 'defend my actions', after which my inbox exploded. Half of my messages were support from people who actually listened to the interview and half were death threats from people who didn't.

## BEING OPINIONATED (AND ANXIOUS)

I am a person who has strong opinions. As I often say, I have no interest in telling people what to think, but I do enjoy making them think. Indeed, as a campaigner, I see it as a crucial part of my job to stick my head above the parapet. This has proved problematic in the past, since I'm also someone with an anxiety disorder. I don't know if people were ever able to have a respectful chat that acknowledges nuance and reasonable ideological difference, but I do know they generally aren't now, in the age of social media.

At times like these, what I like to do is separate Natasha Devon: The Human – wife, daughter, sister, friend and general 'good box' (see *Z: Zero Fucks Given* for an explanation of the 'Good Box Mentality' theory) from Natasha Devon: The Campaigner, who is a public figure and as such has to, as an unwelcome side effect of her job, put up with the bile and bluster of random Twitter users, pundits and columnists. Natasha Devon: The Human and Natasha Devon: The Campaigner then have the following dialogue:

> Human: *The newspapers have misquoted me!*
> Campaigner: *That's what the press do, sometimes. It's their job to look for an angle. Nothing personal.*
> Human: *But everyone hates me based on a misconception!*
> Campaigner: *That's not true, now, is it? A few people are getting what passes for entertainment these days by insulting you via the YouTube comments section. But they also do that to loads of other people you love. Some people slag off Beyoncé online. Beyoncé! A world where Beyoncé is deemed anything less than a wonder is a world in which some people won't like you. Because, whilst I love you and all, we both have to admit you're not quite as fabulous as Beyoncé.*
> Human: *Fair point.*

Campaigner: *Now, what can you extrapolate from this experience? And, more importantly, what wisdom can you impart to others, gleaned from the increasingly ludicrous experiences associated with being Natasha Devon: The Campaigner?*

Anxiety averted, that's when I tend to write. I sometimes I shape my thoughts into my column for the *Times Educational Supplement*. Sometimes I turn them into an amusing anecdote for a speech or presentation. Sometimes I just write an account of my day, like a diary entry. Getting my thoughts onto paper not only has therapeutic value (see *S: Self-Care*) it also helps me learn and to evolve my understanding.

So, in an exercise that I hope, reader, will benefit both of us, I'm going to explain what happened today. I hope that it will teach you something about the media, how it operates and its constant manipulation of narratives that might, in turn, have an impact on your mental health.

Yesterday I presented the keynote speech at the Girls' Schools Association annual conference, an event at which the head teachers of hundreds of single-sex educational institutions throughout the world come together to share ideas.

During my hour-long presentation, I covered all kinds of things, some of which I've written about in this book – social media, how you can develop critical-thinking skills in lessons, healthy coping strategies for academic stress in children, how to listen to pupils' concerns non-judgmentally. And for about five minutes, I talked about sexuality and gender and their relation to mental health. You can read the extended, disco version of my thoughts on these topics in chapters *Q: Queer* and *X: X Chromosome*, but the main thrust of my argument was this:

- A sense of belonging is one of the five fundamental psychological human needs.

- In making sweeping assumptions about gender, sexuality and identity we can create a culture in which anyone who deviates from the established archetypes feels excluded from their community and therefore doesn't have this need fulfilled.

- One way educators could help to avoid this is by using gender-neutral language when addressing groups of pupils.

There are several schools who do this already. They will often ask visiting speakers to refer to year groups as 'students' rather than 'girls' or 'ladies' because they want to be as inclusive as possible. This strikes me as very good practice and none of the five hundred or so delegates in attendance indicated that they thought this was in any way controversial.

After I came off stage, the press officer for the conference asked me if I'd mind a quick interview with a few of the journalists in attendance. One of them asked, 'Can you talk more about the part where you said teachers shouldn't use gender pronouns in case they offend transgender children?'

This was obviously not what I said, but I could see where her line of questioning was leading. So I decided to try and emphasize the benefits of using neutral language for all young people, as opposed to an inconvenient concession we have to make for the benefit of transgender people alone. I talked about how gender archetypes can become oppressive. That's when I made my big mistake. I said the thing that would be turned into headlines in newspapers across the land, the next day: 'I don't think it's useful for children to be constantly reminded of their gender when they're in a learning environment.'

In less than two hours the pieces started appearing online, with increasingly hysterical headlines. The final one I saw before going to bed read: 'Tsar ORDERS Teachers not to Say "Girls" Because it REMINDS Pupils of their Gender.'

This morning, I woke up to twenty-eight missed calls from various media outlets wanting an exclusive interview. The story was on the first five pages of virtually every bestselling newspaper in the country,

The articles featured headlines such as 'GOVERNMENT ADVISOR SAYS WE SHOULD BAN GIRLS AND BOYS' alongside 800-word missives from opinion-piece writers speculating that I was part of the 'transgender lobby', which was trying to 'take away children's innocence' by 'forcing kids to question their sexuality'. A Christian publication even suggested that Satan was speaking through me and that I should be burned as a witch, which was an interesting angle.

Playing a part in the media circus is, arguably, part of my job. Yet here is my real fear: I worry that, for the next few months, if my name happens to be mentioned in a pub, or an office, the next words spoken will be, 'Isn't she the one who says we aren't allowed to say girls or boys anymore? Silly bitch! PC gone mad, that is! Nothing wrong with being a girl/boy!'

And that, in a nutshell, is how the media – for all the magnificent work it does to raise awareness of mental health – shuts down some of the complex conversations we need to have in order to better understand it. This episode served to remind me that, for every news story, there is a context that has, for reasons of word count or sometimes deliberate manipulation, been excluded.

Of course, this isn't my first time on the press merry-go-round, and experience has taught me that time is a great perspective-giver. One day I'll be sitting round a dinner table somewhere with some people I love dearly, saying fondly, 'Remember the gender/Piers Morgan incident when they threatened to burn me as a witch? LOLZ.' But until that day, Natasha Devon: The Campaigner is angry.

## A BEGINNER'S GUIDE TO THE MEDIA AND YOUR MENTAL HEALTH

Two of the strongest and easiest emotions to evoke in people are fear and outrage. In order to generate headlines and the most coveted of modern currency, online clicks, the media often appeals to these fairly base and usually unhelpful instincts.

In a world flooded with news – twenty-four-hour rolling news channels, news websites, news-based social-media accounts – we are having our fear and outrage buttons pressed constantly. This has the potential to put us into a perpetual state of fight, flight or freeze, in turn causing anxiety and panic (see *A: Anxiety*).

The next time you're tempted by clickbait, ask yourself, 'Will reading this prove genuinely useful?' It is, of course, important to keep ourselves informed. Some deliberately outrageous and provocative comments are made by public figures who hold sufficient political power for their views to be significant and our knowledge of them useful. The current president of the United States would be a good example of this. But will your life, your intelligence, knowledge, wellbeing or relationships with yourself and others really be enhanced by finding out what some alt-right rent-a-gob thinks about immigrants? It's not my place to tell you the correct answer to that; I can only trust you to arrive at it yourself.

The sidebar of shame, the screeching, nonsensical headlines, with RANDOM words capitalized like THIS, and the carefully manicured, out-of-context quotations conspire to keep us panicked, afraid and outraged. That's why when you open some newspapers or websites it FEELS LIKE THEY ARE SHOUTING AT YOU. You need a robust sense of Zen to survive them unscathed.

Yet, as consumers of media in the digital age, we have the power to change the narrative. When we click on a piece of media, we are casting a vote for it. We are saying to the invisible algorithms that track unique users and click volume 'more of this, please'. The sites with the highest click volume then get more advertising revenue and can hire more staff to generate more content shaped by what their consumers are telling them they want. We can do our bit to keep responsible, balanced perspective alive by clicking, sharing and (where we can) buying.

## MENTAL ILLNESS IN THE MEDIA

Mental illnesses are conditions that, by their nature, are largely invisible. The media is an industry that is, by its nature, largely visual. Mental illnesses are incredibly complicated and rarely attributable to a single contributory factor. The media is a place where topics tend to be presented in binary ways, using vaguely daft premises to kick-start debate for entertainment value. This makes the melding of the two a tricky landscape to navigate.

When I watch carefully crafted documentaries, deconstructing and examining complex topics, like *Why Did I Go Mad?* on BBC2 examining the link between psychosis and immigration; or listen to Bryony Gordon's 'Mad World' podcasts; or read the beautifully written first-hand accounts regularly featured on the pages of Metro Online's health desk, it renews my belief that mental illness can be described and portrayed responsibly. When I see the double-page spreads of 'before and after' photos masquerading as 'exposés' on anorexia; or opinion pieces about how mental-health issues are being 'faked' by a work-shy generation trying to scam benefits; or headlines like 'Cake Cured My Depression!' my faith is shaken.

There is endless debate over whether the media 'glamorizes' or 'stigmatizes' mental illness. Some argue that the seemingly endless parade of celebrities talking about their mental-health battles is a cynical ploy to garner column inches and downplays the painful realities of living with these conditions. Others say that knowing that someone whose life is seemingly successful and glamorous – say, Fearne Cotton – has been touched by mental illness makes them feel less alone and less of a screw-up.

I've speculated in other chapters (particularly in *O: Obsessive Compulsive Drive*) about where the line might be between normalizing and glamorizing. Crucially, celebrities have helped to bring conversations about mental health to the realms of popular media, meaning greater awareness. Having said that, awareness-raising can be more damaging than helpful if it's not treated with compassion and balance.

I believe progress is being made. I also acknowledge that mistakes are bound to happen during a time when the public's understanding and

perception of mental health is undergoing seismic evolution. The media has a momentous task on its hands. It needs to help people understand that we all have a mental health and convey the distinction with mental illness. It needs to acknowledge that this covers a huge array of conditions, each happening within the context of a unique human being and set of circumstances. It needs to report on the latest scientific and therapeutic developments without suggesting there is a magic cure. And it is faced with the challenge of describing something that is endlessly layered and complicated, invisible and difficult to measure and happens within the confines of the human soul – all in 500–800 words or three-minute slots of airtime, in a way that keeps its audience engaged and interested.

If we want the media to be kind to us, we need to show it some kindness in return and allow the people who work in the industries room for error. We should also give them guidance where we can. Which brings me to . . .

## THE MENTAL HEALTH MEDIA CHARTER

For World Mental Health Day 2017, I created the Mental Health Media Charter. This is seven simple guidelines for media outlets, giving advice on how to report mental-health stories responsibly and without increasing stigma, compiled with the help of the Samaritans, Beat and Mental Health First Aid England. It gives media outlets a steer on appropriate language and imagery, as well as tips like including links to good-quality sources of further support and advice.

When I was a glossy-magazine columnist, I once mentioned in passing to my editor concerns I had about triggering before-and-after pictures on eating-disorder stories. I wasn't talking about *Cosmo* specifically, merely saying how hard it is to report eating disorders accurately in any sort of visual medium.

My editor said that she had taken the time to learn about the 'thinspiration' phenomenon, but prior to that she had genuinely assumed that seeing a shocking image of a severely underweight person would highlight the dangers of, rather than promote, eating disorders. This is a completely reasonable assumption and one that anyone not personally touched by eating disorders could easily make. That's the first time I thought 'Aha! It's not that the media are always trying to create stigma/stereotypes around mental illness! It's that they DON'T KNOW!' It occurred to me that a lot of the problems in mental-health reporting might not be wilful ignorance, but simply habits or misguided intention.

Most charities have media guidelines, but they tend to be lengthy and not particularly user-friendly if you're a journo on a deadline. I realized, therefore, that what I needed to do was to boil everything down and make it as simple as possible, including suggestions for alternative, more helpful ways to report. I contacted the charities mentioned above and conducted an online survey for people currently affected by mental illness, whether directly or via a friend or family member. I compiled the data and extracted the seven aspects of current media reporting that were either considered to be most detrimental or most helpful to an accurate and compassionate portrayal.

For example, it is now considered bad practice to use the phrase 'commit suicide'. One 'commits' a crime and it hasn't been a criminal offence to take your own life in the UK since 1961. This might not seem terribly significant, but when you talk to bereaved families of people who have ended their own lives, or indeed people who have survived suicide attempts, they have found the shame and stigma associated with the word 'commit' damaging. There is also evidence to show that those at risk of suicide who still believe it is a criminal offence are less likely to seek the help they need for fear of legal implications. It's better to say ' died by suicide' or 'took/ended their own life'.

To date, more than fifty outlets, including newspapers, magazines, radio stations, bloggers and YouTubers, have signed up. You can recognize those that have by looking for the 'stamp of approval' below on their website and/or social media. Find us @MHMediaCharter.

is for . . .

# NUMBER 10
# DOWNING STREET

**Up until the summer of 2016, the question I was most often asked in schools or at events was, 'How do I help a friend who has mental-health issues?' Since then, it has been, 'What on earth happened with the Tories?'**

In May 2016, I was unceremoniously fired as the government's Mental Health 'Tsar' and it caused a right old hoo-ha. I've never found a way to convey my experience adequately in the two or three minutes I usually have at events, so this chapter represents my attempt to remedy that. Strap yourself in, reader, for what follows is the inside scoop, the goss, the truth as told through the prism of my blik (see *B: Brain*).

When I first entered the world of mental-health campaigning as an intrepid, newly-in-recovery 25-year-old, I was sublimely apolitical. I hadn't yet exercised my right to vote (for which there is no excuse) and, like many British people, considered politics to be something that happened 'over there' in Whitehall, undertaken by politicians who were entirely unrelated to 'normal' life. My knowledge of what constituted politics was limited to the red-faced, braying show of legitimized bullying and posh toxic masculinity I saw whenever Prime Minister's Questions happened to be on the telly.

I have, however, always had what my parents refer to as an 'overdeveloped sense of fairness'. At school I was forever hounding people to sponsor me for increasingly ridiculous charity endeavours (this was the era when the bath of beans was considered a fashionable way to fundraise), or chewing everyone's ear off in assembly about the injustices of war, famine, climate change or why everyone should be vegetarian (which made me as popular as you might imagine).

In sixth form, whilst the rest of my sexually-repressed-by-years-of-girl-only-schooling classmates began showing up in miniskirts and heels, I did not. I ranted about racism and feminism in the common room and was 'unacceptably' overweight by the standards of image-obsessed Essex. I did not realize at the time that any of these acts were inherently political in their nature. It was only when I began travelling around the UK visiting schools, colleges and universities, and I perceived links between the experiences of the people I spoke to in distant locations that I began to think of my job as inextricably linked with politics.

Spend long enough researching and speaking about mental health and you'll inevitably be drawn into considerations about race, gender, sexuality, culture and affluence. You will begin to ask yourself why, for example, people from black and minority ethnic groups are more likely to become mentally ill but (in the case of people of Afro-Caribbean heritage) less likely to seek help. If, like me, you believe all people are essentially the same at birth, you'll be led to the conclusion that it is impossible to divorce mental health from a person's environment, circumstances and the way they are treated by others.

If, as I was beginning to understand, it was politics that was to a large degree responsible for creating and addressing inequality, and social inequality was a factor in mental wellbeing, then, I eventually realized, I was going to have to start engaging with the strange and scary world of Westminster.

So that, in a nutshell, is how caring about mental health turned me into a political animal.

I believe in justice, fairness and equal opportunity in a way that most often (although not exclusively) chimes with those who identify themselves as on the left of the political spectrum. I think everyone is entitled to a basic standard of living regardless of their financial circumstances. I believe in the National Health Service and the welfare state. I believe a great education is not only a basic right but is the key to the kind of happiness and freedom money can't buy (because discussions about quality of life shouldn't be restricted to financial affluence). I do not think it is right that men are still paid more than women. I do not think it is right that white people are still given more opportunity than people of colour. I do not think it is right to make sweeping generalizations about a person's character or capabilities based on their race, sexuality, gender, shape, size or class.

In essence, I have become what right-wing nationalists would call a virtue-signalling, social-justice warrior and 'snowflake' and I see all of those descriptions as a badge of honour as opposed to a mark of shame.

So, in 2010, aged 29, I not only voted for the very first time but I also joined the Labour party, having concluded at that point that the Liberal Democrat manifesto most supported my idea of how the world should be, but having also bought into the widely held and somewhat-inexplicable notion that they'd 'never get in'.

Around this time I began writing regularly for newspapers, penning pieces with titles such as, 'If I Were Prime Minister' and 'Ten Reasons Why Michael Gove Is the Worst Thing to Happen to Education Since Ever'. So it's something of an understatement to say I was surprised when, in spring 2015, my phone rang and it was a civil servant from the Department of Education, all lovely and sing-songy, saying she had an opportunity for me. The government were recruiting their very first mental-health champion for schools, she said, which meant an opportunity to be a voice for young people at government level and 'ultimately influence policy'. Was I interested?

Michael Gove was no longer Secretary of State for Education, having been superseded by Nicky Morgan, but I assumed they were aware of the games of insult tennis he and I had played in the press over the past couple of years. She assured me that they wanted someone with 'genuine expertise' who would challenge them.

I considered it a great opportunity, but I also couldn't shake this nagging sense that it was a kind of Faustian pact, that being in league with the Tories might sully me and my reputation somehow. Ultimately, I decided it was churlish to dwell on wider ideological differences when the government was showing such apparent willingness to learn and take action on an issue I felt so strongly about.

I accepted the position and asked about the possibility of a salary. I was told it was important for me to remain 'objective' and therefore I could not be paid for my time. Thank our Lord and Saviour David Bowie that this stance was taken − since I didn't sign anything, I was never in thrall to the Department for Education (DfE) and was therefore able to make the decisions I later did.

A press release was swiftly catapulted out into the ether and almost immediately my phone started ringing. People from all over the UK had somehow found my mobile number and were calling to tell me their children were still on a waiting list for therapeutic care despite several suicide attempts, or that they were being shunted between alcohol-addiction and mental-health service providers with neither willing to take responsibility for them, or that they were a teacher whose year group were enduring an epidemic of self-harm and simply didn't know what to do. I had been working in the field for eight years at that stage and still I don't think the national levels of sheer desperation had properly hit me until that moment.

A couple of weeks later I had a meeting with then-Minister for Education and Childcare, Sam Gyimah. He seemed an affable enough fellow, delivering a now-familiar sort of spiel about the government recognizing its duty to address the rising levels of poor mental health in young people and wanting the benefit of my experience as someone 'on the ground'. He asked me how I saw my role, since I was the first ever champion of this nature, which allowed for, I assumed, a certain amount of autonomy in defining exactly what I'd be doing. I said I wanted to be a 'bridge' between government and schools, to bring the concerns of the teachers, pupils and parents I saw every day to the DfE, as well as to report on best practice in the field. He seemed satisfied with that and we went off to have our photograph taken outside Parliament (during which I was instructed, in hushed tones, to stand in such a way as to 'not make the Minister look too short'. I should have known then how things would end).

Over the weeks that followed I attended approximately four billion 'roundtables' with ministers, advisors and various mental-health charity leaders in which we were repeatedly asked the same question: did we think teachers were well placed to spot the signs of poor mental health in their pupils and provide initial care? I always answered in the same way: 'It depends what you mean by "care".' To which the response was usually something along the lines of 'We'll take that as a "yes".'

I was trying to have discussions about the kinds of things initially referred to in my meeting with the Minister and yet kept finding myself, *Groundhog-Day*-style, back at that conversation.

As I now understand it, the way the various governmental departments operate is this: Secretaries of State are appointed across various disciplines without any consideration for the experience they might have in that area. Thus, the Secretary of State for Education will usually have had no actual experience of the sector aside from, presumably, having been to school. This is, I have reflected, much like asking me to take charge of the Bank of England as of tomorrow. I have a tenner in my purse. I think I know broadly how money works. I'd give it my best shot. But I'm probably not the best choice for the role.

Ministers are appointed to serve under the Secretaries of State, again based on apparently not very much. The Ministers and Secretaries have 'special advisors' (or 'SPADs') who, unless publicly disgraced in some way, remain in their positions through various changes of cabinet and, as far as I can tell, are the people who are actually in charge of our country. You can have a meeting with the Prime Minister herself and leave with the distinct feeling that you have won her over with your incredibly innovative idea, but if a SPAD comes in three minutes afterwards and whispers in her ear that it's just not possible, it ain't gonna happen.

I believe the government had already decided, prior to the very public campaign to 'improve' mental health in young people in 2015, that the way to compensate for the £80 million cuts to Child and Adolescent Mental Health Services since they came into power was to get teachers to provide care for pupils with mental-health difficulties, in school. I believe they sought out charities and experts who would provide evidence to support this position. For example, one of the psychologists who presented his findings to the DfE believes that stress is good for children, that the mental-health crisis in young people has been 'exaggerated' and that showing symptoms of mental illness is not the same as actually having one. Now, I'm not saying that there isn't a grain of truth in the last part of that statement. But, if you put his research in the hands of a government whose agenda is to suggest poor mental health in the young is nothing that a lovely chat with their teacher couldn't sort out, it's a recipe for an almighty shit-show.

Skip forward to around March 2016 and I was thoroughly frustrated and radiating anger. The press, in tribute to my self-defined role as an advisor to the DfE, had labelled me 'Mental Health Tsar'. Tsar was a term that suggested I had power over the actions of government, and the DfE did nothing to contradict this impression – I suspect because they knew their policies weren't proving popular and needed a scapegoat. I was fed up of having what I now realized was no real say in anything the DfE did and yet being deferred to whenever the public disagreed with their decisions.

Teachers were, entirely understandably, by turns concerned and furious. Gove's reforms – which called for teachers to fill in mountains of paperwork in a bid to 'improve standards' in schools, along with an increased emphasis on so-called 'core' academic subjects and exams – had already monumentally increased their workload. Now, it appeared, they were being expected to be responsible for the mental health of their pupils as well. They were, they quite rightly pointed out to me in endless emails and social-media posts, not qualified psychologists. Who could they defer to, in the highly likely event that their pupils had needs over and above what they were able to provide?

During this time, despite initial assurances that I would retain total freedom of speech and opinion, the SPADs were doing everything they could to control my public output. I was receiving regular phone calls from the DfE, asking me to delete Twitter posts that were in any way critical of the Tories or their policies, or warning me not to be 'tricked' by the press into commenting on things they thought I might disagree with (like their mooted but abandoned plan to turn all state schools into academies, which they correctly assumed I would think was beyond stupid).

Rules for the sake of rules are anathema to me. The more the DfE tried to silence me, the more mischievous I was determined to be, culminating in that time I called the Behaviour Tsar a bellend on Twitter.

By this stage the government were, to some degree understandably, desperately looking for an excuse to rid themselves of me. They'd allowed a situation to arise where I'd been labelled one of their 'Tsars' and I was behaving in a distinctly un-tsar-like ways, much to the entertainment and delight of multiple education bloggers, who were enjoying the consequent soap opera.

In March 2016 I enthusiastically banged the final nail into the coffin of my brief political career. I was in the audience at a televised conference hosted by Cambridge University and attended by all kinds of important people. Then-Minister for Social Care, Alistair Burt, presented a speech detailing the government's approach to mental health in young people (which can be summarized as: get teachers to handle it) and concluded by declaring that it was a 'symbol of the government's commitment to mental health' that they were 'working with Natasha Devon', thus implying that I endorsed the previous thirty minutes of dreary nonsense. He made the mistake of inviting questions, at which point I raised my hand and explained why I disagreed with pretty much the entirety of what he'd just said, as well as outlining everything I thought the government was getting wrong on mental health, why it was dishonest for them to take the credit for the work of charities and campaigners in the sector, and that if they really cared as much about the mental wellbeing of young people as they purported to then they needed to sort out the lack of funding for services. I also took the opportunity to have a pop at him about student fees, increasing child poverty in the UK, and changes to the curriculum that meant state-school kids were doing less sport, art, music and drama. Because, you know, if you're going to sabotage yourself you might as well go the whole hog.

In that moment, Alistair Burt represented his entire party and was personally responsible for all of their fuckwittery. It can't have been nice, having someone he walked into the room assuming was an ally standing up and contradicting everything he'd just said in such a public way (although, in my defence, my emails requesting a meeting with him had gone unanswered).

Owing to the fact that I have since conducted what's called a Public Access Request, allowing me to see telephone transcripts, minutes of meetings and written communication that contain my name and are held by government, I know that after this conference an email was sent between the Department of Health, where Mr Burt worked, and the DfE which said: 'Appreciate that we didn't want to get rid of her when it looked like we were doing it because she criticized – but it cannot be feasible that she continues when she criticizes . . . 'Which is just brilliantly, gloriously *The Thick of It* in its self-contradictory, 'help-we-don't-know-what-the-fuck-we're-doing-and-we're-meant-to-be-in-charge' type way.

The DfE then concocted a plan to create the position of a salaried, contracted Mental Health Champion (at the time of writing this has not been followed through). They could have total control over the new champion and it would render my position obsolete. They invited me in for a meeting, told me what a fantastic job I'd done, how valuable my work had been over the past nine months but that unfortunately, owing to powers beyond their control, they were letting me go. They were at pains to emphasize that I was no longer authorized to comment as the government's mental-health champion but that they'd also appreciate it if I didn't tell the press exactly what had happened.

The next day, a journalist from the *Guardian* rang me, asking for a comment on an education story that had broken that morning. I, in a fit of righteous indignation, told her I wasn't in a position to comment as the government's mental-health champion any more and, when she asked me why, I said she had 'better ask them'. You might reasonably argue that I was inviting further investigation and you'd be entirely right. I wanted someone to know the truth and was fortunate that the first paper that rang me after my firing was the *Guardian*, a publication that, in my humble opinion, stands head-and-shoulders above most of the rest in its pursuit of publishing truths that don't fit the established, lazy narratives.

What I couldn't have been prepared for was the subsequent media furore. I assumed the press would learn of my firing and conclude, 'Ah, well. This wouldn't be the first time the government got rid of people who speak truth to power. I suppose this was inevitable. There's really nothing to see, here.' How wrong I was.

The next day I had journalists insistently ringing the doorbell of my third-floor flat, whilst I huddled under a blanket in the corner, dodging the constant calls from various media outlets on my mobile, making fervent arrangements to go and stay with my friend Amy out in Richmond so I could work out what I wanted to do. Amy, who in the context of this story is the Elton John to my Geri Halliwell, encouraged me to switch my phone off, come out into the garden with her, sit on her sofa-swing, drink wine and talk non-work-related bollocks in the sunshine until such time as my subconscious gave me the answers I sought. Amy really is very wise. By the time I left the next morning I had decided to give one exclusive each to newspaper, television and radio – the *Guardian*, BBC's super-serious current-affairs show *Newsnight*, and James O'Brien at LBC respectively.

Since then, I've had a more distant and far less fractious relationship with Parliament. I still regularly give evidence to the health and education select committees, so in theory I'm doing what I always set out to do, i.e. ensuring the voices of the people I encounter every day are heard at government level.

People keep asking me if I would ever run as an MP, but my experience of politics suggests that it is more about popularity and power than it is about serving genuine need (although there are of course exceptions – MPs Norman Lamb, Jess Phillips, Justine Greening, Luciana Berger and Heidi Allen spring to mind). Lots of good people are undoubtedly attracted to politics at a local level, but successfully playing the sorts of games that mean I could progress up the political ladder would inevitably mean sacrificing more and more of my integrity.

If the system changes, perhaps a political career is something I would consider. In the meantime, I'm content to campaign on the fringes, for the following principal reason: the Subject Access Request was shocking. (In fact, the original dossier of emails and transcripts I received is covered in brown smudges because I was eating a cornetto when I read it and my mouth kept falling open.) The sheer amount of time and energy the people in charge put into their efforts to shut me up calls into question the impartiality and integrity of every single person advising at government level. It is obvious from the tone of the government employees that very few people have ever stood up to them before in the way I did. This notion is more than a little bit disturbing.

On the other hand, my adventures in government taught me that, contrary to what we are often told, the public are in some ways more powerful than we realize. The Subject Access Request regularly referenced what was being said about me on social media, concluding that I was 'influential' and 'appeal to the masses', and adding in a sinister fashion 'whatever we might think of her'.

## A BEGINNER'S GUIDE TO BEING POLITICAL

First of all, if you're not on the electoral register, get off your arse this very instant and do it. I mean it. Put this book down and go.

You might very well believe that there is no point in registering to vote because there is no one out there worth voting for, and that is an entirely understandable argument. However, it is important that the powers that be know that your vote is up for grabs. If it is not, why should they represent your interests? The political parties can never evolve into something you'd be tempted to vote for if they know you wouldn't vote for them anyway.

There is a reason why, after the 2010 election, austerity measures hit young people to the tune of one third of their overall household income, whilst those aged 55–74 only lost 10 per cent. Cuts might have been announced by David Cameron under the slogan 'we're all in this together', but, on closer inspection, we definitely weren't. Some demographics were shielded from the worst of the measures. That's because during the preceding election only 32 per cent of 18 to 25-year-olds voted, compared with three quarters of 55 to 74-year-olds. Politicians will court the interests of whoever they think will keep them in power.

Once you have made it known you are a political animal, the next step is to make it clear which policies would win you over. Social media is a better forum in which to do this than most people give it credit for, as is writing to your local MP.

At the time of writing, the average local authority only spends a paltry 1 per cent of its overall budget on mental health. If you present to your GP with symptoms of any mental illness, whether that's mild stress or severe bipolar, the length of time you will be made to wait before receiving therapeutic care is dependent on how much money your local council has invested in counsellors, outreach programmes and therapy centres. Waiting times are at present anywhere between six weeks and two years.

Recently, a routine smear test revealed I had pre-cancerous cells on the lining of my womb. (I'm totally fine – this is more common than most people realize and affects around 2 per cent of British women.) The time from my diagnosis to being in a hospital with my feet in stirrups whilst an old Russian guy poked around and froze bits off my chuff spanned a total of one fortnight. I was mightily impressed with the wonder that is our glorious National Health Service.

However, I couldn't help but reflect on the difference between the response when my malady had been cancer-related and when I'd gone to my GP with severe episodes of panic and anxiety two years earlier. In that case, I had been put on a waiting list, received a preliminary assessment over the phone three months later and my first session of CBT after six months.

Incidentally, when I recounted this to a friend of mine who is young, liberal and usually very enlightened, she responded by saying, 'Well, I suppose if they'd left the cancer too long you could have died.' And therein lies the nub of the issue: there is still a widespread belief that mental illnesses can be pushed to the bottom of the pile because they aren't life-threatening. I didn't tell my friend that by the time I was able to access CBT, I'd reached a stage where I'd become suicidal, because social conventions categorize this as inappropriate dinner-party chat (although, interestingly, I was more than happy to speculate on the innermost workings of my lady parts moments earlier).

The urgency gap between mental and physical health isn't so much to do with perceived severity as it is to do with funding, however (although, conversely, you could argue that mental health doesn't receive as much funding because the people in charge of the purse strings don't consider it to be as important as physical ailments). For every tenner spent on mental health, £1,571 is spent on cancer. That's despite the numbers of people affected by mental illness being roughly equivalent to those who will develop cancer – both are one in three or four, depending on which study you read.

The relative lack of mental-health funding might surprise you, since whenever the Prime Minister is challenged on the issue of the crisis in psychological wellbeing amongst young people she usually responds by saying that the government has committed to investing £1.4 billion before 2020. This is, technically, true. However, there are a few things to consider that render it less impressive than it first sounds. Firstly, the promise was originally made in 2015 and £1.4 billion over five years isn't actually that much. To put it into context, Trident (our nuclear 'deterrent') will cost £10 billion over the same period. Secondly, the figure doesn't represent a direct investment as it is dependent on savings being made in other areas. Thirdly, we don't know the money is being spent wisely or effectively. Mental-health services are still stretched to the extent that the government aims to bring waiting lists for severe mental illness in children and young people down to eighteen weeks (eighteen weeks! That's approximately three times their summer holidays!) before 2020. So what, exactly, are they spending it on?

This brings me to the fourth and most important point: the £1.4 billion isn't ringfenced. This means local councils can apply for a chunk of it to support mental-health services in their area but, when they receive the money, they can decide how it is spent. This might explain why the *Guardian* discovered that after the first investment of £76 million between 2015 and 2016, only half of local authorities increased their spending on mental health in real terms. Ultimately, the funding situation boils down to this: the government is able to give the appearance of action without anything having to change in reality.

I met a woman at a conference who runs an organization helping people who have experienced psychosis get back into work or education. This is crucial work, since currently only 8 per cent of people who have had a severe episode manage to reclaim some vestige of the life they had before in the form of employment. Her organization was promised £10,000 – peanuts in the grand scheme of things – by the local authority and . . . it just never arrived. The relevant government department confirmed the funds were sent and as far as they were concerned they have invested that money into helping people with psychosis. Yet because it wasn't ringfenced, the money was somehow lost in transit.

So, as a citizen, what you should demand to know is this: what percentage of the council's health budget is dedicated to mental health in your area? How much of that money is actually getting to where it is supposed to go? And what specifically is it being spent on?

Whatever answer you may receive please read between the lines, question the statistics, look around you and listen to the stories of the people who are accessing the services the government claim to have 'improved'.

And finally, if you don't get the answers you seek, don't be fooled into believing you aren't making a difference when you tweet about it.

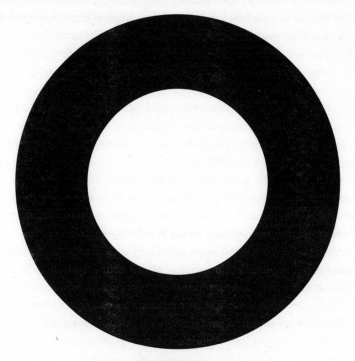

is for . . .

# OBSESSIVE COMPULSIVE DRIVE

**A friend once remarked to me that I essentially have two modes – busy or asleep. I've lost count of the number of times my husband has said 'Will you PLEASE come and SIT DOWN for TWO SECONDS?' or wrestled my laptop or phone from my vice-like grip as I protest that 'I've just got to finish this thing.'**

I find it almost impossible to sit and do nothing. 'Chillaxing' is an alien concept to me. I can do it in groups (I justify it as quality bonding time) or alongside a vaguely productive activity, like walking a dog or cooking, but in solitude I find the notion of pure relaxation perversely stressful.

As someone with a proclivity towards anxiety, I've lost count of the number of times I've been told I 'just need to relaaaaaax'. I've been instructed variously to take lengthy bubble baths, meditate, sit on the sofa and think of nothing, go out with no phone or other means of distraction and sit in a meadow, and other endeavours that, in my case, are akin to asking a fish to recite the complete works of Shakespeare.

A key component of the anxious mind is often a tendency towards perfectionism and to being one's own harshest critic. So, in a turn of events that would be dismissed as laughably 'First-World problem' by most, I began to berate myself for my inability to relax properly. As I sat trying to concentrate on my own breathing, legs jiggling, repeating my mental to-do list like a mantra, I'd see in my mind's eye the disapproving faces of my friends who, in their imaginary forms, were beseeching me to 'practise what I preach' and look after my own mental health.

Was I a hypocrite? According to some of the people I met at events, I was. 'Weren't you just in Scotland/Ireland/China?' they'd ask. 'How can you lecture on the importance of time and space for self-reflection, recreation and relaxation when you yourself hare around like the proverbial blue-arsed fly every hour of the livelong day?'

It was a valid question and it bothered me. It really did.

That was until I had the opportunity to interview a therapist specializing in anxiety, for a piece I was writing. He introduced me to the notion of obsessive compulsive *drive*. I told him about my incessant need to achieve, and how my studies in psychology had taught me that this was indicative of low self-esteem and would inevitably herald disillusionment, burn-out and despair.

'Not necessarily,' was his answer. 'You are a classic obsessive compulsive. You don't have the disorder, but your thinking is that of someone who has those tendencies. You could spend your entire life trying to fight it, but that would be exhausting. Instead, think of it as your driving force. It's an advantage. Without it, you wouldn't have done everything you have done.'

It's important here to highlight what he was careful to emphasize – that I don't have Obsessive Compulsive Disorder. OCD is a potentially crippling anxiety disorder that renders the person experiencing it often unable to function. It's characterized by the endless repetition of rituals, born out of overwhelming and mostly irrational fears (as described in *A: Anxiety*). Obsessive compulsive drive, conversely, is the need for perpetual activity and productivity. Some might describe it as being 'excessively driven'. Indeed, when I first told my mum about my interview she said, 'You have always been that way. All your life I've never had to nag you to do anything.'

Acknowledging my obsessive compulsive drive made my internal life so much more harmonious. My brain was no longer my enemy. I embraced it not just as an essential and indelible part of my nature but also as an advantage to being burdened with a life-spanning mental illness. If my achievements have come from my need to create the illusion of perpetual motion, and that is as much a consequence of my mental illness as the hours I've spent sweating and crying in a corner somewhere, on balance I'd say it was probably worth it.

This philosophy – the belief that there are two sides to the mental-illness coin – is by no means something I invented. The psychological anguish of the artist is, in particular, a well-trodden ideological path.

Here, in no particular order and selected from the available swathe for no other reason than I consider them each to possess extraordinary talent and brilliance, is a list of historical and contemporary figures of cultural significance who are known to have had mental-health issues: Stephen Fry (bipolar), Amy Winehouse (addiction, bulimia), Robin Williams (depression), Virginia Woolfe (bipolar), Winston Churchill (depression – or 'the black dog' as he called it), Sylvia Plath (what was then called manic depression and would now be called bipolar), Sinead O'Connor (depression), Adele (postnatal depression), Marian Keyes (addiction, depression), Nina Simone (bipolar), Zayn Malik (anxiety and eating disorders), JK Rowling (depression), Ozzy Osbourne (addiction), Donna Summer (depression), Elton John (bulimia), Tennessee Williams (depression, addiction), Carrie Fisher (bipolar), Ruby Wax (depression), Princess Diana (bulimia), Anthony Hopkins (addiction), Macy Gray (bipolar), Leonard Cohen (depression), Janet Jackson (anxiety, eating disorder), Ellen DeGeneres (depression), Bryony Gordon (OCD).

The first major research connecting creativity to mental illness was conducted in 1987, when Dr Nancy Andreasen at the University of Iowa demonstrated that there were higher instances of bipolar disorder in study participants who were part of a writers workshop at her university than in a control group. Ten years after that, Dr Arnold Ludwig at the University of Kentucky embarked upon a study that examined the relationship between mental illnesses and those who suffered from them having significant cultural influence. He concluded that, in particular, those illnesses associated with psychosis, like schizophrenia and bipolar disorder, are connected to a higher ability for creative thinking. He concluded it was because these illnesses affect the frontal lobe of the brain, where creativity dwells.

Since then, the perceived link between mental illness and creativity has been the topic of countless psychological studies. Scientists warn us not to mistake correlation for causation, which is to say that simply because many writers and musicians have had mental illnesses, it doesn't necessarily follow, as many have conjectured, that mental anguish is the price one has to pay for one's creativity. Indeed, as I'll explore later in this chapter, that's an idea that can be potentially dangerous, particularly if it leads vulnerable people to conclude that mental illness is in some way 'glamorous'.

There are a number of caveats that I'd apply to the conclusions scientists have reached. Firstly, Dr Ludwig's study was retrospective, i.e. he sought out influential cultural figures throughout history who had mental illnesses to prove his hypothesis and that's a technique fraught with all kinds of difficulty. Mental illness hasn't always been understood and talked about within the same frameworks, so we don't know that someone's experience of, for example, psychosis in 1848 is in any way comparable to someone's in 2018.

Secondly, a study of this nature is bound to be sprinkled with a hefty influence of confirmation bias. Look at the list of people I admire, above. I could have compiled an equally long list of musicians, artists and authors who haven't spoken openly about having mental-health difficulties. You could even argue that the reason I am drawn to those people and their work is because I identify with them as someone who has had mental-health issues myself.

Furthermore, as we've seen many times in the subjects we've covered so far in this book, 'mental health' covers such a wide gamut that it's a little silly to draw conclusions about causation. Linking creativity to mental illness is a bit like linking it to physical illnesses, i.e. spectacularly daft. If I'd said, 'Every influential leader throughout history had a physical illness at some point in their life,' your response would probably be a noncommittal shrug and a bit of an eye roll. Here, knowing that one in three people will experience a mental illness, we should arguably do the same.

Those who beat the 'mental illness equals creativity/success' drum also fail to take into consideration that the chain of causation might work the other way around: if a person operates within a sphere of creative types it is likely that they will feel more able to speak openly about something considered to be peripheral or even unacceptable by mainstream society. Likewise, if you have already achieved an element of success, you may feel that your power and influence is such that admitting to having mental-health difficulties won't damage your reputation or career too severely.

It is just as likely that we have failed to comprehend the true scope of mental-health difficulties as they are experienced by all sections of the population. It's therefore more helpful to think of creative people as spokespeople for humanity than as a peculiar species in their own right.

I spoke to my friend, author Kelsey Osgood about this. Kelsey spent her teenage years in various hospitals across the United States as a result of severe anorexia nervosa. The experience left her with strong opinions about how the medical system gets it wrong when it comes to mental illness, about the double-edged sword of awareness-raising initiatives, and the dangers of contagion.

Unsurprisingly, Kelsey isn't taken with the notion that there are always 'advantages' to experiencing mental illness. She thinks that the fact we don't tend to aspire to 'normal' is a large component in what stops people with delusions of creative genius from seeking help. She says, 'When I was a teenager, I felt like mental illness was shorthand for depth of character, intelligence, creative ingenuity. In a way, I expected my illness to do the work of being creative for me. I didn't have to work hard at being a student or writing – I could just be depressed and my output would automatically look like Sylvia Plath's. Of course, it didn't work that way.'

Naturally, Kelsey is viewing the topic through the prism of having spent a lot of time with people in the grip of anorexia, and a belief that one is 'special' is widely acknowledged to be part of the pathology of that illness. Indeed, Kelsey believes her own ability to recover was an acceptance that she was 'capable of navigating the mundane and often difficult tasks of life.' She concludes that 'All geniuses are a bit mad but it doesn't therefore follow that all mad people are geniuses.'

Kelsey describes herself as 'recovered' rather than 'in recovery' from anorexia. She has left her illness behind completely and has said publicly that the widely held belief that eating disorders stay with you forever is borrowed wisdom from the twelve-step programme, which was designed for drug addicts and alcoholics and is not always directly applicable.

For my own part, however, reconciling myself to the fact that my anxious nature is something I will never be completely free from has been an important component of my recovery. I feel that too often mental illness is presented in one-episode chunks – stories of people who used to be ill but are now better and, apparently, happy ever after. The influence of mental illness upon my life has been much more wave-like in its nature, and there is comfort in knowing when I am struggling that the experience is transient. There is also comfort in the idea that when I am well there is no pressure on me to find ways to cling on to that feeling forever, for that is an impossibility.

Whatever I am going through, whether positive or negative, I am consoled by the notion that it too shall pass. Being introduced to obsessive compulsive drive also impressed upon me the hopeful prospect of a future advantage in some of my darkest hours.

## A BEGINNER'S GUIDE TO HARNESSING
## YOUR OBSESSIVE COMPULSIVE DRIVE

Like the vast majority of things in life, there are multiple ways one can perceive the spectre of one's own mental illness, and the 'right' one is simply that which works for you.

If, like me, you find that your life has more meaning and you are able to function more effectively if you believe that your mental illness has unlocked a psychological or behavioural advantage in yourself, then that is a valid opinion. I would advise caution here, however, in how you might frame that view when speaking to young and/or vulnerable people.

Teenagers often ask me if I regret all the years I spent bingeing and purging during my teens and early twenties. The answer to that question is of course an unequivocal 'yes'. I lost seven of what should have been, by all accounts, the 'best' years of my life. Eating disorders already enjoy an entirely inaccurate reputation for being aspirational. It's irresponsible to fuel that fire. Yet I cannot deny that perhaps part of my obsessive compulsive drive is rooted in the desire to make up for those lost years, and perhaps that might give anyone currently wrangling with their own demons hope.

The crucial thing that is often missed when discussing the 'advantages' of mental illness is that artists, musicians and writers with experience of poor mental health generally produced what are widely acknowledged to

be their best works when they were well. This tells us that, just as Kelsey points out, wellness is something actively to aspire to and recovery is usually tied up with some semblance of routine or what could broadly be termed 'normality'. Yet it also tells us that mental illness can leave us with a little brain-bag of dark and dramatic emotions and sensations to root around in and draw inspiration from, when we are well.

I've concluded that perhaps it is the recovery process, rather than mental illness itself that gives the advantage. Going through recovery forces you to understand yourself and your behaviours better. It gives you an understanding of psychology, which in turn helps in understanding other people. After recovery, people are often left with added empathy and a desire to be helpful.

Most crucially, recovery allows you to separate out which traits belong to your illness and which are your own idiosyncrasies and therefore fundamentally imbedded into the fabric of your unique personality. Whilst the former should be fought, the latter should be embraced. And if you can find a way to use the latter so that it makes you and the people around you happier, so much the better.

is for . . .

**PSYCHOSIS**

**Of all the symptoms of mental illness, psychosis (hearing voices having hallucinations, or having paranoid or delusional beliefs) is perhaps the most commonly referenced. So it's peculiar that the nature of psychosis continues to be chronically misinterpreted and misunderstood.**

Technically, 'psychosis' is an umbrella term meaning a 'distortion of reality'. It is not a mental illness in its own right, but rather a symptom most often experienced by people who have bipolar, cyclothymia (like bipolar but with less severe symptoms) or schizophrenia. Psychosis can also occur as a result of extreme stress, lack of sleep or drug use. It's most common in people aged between fourteen and thirty-five.

'Psychosis' has a phonetic problem, in that it begins with 'psycho'. People are naturally afraid of it and think it denotes 'proper' madness, as opposed to more common-or-garden mental-health issues like anxiety. That the media portrays psychosis as being inextricably linked with acts of terror that the perpetrator believed they have been instructed to carry out by God certainly doesn't help.

In fact, research shows that an episode of psychosis can affect anyone and that most people recover fully. Like all things, psychosis exists on a spectrum. If you have ever been bedbound with flu and been convinced that there was someone in your bedroom only to realize later that you were entirely alone then you could technically be described as having experienced a very small episode of psychosis.

Any enduring problems with, for example, being employed or sustaining a relationship are more likely to be side effects of antipsychotic medication than a direct result of the psychosis itself (see *D: Drugs*). In some cultures where there is a more commonly accepted belief in other spiritual dimensions, psychosis is seen as a gift, in that it enables the person experiencing it to converse with the dead or metaphysical beings.

In many ways, psychosis is emblematic of the conflict at the root of all debate around mental illness – is it 'madness' or simply a way of experiencing reality that differs from the accepted norm? In diagnosing and treating mental illness are we simply forcing people to conform to a certain way of thinking and behaving that fits established social protocols?

In chapter *B: Brain*, I wrote about how we take in around two million pieces of information per second but are only consciously aware of between five and nine. I also detailed how, by the time the brain reaches maturity, it gives more information to itself than it receives from the outside world. In that context, it's not outside the realms of possibility that people experiencing psychosis are just seeing or hearing a different corner of the available reality.

I am, however, a massive hippy at heart and I know these aren't views that would necessarily be shared by most medical professionals. Ultimately, the real question is how much distress is being felt by the person experiencing psychosis and how far is it impacting their ability to function. In my experience, this usually boils down to whether they are able to distinguish what only they can see and hear and acknowledge that it doesn't match everyone else's agreed reality. This is trickier than you might imagine.

Studies have shown that when we hear a sound a completely different part of our brain 'lights up' than when we recall that sound. Logically, it should therefore follow that if a voice is 'in your head', the part of the brain being stimulated is the same part that hears echoes of remembered sounds. However, during an episode of psychosis, the exact same part of the brain comes online when the person 'hears voices' as when they hear any other sound. In layman's terms this means, to that person, what they are seeing or hearing is just as 'real' as anything else.

## BIPOLAR/CYCLOTHYMIA

These conditions were once referred to as 'manic depression' because their defining characteristic is dramatic mood swings – periods of mania followed by periods of severe depression.

When a person is manic they tend to have excess energy and will find it impossible to relax. They'll often find that they require much less sleep than usual. They might seem both incredibly cheerful and upbeat and simultaneously irritable, speaking and moving more rapidly than usual. They are likely to lose their inhibitions, which is why both sexual promiscuity and a tendency to overspend are both symptoms associated with the condition.

Mania also causes grandiose delusions and a lack of concern for personal safety. People who are manic tend to think they are invincible. Because they are spontaneous and prone to adventure, manic people generally represent a 'good night out' and tend to be popular. However, you'll often hear them say that they have difficulty sustaining friendships. This is because what goes up must, inevitably, come down, and mania is followed by depression. This is the same as 'regular' depression, which means that bipolar is often initially misdiagnosed.

## SCHIZOPHRENIA

This is a term still used interchangeably (and totally erroneously) with having a 'split personality'.* In fact, it simply describes a psychotic illness in which symptoms have been present for a period of more than six months. Over the past decade, diagnoses of schizophrenia have reduced. Experts have theorized that this is because of the decreased stigma around psychosis, which allows people to seek help earlier and thus improves their chances of making a swift and full recovery.

## WHAT CAUSES PSYCHOSIS?

At its root, psychosis is caused by a combination of underlying vulnerability and increased stress. Vulnerability is most often the result of past trauma. When we think of 'trauma' we tend to conjure up images of abuse or living in a war zone, and whilst these would probably make a person vulnerable, more common occurrences like bullying and bereavement can also cause trauma. Ultimately, it depends on the broader context of that person's life experiences. Lack of 'attachment' (feeling supported and cared for during formative years – see *Y: Young People*) can also make a person vulnerable.

Additionally, there is a genetic element. You can't 'inherit' psychosis in the same way you can with physical conditions, but it has been shown that people who have a parent affected by psychosis are more likely to develop it themselves. With schizophrenia, for example, the risk across the general population is around 1 per cent, but for people with a close relative who has the condition this jumps to 6.4 per cent.

Some assert that cannabis use 'causes' conditions like bipolar. I'll explore this more fully in chapter *W: Weed*, but it isn't that simple. Cannabis affects levels of dopamine in the brain, which is essential to healthy function and has a role to play in all mental illness. Therefore, if you have a personal or family history of psychosis, you should probably avoid using cannabis, but it is a catalyst more than it is a cause. Hallucinogens and stimulants can also produce symptoms similar to psychosis, i.e. seeing or hearing things others can't, and have been shown to trigger enduring mental-health problems when there is an existing underlying vulnerability.

---

*At the time of writing, there is a lot of debate over whether personality disorders should be placed under the umbrella of 'mental illness', or are conditions in their own right. I have elected not to include them in detail in this book, firstly because I don't feel as though I have done a sufficient amount of research into them and secondly because, whilst they are undoubtedly related to mental health, they probably deserve a book of their own.

## A BEGINNER'S GUIDE TO PSYCHOSIS

It's pretty much impossible to predict whether or not a person will experience an episode of psychosis. If it has happened to you already and you therefore know you have a vulnerability to psychosis, ongoing management is all about recognizing and dealing with the early signs. Use regular self-care to minimize stress (see *S: Self-Care*). If you have bipolar or cyclothymia recognize that, whilst mania feels good at the time, there is just as much need to curtail and minimize it as there is depression. Stabilizing your mood reduces the risk of psychosis.

If you see or hear things you know others can't, but they aren't distressing to you and you're able to function effectively, it's still important to have some medical supervision. Build a safety net so that if your symptoms change there are interventions already in place. Remember that psychosis is more treatable the earlier it is identified.

It's also crucial that the people around you understand how to support you. Some local authorities have early-intervention teams that work with families where one or more people have had an episode of psychosis so that everyone knows what they can do. It's worth asking your GP what's available.

If you are communicating with someone experiencing psychosis, the most important thing to acknowledge is that what a person sees, hears or touches during the episode is real for them and that what they are saying makes sense to them. Straightforwardly challenging their world view is therefore only going to result in further confusion and potential conflict.

If someone seems to be in the grip of a belief that seems nonsensical, paranoid or delusional, I have often found it useful to calmly ask the person how they got there. In talking through the process that gave birth to the unusual thought, you'll usually be able to identify where they took a 'left turn'.

It's important to be authentic in all communication, so never agree that you can see or hear something if you can't. However, do acknowledge that they can and don't laugh or ridicule them, however ridiculous their beliefs might seem to you. For example, if someone asks you if you can 'see those demons in the corner', an appropriate response would be, 'I can't see them, but I believe that you can.' You can then move on to unjudgmental listening techniques (see *U: Unjudgmental Listening*) by asking an open question like 'what are they doing?' or 'describe them to me'.

is for . . .

QUEER

**At the time of writing, I have been reliably informed by my friends who campaign in the area that the most acceptable term for the community of people who have an 'alternative' sexuality (by which I just mean 'not straight and/or cisgender'\*) is LGBT+. This stands for lesbian, gay, bisexual, transgender, with the plus sign in recognition that there might be people who aren't necessarily straight who don't fit neatly into any of the aforementioned categories.**

Increasingly, I see LGBT+ people describe themselves as 'queer'. I love the word queer for a multitude of reasons. First and foremost because, much like 'mental', it was once a word used to denigrate the people it described. Queer's original meaning is 'abnormal' and it was often used euphemistically to describe gay people, usually in hushed tones, before even having such a conversation was considered socially acceptable. The word has now been reclaimed. Hurrah! I also love it because it is only one letter different from 'Queen' and for that reason I associate it both with Freddie Mercury and with a sense of defiance and pride. We're here. We're queer. Get over it.

Sexuality, gender and mental health are inextricably linked (see *X: X Chromosome* for some thoughts on traditional male and female gender identities and their impact). A shocking 48 per cent of transgender people have attempted to take their own life. Depression is four times more prevalent in LGBT+ people than it is in the wider population. According to the *Guardian*, 86 per cent of the people who work at Stonewall, an organization dedicated to campaigning for equal rights for LGBT+ people, have experienced mental-health issues.

The traditional (and valid) argument has always been that homophobic bullying is to blame. We know there is a direct, empirical link between bullying and depression. Being a victim of bullying doubles your risk of developing depression in later life. Whilst homophobic bullying undoubtedly plays a role, the term does conjure up an image of something that is both deliberate and affirmative. Having dedicated the past year to researching the link between sexuality and mental health, I have concluded that there is something more subtle and, in many ways, sinister going on.

All human beings, regardless of race, age, background, gender or sexuality have five fundamental human needs. Without having these needs

---

\*Cisgender is the term used to describe people whose gender matches their sex, e.g. they were born with female genitals and identify as a woman.

met, it is largely impossible to attain or sustain good mental health. These needs are:

- Love

- Belonging

- Purpose

- Achievement

- To be heard and understood

It is, I believe, that second need – belonging – that LGBT+ people are at much greater risk than straight people of not having met. (Interestingly, immigrants are also at greater risk of not having this need met and also suffer disproportionately with poor mental health.)

Some people, let's call them 'homophobes', ask why gay people 'insist' on talking about their sexuality 'all the time'. After all, the homophobes reason, if they were asked to give three pieces of information about themselves one of them would not be 'I'm straight', so why the need to make these constant references? These types of people also tend to conclude their thoughts with the phrase, 'I don't care what they do as long as it's behind closed doors.'

Anyone with any sense of compassion can see that the reason LGBT+ people have to come out not just once but over and over again in various social and professional situations as they progress through life, is because they live in a world where, tragically, they have to check that they are accepted. Our sexuality, whilst it does not completely define us, is a huge part of who we are. In order to feel that we belong, we must therefore know that our sexuality is acknowledged and accepted by the people around us. If you are straight, you can assume your sexuality is accepted and so you don't need to declare it in the same ways.

The upshot of all of this is that, the way things stand at present, LGBT+ people cannot truly have their essential 'belonging' need satisfied until they have come out. Of course, they shouldn't have this obligation placed upon them. If you want to declare your sexuality to the world in an act of celebration, that's brilliant, but no one should feel compelled to do so. Unfortunately, in the absence of actively telling people you're LGBT+, it will be assumed you are straight and, as such, you are automatically living a lie – a state that is not conducive to the enjoyment of good mental health.

The problem here is a little bastard of a thing called 'heteronormative assumption' and it is, in many regards, even more damaging than homophobic bullying. People tend to assume everyone they meet is straight, cisgender, wants to get married and have babies unless they are specifically told otherwise. This isn't helped by advertising that, in deference to the fact that the majority of the population identify as straight, often use the concept of heterosexual sex to sell products that have no relation whatsoever to sex or romance. Thus, a repetitive unconscious narrative is created whereby these biases are constantly confirmed.

In a school setting, where I spend the majority of my time, heteronormative assumption manifests itself in the 'LOOK! THIS PERSON HAS COME OUT' year-group assembly. One very brave person in Year Nine (I don't know why it's Year Nine, but it always is) comes out, usually as gay. The school is then seen to 'panic' in the eyes of their students. An assembly is hastily organized, during which a representative from an LGBT+ rights organization is called in to emphasize the importance of not being homophobic bullies.

Now, this assembly is necessary and homophobic bullying is a topic that can and should be tackled with children as young as possible (see below for more thoughts on this). The problem here is the lack of any preceding context. For many of the pupils in the assembly, this will represent the first time they have heard about LGBT+ issues in anything other than a negative way.

For the person who has come out, they have effectively just had a spotlight put on them. It's likely to be a fairly emotionally turbulent time for them anyway and the creation of an event where everyone is aware that they are coming together as a direct result of them is likely to make them feel even more scruntinzed and isolated. It creates unnecessary drama. For the estimated 10 per cent of the rest of the year group who are LGBT+ but haven't come out, the message is 'LGBT+ people inevitably endure a lot of shit', which is likely to lead to increased fear and apprehension about not being accepted.

And it's that 10 per cent who are the crux of the matter, really. Statistically, one in ten people will self-identify as LGBT+. Within the context of a still very homophobic society that's a conservative estimate. In an average classroom of thirty students that is three young people. That's five people in the pub, sixty people in your office block, six people in a crowded Tube carriage. LGBT+ people are part of our communities and it's incumbent upon everyone to let them know that they are welcome. This is, like so many things in this book, often just a simple case of language.

I still clearly remember the lesson in which our rather brilliant drama teacher, Dr Peter Cochran, casually said whilst we were rehearsing Shakespeare's *The Merchant of Venice*, 'Of course, Bassanio is bisexual, like most intelligent humans are.'

This was in 1997, six years before the repeal of Section 28, a disgusting piece of legislation introduced by Margaret Thatcher a decade previously, dictating that no teacher could 'promote' homosexuality in the classroom. Dr Cochran has passed now, so no one can come after him retrospectively for breaking what was, at the time, the law. Contrary to what Thatcherites feared, his statement didn't immediately turn us all into lesbian nymphomaniacs because, as we now know, sexuality isn't a choice.

What it did do, however, was make the gay and bisexual pupils in our class feel acknowledged and accepted. I know because I was one of them. Sort of. I've done a quick calculation and 17 per cent of the people I've had a sexual relationship with during my life have been women. I sometimes self-describe as bisexual, because it's the closest available thing to an accurate label, although I suspect I'm probably representative of quite a large number of women who identify as broadly straight and 'dabble'.

Even though I've always known I'm not gay, I had anxiety about my occasional attractions to women from a very early age. I remember vividly a picture of Dannii Minogue on the front cover of pop magazine *Smash Hits* giving me peculiar feelings at the age of ten. This was a full year before my first proper boy-crush (Taryll Jackson from 3T, in case you're wondering).

I went to a fairly progressive all-girl secondary school, full of broad-minded-for-their-time, middle-class, boho-yup-yup types. I dread to think how all-consuming my worries about my not-quite-average sexuality would have been if I'd gone to the co-ed comprehensive down the road, where I regularly saw pupils being caught in headlocks and kicked over the yellow lines by the railway tracks for perceived transgressions like giving their friend of the same sex a hug.

This brings me to the topic of 'banter'. I've come to understand that 'banter' means different things depending on who is using the term. For example, I do some work with the Men and Boys Coalition, an organization dedicated to reducing the suicide rates amongst men and to finding out why working-class white boys underperform at school compared to their peers. When the Men and Boys Coalition say 'banter' they mean the way masculine-minded people use humour to test the safety of discussing certain potentially thorny and emotionally difficult topics. I don't mean that sort of banter, which can be used in positive ways.

When I say 'banter' I mean the sort of language or behaviour which would, in any other circumstances, be called plain old-fashioned bullying or harassment. 'Sorry I touched your arse in the lift! Banter!' 'I didn't mean to call you a poof in front of the entire rugby team! Banter!' 'Come on mate, stop complaining, it's banter!' When 'banter' is used in this way, it's implied that any consequent upset is indicative of the victim being oversensitive rather than the perpetrator being a total knobcheese.

Homophobic 'banter' is still incredibly prevalent and it's mostly not categorized as bullying because it doesn't tend to have a direct target. Calling a salad a 'gay' choice of dinner, for example, isn't going to hurt the salad's feelings. It is, however, most often said with disdain, as though the salad isn't 'real' food, implying it's a poor choice compared to other, heartier, more delicious, straighter things. Bearing in mind that LGBT+ people are everywhere and the speaker might not be aware of their presence, this kind of insidious rhetoric has huge potential for damage.

I heard an interview with one of the few openly gay football players on the radio once, in which he said when he came out to his teammates they all immediately apologized for their previous locker-room 'bants'. If they knew he was gay, they maintained, they never would have said some of the things they did. I'm sure they didn't mean it in that way, but what I heard was his teammates telling him their homophobia was his fault.

'Why didn't you tell us?' is the last refuge of a person who has realized they have been a douchenozzle. 'I'm so sorry for how I acted' would have been a much better response.

We're none of us infallible. I'm sure there is terminology I have used or opinions I have expressed in the course of this book that I will, at some point in the future, owing to having gained a better understanding, come to see as unacceptable. But I'm always coming from a place of kindness. And I'm prepared to listen and to change. That's all anyone can promise.

## A BEGINNER'S GUIDE TO BEING QUEER

I read a fantastic book when I was at university called *Sugar and Slate* by Charlotte Williams, which made me think about identity. Charlotte grew up in a small Welsh mining village with a white mother and a black father orginally from Guyana, who was often working away in north-west Africa.

Being the only visibly mixed-race children for miles, Charlotte and her siblings never felt as though they entirely fitted in, in Wales. Similarly, when she accompanied her dad on work trips to Africa, the very dark-skinned children in the particular region where he worked used to point at her for being lighter-skinned than they were. All Charlotte's life, she thought if she could just get to the West Indies she'd finally feel at home. When she finally made her pilgrimage to the Caribbean she had the realization that, actually, she's Welsh.

It was an important and necessary journey for the author to have gone on, but it does highlight the danger of believing that if you can just [insert x] everything will fall into place. To come out, or transition, or to find a community of people who understand you are all huge, monumental, life-changing things. But at the end of it you'll still be human and life will still throw you curve balls and challenges. Things won't be perfect. They never are.

Equally, you might feel a sense of anticlimax. I referred to myself as bisexual during a speech in Parliament once and didn't get chased out with pitchforks or anything. In fact, no one batted an eyelid. I was half incredibly encouraged and half disappointed – not because I wanted the people governing our country to be intolerant, but because it was a momentous moment for me to self-describe in such a way and the lack of drama, or even any acknowledgment, didn't match up.

Try not to be angry with people for not knowing as much as you about gender and sexuality. It is frustrating and your anger is valid, but also consider that your circumstances have probably led you to research the issues and understand them in more depth. You're going to need patience when you're explaining that sex lives between the legs and gender between the ears for the eighty-seventh time, but if it helps one person become better informed and more tolerant, it's worth it.

I always advise people who say to me they're confused about which pronouns to use, or how they should treat their LGBT+ friends, to simply ask their friend if there is anything they can do to make their life better. Consider changes the people around you could enact that would make you feel included and respected, so you're prepared for this question.

Equally, however, don't feel you have to be the ambassador for 'your people'. The only person's feelings or experiences we can ever know with any real, meaningful reliability are our own. If someone asks you to answer on behalf of gay people, make it clear that they probably need to take a bigger sample size for whatever study they're trying to do. (This is, incidentally, something my mate Jake, who is gay and very active in LGBT+ campaigning, very lovingly and gently said to me the day I texted him saying, 'What about Ru Paul? Would he identify as gender fluid?'. Jake replied 'I am not the gateway to all gender labels. You need to ask Ru.' Fair point).

## A BEGINNER'S GUIDE TO SUPPORTING THE QUEER

It's not enough to not be actively vile to a person you know is queer. We are all responsible for creating the community in which LGBT+ people exist and it's our responsibility to ensure they know they are accepted, celebrated and belong.

### Step 1 – Don't make heteronormative assumptions

Unless you know for sure, don't assume the person in front of you is straight. Say 'partner' rather than 'husband' or 'wife'. Don't walk into a room of people who appear to be female and call them 'ladies' or 'girls' because some of them may be transgender. (Also, it's annoying and patronizing.)

### Step 2 – Get your terms right

There are important distinctions to be made between gender, sex and sexuality. Of course, in utopia we won't need labels and everyone can just be themselves without fear of judgment or needing to explain. Until that time, it's important to understand the technical meanings of different terms. As a general rule, remember that gender resides in the mind and sex resides in the pants.

**Gay** – attracted to the same sex; can be used to describe either men or women

**Lesbian** – same as above but usually only applied to women

**Bisexual** – attracted to people of different sexes

**Transgender** – the gender of the person does not match their biological sex

**Gender-fluid** – can present as either male or female

**Androgynous** – has both feminine and masculine physical characteristics

**Non-binary** – person who does not identify with either the male or female gender

### Step 3 – It's not about you. No, really. It isn't. Get over it

A few months back, I was watching an episode of *The Big Questions* or, as my husband calls it 'The Sunday Morning Shoutathon'. The show involves about five pundits discussing the big news stories of the week, only one of whom usually has anything that could be described as a 'balanced, reasonable view'.

In this particular instalment, the token reasonable person was a 25-year-old non-binary campaigner who asked to be called 'they' instead of 'he' or 'she' because they did not feel that 'he' or 'she' accurately described their gender identity. The only objection anyone could have to this is that the grammar is wrong. Other than that, the intelligent, human response is to say, 'Cool. I might slip up because I'm so conditioned into saying "he" or "she" but I'll do my very best to call you "they" from now on because it would make a tangible, positive difference to your life and makes absolutely sod-all difference to mine.'

Their opponent in the debate was a woman from some organization with 'Conservative' in the title who appeared to have styled herself, both physically and intellectually, entirely on Margaret Thatcher. I have never seen anyone so angry about anything. She was apoplectic, insisting in tones of increasing pitch and volume that there 'ARE ONLY TWO GENDERS AND LANGUAGE MUST REFLECT THAT REALITY.'

My question to that woman, had I been in the studio to ask it, would have been 'Why do you care so much?' Nothing, for her, had to change. She could carry on being a cisgender straight person in a Thatcher-style skirt suit with helmet hair for the rest of her natural days, completely unencumbered. No one was trying to take those rights away from her.

People are naturally reticent to change. But the next time you find yourself thinking, 'That's silly! PC gone mad,' consider where doing things the way we have always done them has brought us. In the case of our attitude towards and treatment of LGBT+ people, we have arrived at a point where they suffer disproportionately with the anguish associated with depression, suicidal thoughts and behaviours.

So, if an LGBT+ person says, 'By doing this, you can help me and people like me,' consider listening. Consider adopting the relatively tiny inconveniences making that change would involve.

Consider how much better the world would be if everyone knew they belonged.

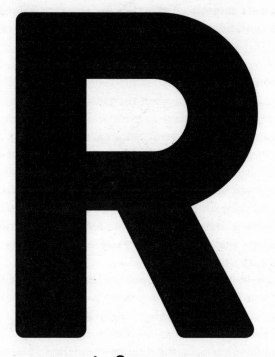

is for . . .
**RECOVERY**

**One of my closest friends is called Adrian Warwick. Adrian works in sales and he bears all the stereotypical hallmarks of his trade. His immaculate, slightly flashy attire and abundant reserves of confidence are sometimes mistaken for arrogance. Yet it only takes the most tentative scratch at his shiny surface to reveal a solid diamond.**

Adrian and I met in 2005, when my eating disorder had succeeded in consuming almost every aspect of my personality. I'd spend every night bingeing, purging and drinking to excess in a futile attempt to blot out the persistent, intolerable anguish tht characterized my existence. I'd snatch a few hours of poor quality sleep before getting a train from where I lived in Hertfordshire to where I was working as a legal secretary in Cambridge. The journey was about an hour and I was always so exhausted I'd fall asleep straight away, waking up a couple of stops before my destination and frantically wiping dribble from my chin, fixing my make-up and making plans to imbibe industrial amounts of coffee in an attempt to present in a suitable state for work.

I was newly single and, despite my enduring emotional turmoil, I couldn't fail to notice that, by the time I awoke, a tall, handsome, dapper bloke was usually sitting opposite me. He'd normally have a wry smile on his face, which I attributed to the almost-certainty that I'd been either snoring or muttering embarassing things in my sleep. I began to enjoy this this little routine – it represented a small slice of certainty in a life that was, at the time, defined by its chaos. I even spoke to some of my friends (or I should say drinking companions – I didn't really have any friends to speak of then) about him and we awarded him the hugely imaginative moniker 'Fit Train Man'.

One morning I woke up to find Fit Train Man wasn't there, which was more than a little disconcerting. I blinked in consternation, mentally chiding him for being so selfish as to have a day off, when I heard a voice say, 'So, do you like waking up next to me, then?' and realized I'd been asleep on his shoulder.

Yes, it was the cheesiest line that has ever been uttered in the history of humanity, but it was the start of an enduring friendship (once we had done the inevitable dating and realized we weren't romantically compatible, of course).

Six months later I moved to Cambridge in a bid to reduce my commute, but bulimia now dictated every waking decision and every unconscious action, meaning I wasn't a reliable or professional employee and the law firm let me go. I took a job waitressing (in a cocktail bar, whooaaa) and that's when my life nosedived with terrifying rapidity into an unmanageable clusterfuck.

I had no routine, no incentive to get out of bed in the morning and no sense of self-worth. All my spare money went on food and booze for binges. All my waking hours were spent in a vortex of self-loathing and self-medication. This made me toxic company. It wasn't that I was deliberately trying to be a dick, more that it was an inevitable side effect of not meaningfully inhabiting my own brain or body. I'd delegated control of myself to my mental illness. I had been relegated to passenger.

The initial part of my recovery involved enduring all the worst aspects of mental illness with the added effort of taking active responsibility for it. It was like walking into a room full of screaming, feral children who are hyperactively decorating the walls with their own faeces, and bellowing 'Right, I'm taking charge here, we're all going to calm down and clean this place up!' over the din. I was both the exhausted, world-weary adult and the inconsolable child for whom they were attempting to care during that time. Needless to say, it was less than fun for the people around me.

Recently, I asked Adrian why he stayed friends with me. 'Because you were always you,' he said. 'It was really hard to see sometimes. But I remember when I first met you I thought, "Wow. I'd better up my conversation game because this girl is really smart and interesting." And then I realized you had something special about you – something that was worth sticking around for. And I'm glad I did because . . . here you are.'

See, I told you he was a diamond.

Recovery is the gradual peeling-away of the layers of dysfunction and toxic belief that we initially adopt as coping mechanisms and which then gradually erode the self. In Adrian I'd found a friend who was able to see that there was a phoenix waiting to rise from the ashes of my mental illness. How he did that I'm not entirely certain. I was a right pain in the arse.

Recovery involves a combination of desperately clawing yourself out of a hole whilst learning the necessary strategies to ensure you don't slip straight back down again. Physically, I'd liken it most to the healing of a wound, in that mental illness always leaves indelible scars. There are two ways of thinking about this: either the scars are points of vulnerability – places where, if we aren't careful, we can be opened up again – or they are places where we have reinforced ourselves and have therefore become stronger. In my experience, they are simultaneously and paradoxically both.

For me and countless others I've spoken to, recovery has happened in stages. If the mental illness involves an element of addictive behaviours, as in the case of eating disorders, self-harm, drug or alcohol dependency, then the first step people usually take is to address them. Whilst this is an understandable approach, as we learned in chapter *J: Just Attention Seeking*, self-harming behaviours are often a coping strategy, and therefore seeking to remove them without addressing the underlying causes increases risk of suicide.

There's also the danger of simply replacing one unhelpful coping strategy with another. In chapter *F: Food*, I described how I glided seamlessly from anorexia to compulsive eating to bulimia. The emotions that fuelled my distress remained mostly consistent; it was the mechanisms by which I expressed them that changed.

Having said that, in the case of drug and alcohol dependency, it is usually necessary to stop the substance misuse first, since a person who is intoxicated cannot engage meaningfully with therapy. Similarly, people who are severely malnourished do not have the necessary cognitive capability to think clearly, which is why those who have had anorexia for extended periods of time are often force-fed before the recovery process can start in earnest.

Ultimately, whilst it is almost impossible to achieve in solitude, recovery is an incredibly intimate, personalized experience. Just as there are myriad ways for a person to be psychologically dysfunctional, there are as many ways to tackle it. It's futile, I believe, to argue about which methodologies are the most effective, when it's far more pertinent to ask what works for you.

## A BEGINNER'S GUIDE TO RECOVERY

I can only speak from what my personal and professional experience has taught me, but if you or someone you love is embarking on the recovery process, here are a few things I believe you should know.

### What's your 'primary'?

Mental illnesses tend to 'borrow' risk factors and indicators from one another. This means that if you saw a person's circumstances and symptoms written down, you'd be unlikely to be able to distinguish absolutely whether they had depression, anxiety, were self-harming or had an addiction issue. Similarly, long-term physical illness can lead to mental-health issues and vice versa.

This can present difficulty when it comes to finding the right help. A story I hear regularly, for example, is that of a person who is ping-ponging indefinitely between mental-health and alcohol-dependency services, since NHS mental-health services won't work with you until you stop drinking and (for reasons that are beyond me) alcohol-dependency services often won't treat you if they suspect that the reason you're drinking to excess is mental health related (which it usually is).

In private facilities, where they have sufficient time and resources to acknowledge that you're a human being and therefore quite complex, they speak in terms of 'primaries'. Do you drink because you are depressed? Or is your low mood a result of drinking too much alcohol, which is known to be a depressant?

It took me more than a decade to figure out that my eating disorder was a manifestation of underlying anxiety. As such, I went through a lengthy (and expensive) recovery process for bulimia that, whilst it did technically rid me of my eating disorder, didn't do anything to make me healthier mentally. If I had tackled the anxiety first it's likely that the eating disorder, which was my coping mechanism, would have responded better to the initial therapy I sought for it.

Identifying your 'primary' can be difficult, but it's worth investing some time in, particularly in a climate where your GP is likely to be so overworked and undertrained that they'll be guided toward diagnosis by whichever symptoms you are able to describe to them during your allotted six-minute slot (see *G: GP*).

### There's no magic cure

Recovery is rarely down to one thing. Medication might initially put you on an even keel, but it's not going to address the circumstances that led you to mental illness in the first place. The right therapist is a gift from the heavens, but their efficacy is increased a hundredfold if you have a supportive network of friends and family around you.

If a 'quick fix' seems too good to be true, it probably is. I misguidedly believed a practitioner when he told me that three sessions of NLP (neurolinguistic programming) was going to cure my bulimia. It appealed to me because he said they didn't want to know anything about my past, which in turn meant I didn't have to delve into difficult emotional territory. Whilst the combination of hypnosis and other techniques did abate my bingeing and purging for a good year, it wasn't long before I was back repeating those behaviours. That's not to say NLP has no value (see

*T: Therapy*) but I should have used it in conjunction with other, supporting techniques. NLP did sort out my superficial symptoms, but it left a bag of poison inside me. Sooner or later, something was going to pierce that bag and leave me full of toxicity again.

### It's like knitting

Too often, mental-health stories are presented in binary terms: here is a person who used to be really fucked up but thanks to [insert whatever medicine, therapy or vaguely hippie-esque wonder-technique here] they are now better! I have lost count of the number of times I've had to counsel a young person who is distraught because, having bought into the narrative that the options are either eternal illness or wellness, they think a setback in recovery has left them 'back at square one'.

As we go through recovery, we are learning through trial and error. Each stage leaves us with more information and psychological tools at our disposal than we had before. A setback, be it a drinking binge, an episode of self-harm or the odd day where getting out of bed seems like an impossibility, is therefore like 'dropping a stitch' in knitting. Just because the stitch has been dropped, it doesn't mean you haven't already knitted a row.

### Your social landscape will change

The vast majority of human communication is non-verbal and invisible to the naked eye. I like to think of it in terms of vibrating on a certain frequency, meaning that we will in turn attract people who are tuned into that frequency, a bit like the CB radios everyone used to have in the 1980s.

When we're in a dark psychological space, it isn't long before we find ourselves surrounded by people similarly burdened. They might not be ready or willing to get better and their presence in your life will hold you back. We're so conditioned into believing that 'true friendship lasts a lifetime', most of us think that losing friends represents a personal failure. Yet the fact that a former friend or lover's presence is no longer compatible with the person you want to be, or the life you want to live moving forward, doesn't diminish the relationship you had.

### Don't wait for someone else to save you

Being something of a closet romantic, I had various partners throughout my recovery who I fervently believed were going to make everything better. For me, my white knight and saviour wasn't someone who was going to relieve my financial burdens, or help me escape my wicked stepmother (chiefly because I don't actually have one), but a person who would provide the key to lasting mental equilibrium.

Infatuation is a powerful force. When you're in its clutches, everything else appears suspended in time. It's easy to mistake the heady combination of hormones and wishful thinking that characterizes the first throes of a romantic relationship for miraculous recovery. It isn't. Your problems will still be there waiting for you once the lust has worn off.

I, like everyone, am still very much a work in progress, but I don't think it's a coincidence that I met my husband at a time in my life when I had finally reached emotional self-sufficiency. After all, your partner should always be someone you want, rather than need, to be with.

You are going to need help, both personal and professional, in order to recover. Love, in whatever form, absolutely makes recovery easier and life more bearable generally. Yet the only person who can do it is you. There is both terror and solace in that notion. Choose to focus on the latter.

### It's an absence, not a presence

In the context of an aggressive, consumer capitalist culture (see *C: Capitalism*), the idea that you need something additional in order to 'achieve' recovery can be a dangerous one. It is yet another slosh of fuel on the fire of our unconscious beliefs around not being good enough and requiring 'stuff' in order to fix us.

For me, recovery was less about acquisition and more about absence. Slowly, I realized I was beginning to emerge. The pain diminished, the compensatory behaviours began to slow, the incidents during which I felt like I was watching myself act strangely or hurtfully dwindled, until I could finally breathe.

The best thing I can liken it to is bereavement. When you have lost someone, the heartache is so all-encompassing you cannot fathom that you will ever feel 'normal' again. Yet, one day, you realize you got through an entire morning without crying. Later, something makes you laugh. Whilst the pain will always lurk somewhere within you, eventually it becomes manageable and you are yourself again.

### There are three vital components

Almost everyone I've encountered who has been through recovery has found it entails a combination of at least three things:

**1.** Therapy and/or medication (see Chapters *D: Drugs* and *T: Therapy*)

**2.** A creative outlet

**3.** A supportive friend or mentor

Whether the people you choose to rely on socially during the stages of recovery are those who have personal experience or not is an incredibly personal thing. I found in relation to my eating disorder that there was value in talking to people who wouldn't normalize my problem by telling me they'd been through it, too. I wanted to be surrounded by people who thought making yourself sick was bizarre and illogical – something they could never imagine themselves doing in their wildest fantasies – to connect me to a vision of life outside my issue. When it came to anxiety, however, I needed friends who understood the abject horror of a panic attack and why someone as apparently 'confident' as me can be incredibly socially awkward.

### Recovery forces you to do what everyone should

Recovery involves understanding your drives and motivations and how they affect your emotions and behaviour. It necessitates understanding the impact you have on the people around you and the tools you are going to need to survive modern life. Ultimately, you emerge more 'sane' than people who never had a mental illness in the first place.

I'm wary of perpetuating the myth that mental illness is a 'blessing' (see *O: Obsessive Compulsive Drive*) but certainly, at least in the sense that it pushes you towards a process that will lead to higher levels of self-awareness, it's an advantage.

### Never give up

There's a lot of bad advice out there (see *I: Internet*). There's also a lot of good advice that simply won't work for you. Hardly anyone manages to stumble upon the exact combination that will facilitate their recovery first time round.

If you don't think your GP has the right training, ask to see another one. If your therapy or drugs aren't working, try a different type.

Above all, never give up on the belief that you can (and deserve to be) the very best version of yourself.

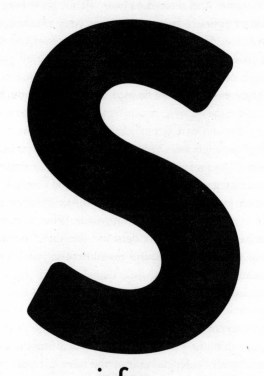

is for . . .

# SELF-CARE

**Georgia Dodsworth, otherwise known as the 'self-care queen' is the founder of worldofselfcare.com. She has a diagnosis of borderline personality disorder and describes how, although therapy has been helpful, it didn't prepare her for the everyday challenges of living with her condition. This in turn led her to discover the importance of self-care in both recovery and maintenance of good mental health. Georgia describes self-care as 'A daily practice of taking the time out of your everyday life to look after your mind, body, spirit and soul'.**

I feel compelled to begin this chapter by stating the following: you know those 'inspirational' memes on Instagram and Facebook? The ones that tell you how important it is to take some time out for yourself to relax and unwind – hashtag because you are worth it? I hate those as much as you (probably) do. Particularly when I'm feeling anxious and overwhelmed, I find them patronizing and can't help but detect a hint of accusation – a touch of 'if you just looked after yourself better you wouldn't be in this mess, would you?' sentiment. Like many modern phenomena, these snippets of online 'advice' represent a hugely watered-down version of what was once a valuable truth twisted, sugar-coated and commodified until they have become virtually unrecognizable.

Having said that, the fact is that self-care is a crucial building block of good mental health. So, let's not throw the baby out with our lavender-scented, relaxation-inducing bathwater.

### THE STRESS BUCKET

In 2002, Brabban and Turkington produced a diagram of a 'stress bucket' that is used by Mental Health First Aid England in their training. As an instructor for MHFA, I've shown the diagram to countless audiences of people from hugely diverse backgrounds and I've never met anyone who didn't relate to it.

The model works on the basis that we all have a stress bucket (or 'stress container' as you are advised to say when working with teenagers, since they seem think 'bucket' is a euphemism for vagina), the size of which differs according to our 'resilience'. Those who have experienced a large amount of personal trauma are likely to have a small stress bucket that fills up relatively easily.

It's important to acknowledge that stress is both inevitable and unavoidable. Mundane happenings such as a difficult professional or

personal confrontation, a household appliance breaking, a nightmare commute, a presentation to colleagues, the house being a mess – these aren't events that would engender too much sympathy from the casual observer, but they do represent a potential incremental rise in the amount of stress in the stress bucket.

If our stress buckets overflow, we potentially enter fight, flight or freeze mode (see *A: Anxiety*). Stress also causes our brains to flood with a chemical called dopamine (see *Y: Young People* for what this is and does). The net result of this is that stressed people cannot think clearly and generally do not make good decisions.

Another potential consequence of stress-bucket overflow is 'snapping', which is when we do or say things in the heat of the moment that we aren't particularly proud of and wish we could take back. This can, in turn, have a negative impact on our friendships and relationships. This is responsible for the 'straw that broke the camel's back' phenomenon whereby something that appears to be relatively insignificant engenders a disproportionate emotional response.

What healthy people have, therefore, is a tap on their stress bucket. This is a relaxing and/or endorphin-producing activity that they incorporate on a regular basis and that allows stress to drain out of the bucket, meaning that it never gets to the point of overflow. I realize I am making this sound incredibly simple – and indeed it is, in theory. However, human beings are infinitely complicated and will therefore find a hundred distinct ways to fuck up their own stress-bucket system.

One of the primary barriers to healthy stress-bucket management are coping strategies which 'block the tap'. Classic self-harming behaviours would be an example of this (see *J: Just Attention Seeking*). Self-harm is, in its most basic form, a survival mechanism – a way to temporarily alleviate stress. Whilst it brings a sensation of release, it also ensures more stress flows into the bucket, resulting in an overall excess.

Most people indulge in some form of tap-blocking behaviour in one form or another. If you cast your mind back to the last time you had a stressful day and think about what you did at the end of it, you'll be given a clue as to your instinctual coping mechanism. If it involved something that ultimately has a negative net impact, then your coping strategy is a stress-bucket blocker.

This book is a judgment-free-zone. I'm not for one moment suggesting the odd glass of pinot grigio or slice of chocolate gateau is going to kill you (unless you have severe allergies). The danger, however, is when sustained stress leads to unconscious coping mechanisms that are instinctually sought on a regular basis.

According to practitioners of CBT (cognitive behavioural therapy – see *T: Therapy*), it can take as little as two weeks of doing something regularly for the activity to migrate from the realm of the conscious (i.e. a 'decision' to have a glass of wine in direct response to stress levels) to the unconscious, where it becomes a habit. Once an activity is habitual and unconscious, its 'trigger' is no longer the difficult day, but rather a time or location. The unconscious brain associates, for example, being in the kitchen at seven o'clock with the wine habit. It sends an instruction to have the wine which feels like a compulsion. The willpower to avoid the habit dwells in the (much smaller) conscious mind. This is one of the mechanisms by which addiction can begin (see *W: Weed*).

You wouldn't wait until you were falling to begin building a safety net. Bearing in mind that we all inevitably encounter emotions that are toxic for our wellbeing, like anxiety and stress, it therefore follows that we all need coping strategies in place to deal with these. If we practise good coping activities regularly they will become unconscious, oiling the wheels of an effective stress-bucket management system (a bit of mixed metaphor here, but you catch my drift).

Self-harming behaviours like drinking, taking drugs or overeating are potentially unhelpful ways of seeking what are, in actuality, human needs. The first of these is distraction. We can't think about our problems all day – it would quite literally send us mad – so we engage in activities that focus us on the moment. However, distraction alone doesn't release stress. The second is self-expression. These are physical manifestations of our internal stress, so that you literally feel as though you have 'got it out of you'. The third is endorphin production (see *E: Endorphins*).

Creating an effective 'tap' on the stress bucket therefore involves identifying and incorporating activities that provide distraction, self-expression and endorphin production, but in a way that does not have harmful side effects.

## SPORT AND EXERCISE

Exercise is an obvious example of a healthy way to create endorphins. It's important, however, that there isn't a professional – or any kind of crushingly competitive – element to the physical activity. It's fine to be playing tennis and passionately want to defeat your opponent for the duration of the game. If, however, the victory represents your funding for the next year (because you're a professional athlete) or your parents' approval, or your sense of self-worth, that's a stress-creating, as opposed to a stress-bucket-emptying, activity.

I am not particularly good at sport. I'm quite strong and I 'throw like a man' according to my dad's rugby team (since they say this in an admiring way I have yet to give them a lecture on gender stereotyping) but I'm not by any stretch a natural athlete. For people like me, an element of self-care is being kind enough to allow ourselves to enjoy activities we aren't objectively 'good' at. In my case, that's sport. I'm never going to be the swishy ponytailed person, barely breaking a sweat as they effortlessly spring through the park on a run, but that's okay. As my mum says, 'you can't be good at everything.' It's only relatively recently I realized that shouldn't stop you giving it a go and risking making a tit of yourself anyway.

## THE ARTS

Distraction, self-expression and endorphin-production can also be achieved through music, drawing or painting, craft, creative writing, dance and other artistic endeavours.

In 2017, the All-Party Parliamentary Group on Arts, Health and Wellbeing produced a report exploring the psychological benefits of creative activities. In it, they acknowledge that 'wellbeing' is a difficult thing to measure. However, by collating evidence from a wide range of practitioners, they concluded that there is a consensus in the field of psychology that creativity is essential to mental health.

Art therapy is often used alongside more traditional methods to aid the recovery of people with mental illnesses. However, there is value in creativity for people at all points on the mental-health spectrum. This is not least because art and music are often more effective ways of articulating complicated emotions, given the inherent limitations of language. They represent a way to be heard and understood that transcends the confines and potential inaccuracy of words.

## MINDFULNESS

We tend to associate mindfulness with meditation and that is one way it can be achieved. However, the term 'mindfulness' is a description of a headspace in which one is neither dwelling on the past nor worrying about the future. It doesn't mean that you have no thoughts at all, but that the thoughts you do have are acknowledged and let go as opposed to 'locked down' and analysed.

The classic exercise done during 'introduction to mindfulness' sessions is to sit in a chair and focus on each part of the body in turn, beginning with the soles of the feet and the sensation of them against the floor. This is designed to turn focus to the realities of the moment and to quiet the part of our brain that is constantly spinning yarns, creating narratives around our experiences and trying to work out what it has learned in order to anticipate future challenges.

Mindfulness has enjoyed a huge surge in interest over the past few years along with an inevitable backlash, with seemingly endless arguments surrounding its effectiveness. Critics of mindfulness are usually people who have been told to go on a one-hour course as an antidote to their hugely stressful and demanding jobs and (understandably) remain unconvinced that 'feeling their feet on the floor' is going to combat this effectively.

Equally, a lot of teachers (also understandably) resent the idea that mindfulness is being presented as a sticking-plaster solution to record stress levels (according to the BBC, 70 per cent of teachers have had a physical- or mental-health issue they relate directly to the stress of their job in the period 2016–2017), as opposed to, say, reducing their workload. I get that.

None of this, however, means mindfulness isn't valuable. An essential component of mental wellbeing is to understand that there is no such thing as objective reality. The brain doesn't like incomplete stories, so fills in any blanks in our experiences to create stories that in turn inform our sense of identity. This began as a survival technique but in a modern context this propensity is likely to manifest itself in thought sequences such as, 'Sarah didn't put a kiss at the end of her text. Maybe it's because I was late sending her birthday card. OH GOD, WHAT IF SHE HATES ME AND IS AT THIS VERY MINUTE TALKING ABOUT WHAT A HORRIBLE PERSON I AM? WHAT IF EVERYONE IS ONLY PRETENDING TO LIKE ME?' Mindfulness represents a path out of this type of self-esteem-bashing inner monologue – a way to remind yourself that, right now, everything is okay. There is no immediate danger. You're fine.

### SLEEP

Getting the right amount of good-quality sleep is absolutely crucial to mental health. On average, an adult needs between seven and eight hours per night, with adolescents generally requiring slightly longer. Both too little and too much sleep can disturb our mental equilibrium.

You can never compensate for a lost night's sleep in a basic, transactional way. Each night's sleep is its own entity and as important as the one preceding and following it. There's a lot of evidence to show that inconsistencies in sleep patterns are as damaging as not getting enough and that the healthiest people go to bed and wake up at the same time, even when they have the day off work (which is, I must confess, a skill I have yet to master).

I like to think of sleep as 'worry flossing'. On a physiological level, it's when our nerve cells clean themselves. They cannot do this while we are awake. So if you're tired, you essentially have a dirty mind (snarf). In terms of learning, sleep is when information is 'downloaded' into our long-term memory banks. That's why it's generally more advantageous to get a good night's sleep before an exam than to spend all night up cramming. It's also when our unconscious untangles all our niggling anxieties.

The enemy of sleep is overstimulation. In recent years, this is most likely to be in the form of technology. Phones and tablets emit blue light, which in turn suppresses our secretion of melatonin, a hormone we need to drift off. It's recommended that we do not interact with any kind of technology, even television, for two hours before bedtime.

Some devices have an option to switch off the blue light, so that the screen takes on a kind of sepia hue, at a designated time. However, the intellectual stimulus we're exposed to on social media can still mean we are too anxious or overwrought to relax into sleep.

In some of the schools I visit, the parents of a year group have taken a joint decision to instil a curfew on phone use, putting all family smartphones on a charging doc in their kitchens overnight and banning them from bedrooms. That way, no one suffers from the dreaded FOMO (fear of missing out). This not only prevents anyone feeling singled out for punishment, it also presents a way to bypass feelings of guilt for not responding to messages or notifications. You're not ignoring your friends, merely adhering to a family rule about phone use.

## A BEGINNER'S GUIDE TO SELF-CARE

You may already be practising self-care without realizing. I tend to wake up a little earlier than technically necessary because I like to 'potter' in the morning. The first thing I usually do is put on a facemask which I keep in the fridge, because the coldness helps me wake up. I then put on a pot of fresh coffee, take a long hot shower and sit at a table by a window overlooking the gardens in our block of flats, before spending a good fifteen minutes carefully and slowly applying my make-up. This represents for me a glorious period of stillness before the inevitable mayhem of my day begins. Make-up application is one of my mindfulness activities. It's difficult to worry about anything else when you're trying to ensure your eyeliner isn't wobbly.

When I asked self-care queen Georgia Dodsworth about her forms of self-care she responded with similar suggestions:

> My simplest forms of self-care, of which I aim to practise at least five every day are: morning pages (stream-of-consciousness writing), taking a shower, brushing my teeth, getting dressed, having a cup of tea, listening to music, taking ten minutes to sit down and practise a guided mindfulness exercise, hugging a friend or a family member (human contact soothes me), drinking water, eating three meals per day, and smelling lavender.
>
> My advanced forms of self-care, which I treat myself to once I have practised the simplest forms, are: buying a bouquet of flowers, treating myself to a bar of chocolate, taking myself on a solo date to explore something I'm curious about, buying a facemask and booking a massage.

The barriers to the practice of self-care are pace of life and underlying feelings of constant, low-level guilt that can accompany it – the sense that there is always something more 'productive' and 'useful' one could be doing. Yet the best gift we can give ourselves is permission to carve out pockets of time in our day to do the things that empty our stress bucket in the knowledge that, without our mental health, any other achievements are meaningless.

is for . . .

# THERAPY

**Owing to the nature of my role as a campaigner, I am far more likely to hear about negative experiences of people with mental illness than positive ones. Please bear in mind whilst reading this chapter that thousands of people have accessed state-funded mental health services and found them extremely helpful. This does not represent my attempt to 'put you off', merely to highlight some of the issues with access to therapy within the National Health Service.**

### THERAPY ON THE NHS

As discussed in chapter *D: Drugs*, adequate therapeutic care is increasingly difficult to access expediently, free of charge. Most experts I've spoken with agree that, if the system worked perfectly, antidepressants would only be prescribed where therapy is either not an option or has not proven effective. In reality, you're much more likely to find yourself given a prescription for medication and put on a seemingly indefinite waiting list by your GP.

The length of waiting times depends on how much strain your local authority's services are under, as well as how urgent your case is deemed to be. The average is, according to the latest information garnered by UK-based charities, around six months. Half a year of emotional pain is an eternity.

At the time of writing, the government has just published a green paper proposing waiting times for young people with severe mental illness should never be longer than four weeks, and pledging to put this rule in place by 2022. Whilst this is, as my nan would (somewhat inexplicably) say 'better than a smack in the mouth with a wet kipper', it's been deemed too little too late by most mental-health campaigners.

What concerns me is whether the waiting time relates to the point between diagnosis and when the therapy actually commences, or just the 'initial assessment'. Before your therapy can begin, you'll be scheduled for an assessment, which will usually take place over the phone. During the conversation you'll be asked a series of questions designed to ascertain which form of therapy you will best respond to. You will then be placed on another waiting list for whichever therapy is thought to be most appropriate.

If you are under eighteen, you will be referred to CAMHS (Child and Adolescent Mental Health Services). If you are an adult and it is considered that short-term therapy is the best solution for you, you'll see IAPT' (Improving Access to Psychological Therapies) services. A complaint regularly made by service users is that the environments these therapies are practised in can be intimidating and unwelcoming, particularly in adult services. This has in turn led to a high proportion of teenagers 'dropping off the radar' as they transition between CAMHS and adult services (see *Y: Young People*).

However, interviewing some contributors from countries who don't have state healthcare has reminded me how lucky we are. Comedian Felicity Ward, who lives in Britain but is originally from Australia, popped up on Twitter once to chastise me for my constant rage against the NHS machine. She said, simply, that without NHS-provided CBT services prescribed for her severe anxiety, she wouldn't be here. Which brings me to . . .

## CBT

For the most common mental-health problems – depression, anxiety and stress – the NHS recommends Cognitive Behavioural Therapy. The aim of CBT is to identify patterns of thought and behaviour that are damaging to the patient and to change these using a combination of talking therapy (which is exactly what it sounds like) and consciously managing behaviour. CBT is appealing for a lot of people because of its 'one day at a time' philosophy. It has a knack of taking seemingly insurmountable issues and giving the patient control over them with easy-to-implement techniques.

I used some CBT exercises during my recovery from bulimia and found them incredibly effective. I was asked to keep a food/mood diary, which allowed me to identify patterns in my behaviour as well as 'trigger' foods, locations and times of day. I had to prepare distraction activities for the times and locations where I was most vulnerable and avoid foods that set me off on a binge–purge cycle.

I was initially alarmed by the idea of avoiding certain foods, not least because my experience of anorexia showed where excluding 'forbidden' foods could lead. One of the foods that would almost always induce a binge for me was bread, and the prospect of never eating it again disturbed me deeply. Happily, I only had to avoid bread for about six months in the end.

In order to prevent me bingeing, I was asked to always present my food in an aesthetically pleasing way, place my knife and fork down for three seconds between each bite, divide my plate into quarters and to leave at least a quarter of my meal.

As I typed the above, I realized that all of these behaviours have since become an unconscious part of my normal routine. It's a running joke amongst my friends that I refuse to eat snacks out of packets, preferring instead to decant them into an 'appropriate receptacle'. Similarly, I now habitually register if I am eating too fast (which usually indicates that I am anxious about something).

What CBT didn't help me with was anxiety. This could have been a reflection of the fact that I had a different therapist, who I didn't 'gel' with quite as well. In my own experiences – and this is of course by no means all-encompassing – I've found CBT to be naturally more effective for mental-health problems that have a strong behavioural element. Essentially, I found it much easier to physically put my knife and fork down than to let go of the worries in my head.

## PRIVATE THERAPY

Whether through choice or desperation, private therapy is becoming an increasingly popular option for those languishing at the pointy end of the mental-health spectrum. Once my NHS CBT practitioner declared that I was 'cured' of my anxiety (I wasn't), I went on the search for a private counsellor. I sought recommendations from my network and eventually found a person who I felt safe with and who 'gets' me (or at least does a great impression of somebody who does).

A quick note for anyone whose job involves a lot of dealing with humans in emotional difficulty: it's a really good idea to avail yourself of weekly therapy sessions if you can afford it. Therapists themselves have 'supervision', i.e. another therapist they visit to offload and ensure they don't absorb all of their clients' sorrow like a sponge and end up entirely mad and more than a little soggy. Since so many other jobs now involve an increasing element of social care, it's probably true to say we should all have this kind of supervision. You may even find that your employer will pay for it. (I am self-employed so my employer immediately agreed with me that counselling was a necessary expense.)

Here are a few things I consider noteworthy about the experience of having private therapy:

### More expensive does not necessarily equal better

I pay £75 per therapy session, which is about average. If a therapist is very expensive it simply means they are in demand. This might be because they are fantastically gifted at their job and have a success rate to match, or it might be because they're in a convenient location, or come up first on a Google search. Trust your instincts.

YES, THEY'LL HAVE THE 'PSYCHOLOGICAL INSIGHT', HOLD THE SELF-LOATHING DRESSING... AND A BOX OF TISSUES.

## Your therapist is not your friend

Because my work involves activism, lots of the people I meet are awesome human beings one naturally craves proximity to. It's therefore really difficult for me to distinguish a professional relationship from a friendship.

When it comes to therapy, however, it's important those lines do not become blurred. Most therapists will ask you to sign a contract, detailing what happens if you don't show up, or if you are clearly intoxicated. They'll also outline the protocol if the two of you see each other outside of therapy – for example if you bump into one another at the supermarket. Most therapists will agree to acknowledge you, but not to engage in any further discussion. Knowing you in context makes your therapist less good at their job. Knowing them in context means you will see them as a fallible human (because everyone is), which might make you trust them less.

## Sessions have time limits

There is an inherent imbalance in the dynamic when you see a therapist, in that you are often probing and recounting deep-buried, painful and traumatic experiences that have had a profound impact on your life while your therapist is having a normal day at the office. The first time your therapist says, 'Okay, that's fifty minutes and the end of the session,' it can seem heartless. Remember, though, that they have to keep to time.

It's also wise to prepare yourself for having an unresolved feeling of 'NNNNNGGGFFF!!' following your appointment. I usually have the urge to 'walk off' my counselling sessions and schedule in an extra half an hour to march around both determinedly and aimlessly until the uncomfortable sense of everything not being quite right with the world has subsided.

## Consider neurolingiustic programming

As well as CBT and talking therapy, an increasing number of private therapists practice NLP. This is, as far as I can tell, a combination of hypnotherapy and common sense. It works on the basis that we all have an inner monologue (true) and that these patterns of thought and belief systems can either work to our advantage or hold us back (again true). Practitioners of NLP hypothesize that the unconscious mind (comprising 91 per cent of our brain's capacity for thought, as detailed in chapter *B: Brain*) can be accessed using techniques such as repetitive positive affirmations, visualizations and hypnosis. This is where we enter more controversial territory.

NLP has an inconsistent evidence base. You'll usually therefore find people are either utterly convinced of its efficacy or declare it to be a load of old hokum more suited to a magician's act than a therapy room. (Derren Brown uses NLP techniques. I don't know what that proves.) I'm unusual, in that I remain unconvinced either way.

For me, NLP changed my understanding of my mind for the better and it also provided a temporary fix for some of my more toxic behaviours. For others, it has been transformational and life-affirming. My advice would be to suck it and see.

## Complementary therapies

'Alternative medicine' describes anything used in healing that has not been, or cannot be, proven to work using traditional scientific methods. For this reason, they tend to attract a lot of derision. Homeopathy, the process of distilling tiny amounts of medicinal substances into large amounts of water in the belief that it somehow 'increases' their strength, seems to attract the most scorn (and I understand why).

Having said that, I've had reiki (a sort of bizarre massage where the person conducting doesn't actually touch you) and it made me feel better. I don't know why, but being a pragmatic type, how something works is a secondary consideration after the fact that it does. My reiki practitioner told me that a healthily functioning body has one 'circuit' – a steady flow of energy that circulates around the body. In my case, according to him, I had two circuits – one flowing around my head and one around my body from the neck downwards. My mind and body had disassociated.

This happened just after my emergency hospital stay when my spleen exploded (see G: GP), an incident that was both traumatic and painful. It therefore made total sense to me that my mind would detach so it didn't have to acknowledge the realities of what was happening in my body. In fact, this 'disassociation' is an acknowledged side effect of trauma. The reiki practitioner had just found a different way of articulating that phenomenon.

Modern science is brilliant, yet a lot of the time it's just finding a way to place into empirical, measurable terms what wise people have mysteriously known for ages.

Complementary medicine probably isn't going to cure a mental illness, but it can boost mental health. Similarly, if relaxing, stress-bucket-emptying activities such as yoga, reflexology, acupuncture or Indian head massage help you successfully navigate your short time on this ludicrous planet, just do it. Western science will eventually, I am confident, discover in concrete terms why these things are much more beneficial than we originally gave them credit for.

## A BEGINNER'S GUIDE TO THERAPY

Countless studies have proved irrefutably that the most important component in ensuring efficacy in therapy is your relationship with your therapist, as opposed to the methods they practise. Like most things in life, the objective success of therapy depends on the immeasurable presence of 'connection'.

Just as with finding the right partner, finding the right therapist involves trial and error, effort and compromise on both sides, and you shouldn't hesitate to get out of the arrangement if it isn't working. Amie Sparrow, who works for Counselling Directory (a national database of therapists, giving details of their training, expertise, fees and contact details), told me that she didn't think it was necessarily helpful or relevant to get too bogged down in which discipline a therapist uses. She said, 'A counsellor isn't going to ask you what approach you want. It's kind of like going to a mechanic and asking what tools they use. The professional should look at your issues and personality and make a decision.'

Of course, it's important to ensure your counsellor or psychotherapist is a member of a regulating body. It's also worth noting that 'psychotherapist' and 'counsellor' are often used interchangeably and are roles that don't require a specific qualification (although they will have individual training), whereas psychologists and psychiatrists have completed specific training that allows them to use those job titles. All might be described as a 'therapist', rendering it a very general term that will have different meanings to different people.

How many sessions you need will depend on what you're seeking help for. Amie recommends finding a therapist with experience working with people who have similar issues. On the NHS, you'll generally be given six sessions of CBT. This isn't to say that you'll be 'cured' at the end of this process, or that you shouldn't continue if you believe there's more ground to be covered. It's a good idea to set down some 'markers' with your therapist, however, so that you can review your progress and identify anything that needs to be tweaked.

Ultimately, there aren't any rules when it comes to therapy, only guidelines, and there definitely shouldn't be any judgment. I have friends who get their fingernails buffed and painted once a week because it makes them feel better, springier and more able to take on the world. I choose to invest in a weekly session of exploring my brain with a professional for exactly the same reasons.

is for . . .

# UNJUDGMENTAL LISTENING

**The central conceit of this book is that English provides a limited and often inadequate supply of linguistic tools with which we can successfully navigate an issue as wide-ranging in its scope as mental health. Multiple and/or ambiguous meanings lead frequently to misunderstanding and miscommunication, which in turn hinders progress, education and recovery.**

I've discussed this with countless audiences of young people and adults from a huge variety of backgrounds and they always agree. Except for one fourteen-year-old, who stuck his hand up when I was mid-flow on the inherent frustrations of being an English speaker and said 'I don't agree'. I secretly love it when teenagers disagree with me, principally because it shows they're applying critical thinking skills but also because I revel in the sorts of juicy debates you only get in a school, college or university environment.

This pupil's hypothesis was that the stunted nature of the English emotional vocabulary is in fact an advantage, because it forces the speaker to elaborate and explain what they mean, thus encouraging exploratory mental-health-based conversations. This is an interesting point and, I grudgingly conceded, potentially correct. In theory.

His theory does, however, fail to acknowledge a few fairly major conversational obstacles arising from the nature of humans and, in particular, British ones. The first is that we are naturally fearful of anything unfamiliar or that might result in our discomfort. More often than not, when a person hints at some kind of vulnerability that might result in them 'causing a scene' or calling upon us to demonstrate skills we're not sure we are capable of, our instinct is to avoid the situation.

The second is our tendency to simply assume that people mean the words they are using in the same way as we would – rather than to enquire after the speaker's meaning. I watched an incredible lecture once, during a visit to an international college in Shanghai, by an English professor called Stephen Jacobi.

Working in an environment where everyone spoke a decent level of English but had been taught the language in a variety of far-flung locations around the world had shown Stephen the extent to which a group of people can hear the same word and extrapolate a large number of contradictory meanings. Some words depend on the listener having a certain cultural understanding. Others have negative connotations in some countries that inhabitants of others would find really difficult to fathom.

Stephen gave the humorous example of a child from Hong Kong asking him what 'bosom' meant. Take a minute to contemplate the word 'bosom'. On the most basic level, it just means 'breasts'. Yet it's more than that. The word conjures up images of the ample chests of milkmaid types with braids in their hair. A bosom is comforting and fleshy and abundant. A bosom is a place one goes to seek refuge. To be welcomed into the bosom of someone or something is to be accepted. There are all kinds of associations that simply saying 'tits' wouldn't adequately convey.

When it comes to mental and emotional vocabulary, the linguistic landscape becomes even more fraught with hazards because of the strong, individual associations we make with words.

Take, for example, the word 'grief'. Hailing, as I do, from the eqully glorious and ludicrous county of Essex, my mind associates 'grief' with minor quibbles resulting from disputes over a bill or stupid, drunken arguments in a pub near closing time. I hear it as 'that bloke in there was giving me a load of grief.'

Say 'grief' to a recently bereaved person, however, and it will most likely bring to the surface altogether different emotions. They'll associate it with their loss and the ensuing conversation will be influenced in no small measure by overwhelming and complex emotions that have been conjured up.

As if that wasn't enough to consider, there is then the way that people misuse clinical terms because they are the closest thing to an accurate description of what they have experienced. Let's take as an example 11 January 2016, the day I learned that David Bowie had died (and also, coincidentally, my husband's birthday). I should probably preface what follows by making you aware that 'fan' doesn't effectively describe my relationship with Bowie. It isn't unnecessarily hyperbolic to say that Bowie's music has saved my life on more than one occasion. If you are my friend, you will possess at least one homemade mix CD of Bowie tunes that I have agonized over, based on my understanding of your present musical taste, because that's how much I want you to love him too. For my first four years in London I had a shrine to him in my bedsit, which really freaked out anyone I brought home for shenanigans. My husband proposed in front of Hansa studios in Berlin, where Bowie famously recorded three of his most iconic albums. On the last UK-wide census form, when asked to state my religion, I wrote 'Church of Bowie'.

My husband was awoken on the morning of his forty-fourth birthday not by the brandishing of a cake and cheerful singing as would be customary, but by me trying to burrow into the crook of his armpit, letting out small, sniffly sounds and being, thanks to sodding Nigel, completely incapable of telling him what was wrong. After about five minutes he established that Bowie had died and I spent the remainder of the day, and indeed the following few weeks, feeling curiously empty. My overwhelming thought was that the world would now, in the words of Emma Thompson in *Love Actually*, 'always be a little bit worse'.

Now, what do you call that? I wasn't bereaved because I didn't know Bowie personally and to use that word would be grossly insensitive to the people who did. I wasn't 'depressed' in the medical sense – there was a clear and understandable reason for my sadness and it lasted an appropriate amount of time. I wasn't just 'sad', either. 'Sad' is when you realize you've missed the boat and that gorgeous pencil skirt you saw in the window of Topshop has sold out. Or, perhaps more relevantly, when a well-known figure you quite admired but didn't actively adore dies.

'Devastated' suggests that I was rendered incapable of functioning, or that my whole life immediately went to shit, neither of which is true. Plus, it's melodramatic in a way I'd find irritating if I heard someone else use it in that context.

If I didn't work in the sphere of mental health, I'd probably settle on 'depressed' as being the best approximation of my feelings over the loss of Bowie. Yet if I said it within earshot of someone with experience of clinical depression, they'd understandably take umbrage.

The conclusion we can draw here is that if someone says to you 'I feel depressed', you probably have no idea what they mean. The statement could be used to indicate anything from 'my favourite character in *TOWIE* has just left the series and I'm kinda bummed' to 'suicidal'. Or any myriad, uniquely tailored meanings in between those two psychological standpoints.

The act of non-judgmental listening is, at its core, simply an attempt to attain a better comprehension of what the other person means by the terms they are using, knowing that it is unlikely their understanding will match yours. Of course, it means not actively judging by saying things like 'what do you have to feel depressed about?' or 'you should go and live in a country where they don't even have food to eat', or some other relativist, dismissive hokum, but it also involves a desire to truly gain a compassionate understanding of what has brought the other person to this point.

Non-judgmental listening is about, above all, being present. By this I mean it is not another task that can be ticked off your to-do list between basting a chicken, putting a wash on and writing 2,000 words of your thesis. It involves halting the momentum of your day and giving the other person the full force of your attention.

Sometimes, non-judgmental listening can bring you to a place where you are sitting in silence with someone and, if you're anything like me, you will find this absolutely excruciating. Most of us have a compulsive need to fill awkward silences with babble, yet any journalist will tell you that being unafraid of silence is the quickest way to make someone talk.

Creating a metaphysical safe nook of compassion and non-judgment in which you and your listenee can shelter not only greases the wheels of conversation, but it also has a measurable benefit in creating healthy brain chemistry.

Neurobiologists talks about the role of dopamine in bringing about an optimum chemical balance in the brain during therapeutic situations. The aim of a mental-health-based conversation is usually to allow the person to calmly reflect on what has brought them to the point they are at and what they might do in the future to change it. In order to do this effectively, it's absolutely crucial to control their levels of dopamine secretion. 93 per cent of dopamine production happens in the limbic brain, which is our emotional control centre. This is, in layman's terms, the brain's heart. Creating an environment where a person feels genuinely listened to and understood is the first step in engaging their limbic brain. Or, in the words of neurobiologist Dr Andrew Curran, 'This comes down to the oldest algorithm in the book: love'.

## A BEGINNER'S GUIDE TO LISTENING NON-JUDGMENTALLY

You might be tempted to think that listening is a pretty basic skill, hardwired into us from the necessity of having to hear things. Unfortunately, active listening is a little more complex than 'hearing' and it's a skill that, whilst arguably inherent, is often forgotten and has to be relearned in later life. Author and speaker Simon Sinek once said, 'There is a difference between listening and waiting for your turn to talk.' It is this ethos which lies at the heart of the non-judgmental listener.

The first step in developing your nonjudgmental ear is to ensure you remain calm yourself. You might wish to follow some of the breathing recommendations in *A: Anxiety* to relax and, in turn, reassure the person you are talking to. One of the things I hear most often from teenagers is, 'I can't tell my mum/dad/teacher, they'll freak out.' I believe most people think that if they reveal an emotion they've been struggling to contain it will unleash unbearable chaos. Your first task is to assuage that fear.

It's also helpful to bear in mind that different people respond to different levels of intensity during the conversational process. Some people see a lot of eye contact as a sign that the person they are talking to is genuinely interested and is being honest with them. Others find it awkward. However much eye contact they are making, try to mirror that.

There is evidence to show that people who fall at the masculine end of the gender spectrum (see X: *X Chromosome*) don't generally tend to want to sit down and talk for the sake of it. They're far more likely to open up alongside another activity, some of the reasons for which are outlined in chapter E: *Endorphins*.

By far the most important skill in active and unjudgmental listening is the asking of open questions. These are characterized as enquiries phrased so as it's not possible to give a 'yes' or 'no' answer. They should also be asked with the aim of understanding what precisely is meant by the words that are being used, as detailed above. Examples include, 'What does that feel like?' 'When did you first notice you felt this way?', 'Can you feel it anywhere in your body?' and, the cliché-for-a-reason catch-all employed by therapists, 'How does that make you feel?'.

Conversely, assumptions are anathema to an honest conversation. I once heard a school nurse say to a Year Nine girl who had several angry looking slashes on her upper arm, 'What have you done that to yourself for? Think what you'll look like in your wedding dress!' The question was rhetorical and therefore 'closed', the tone was judgmental in that it suggested she had complete freedom of choice when she 'did it to herself' and then, just to add some crud icing to an already shitty cake, she made the further assumptions that the girl in question had aspirations to marry, would wear a dress when she did it and that her scars would detract from her perceived mandatory bridal 'perfection'.

Remember also that you aren't there to provide a solution to their problem. That goes beyond your remit (see *K: Knowing Me, Knowing You*), although you can bring them closer to solving it themselves, or at least identifying what help they might need. In that spirit, below are some open questions I have found particularly useful.

### What would you like to happen?

This question forces the person to stop dwelling on the problem and start thinking of potential solutions. Encourage them to articulate these solutions (however unlikely they consider the possibility of them becoming a reality) as there might be an option they haven't yet considered.

**Okay, what out of that list do you have the power to change?**
We have a tendency, as humans, to collect problems. Rather than considering each challenge individually, we allow them to spiral into one giant, insurmountable uber-dilemma. You have probably had a conversation with a friend along the lines of:

You: *How are you?*
Them: *Not great. My boss is being a nightmare, I think Jake is allergic to something, plus I have a huge pile of paperwork to complete, the front porch is crumbling around my ears, the dog got a thorn stuck in its paw and the vet bill is huge, and then there's the destruction of planet Earth and our inevitable demise as a species.*

In this instance, your friend has harvested their individual worries and combined them into one gigantic problem, that seems insurmountable. We all have a proclivity for this type of thinking. When our stress buckets (see *S: Self-Care*) are being slowly and incrementally filled by a constant deluge of challenges of various sizes and urgency, our minds (which like to create narratives) will assume we're having a spell of 'bad luck' and that it's all connected. This is what practitioners of NLP call 'living below the line', and it can become a self-fulfilling prophecy, as we start actively looking for ways to confirm our 'world is against us' blik (see *B: Brain*). It's crucial to gain some vestige of perspective, to remember that we aren't 'cursed', and that sometimes life's random problem-generator simply creates an almighty clusterfuck.

Clearly, in this example, the first thing your friend should do is to separate out those problems they have control over, then put them in order of urgency. Often, just the act of making an emotional to-do list makes life seem brighter and more manageable.

**Who can help you with that?**
I'm staggered by the number of people I meet who believe that they have to do everything themselves – as though such a thing were even possible. We're pack animals, evolved in such a way that it forces us to rely on one another. Everyone should have a network of trusted people they can defer to for advice and assistance, and this question can provide the first step towards identifying who those people might be. It can also prevent a situation whereby a misguided expectation is placed on you as the nonjudgmental listener to provide a comprehensive solution.

**How much of your time are you spending thinking about that?**

Sometimes, people have a vague sense of unease and their brain wants to attribute it to something tangible. So in response to the question 'what's wrong?' they reply with a fear that seems logical, in the absence of any notion of what's really bothering them. The above question is a good way of distinguishing the former from the latter.

**What's the worst that can happen?**

Within the confines of their head, an anxious person's worries take on a resonance they don't merit. If they try and ignore them, the brain magnifies and intensifies them because the amygdala believes it is being ignored (and, being a petulant sort, it really doesn't like that). The act of articulating frightening ideas can put them into context. Said aloud, they often they seem really, really silly.

I have this conversation most weeks with my counsellor, who has a brilliant habit of saying 'and so what?' when I verbalize fears around making an arse of myself, being laughed at or making mistakes. After all, as Jane Austen said, 'For what do we live if not to make sport for our neighbours and laugh at them, in our turn?'

**Now, crucially, what is the best?**

Many people unconsciously abide by the old adage that if you always expect the worst you can never be caught off guard. This makes sense from a survival point of view, but does nothing for the mindset over time. It's important for them to remember that the worst consequence is only one of a range of possible outcomes.

**What advice would you give to a friend**
**who came to you with this dilemma?**

Usually, people are much harder on themselves than they would be on other people given the same circumstances. Applying the same amounts of balance, forgiveness and kindness to ourselves that we would to a friend is the ultimate soothing balm for a troubled soul. After all, listening non-judgmentally isn't a skill that should be confined to our conversations with others, it is something we should apply to our inner monologue.

Whilst it won't cure mental illness on its own, non-judgmental listening is the psychological equivalent of checking a person's airways and putting them in the recovery position: done right, it can save lives.

is for . . .
**VENTING**

**In my parents' house there is an armchair covered in fabric depicting flying ducks. It's tucked away in the corner of the sitting room, usually cosily covered with a casually draped knitted blanket, a volume or two of whatever my mum is reading or occasionally the family pooch, Mae. (Mae 'isn't allowed' on the furniture. Naturally, we all let her on the furniture, believing that no one else does and it's our uniquely 'special treat' for her. She has therefore surmised, quite reasonably, that she is allowed on the furniture so long as a maximum of one person has noticed.)**

On a fairly regular basis, one of us will declare that we are 'going to the duck chair' and everyone has to stop what they're doing and listen. 'Going to the duck chair' means that we have been sufficiently moved to annoyance that we simply must have a rant to get it off our chest. Whoever is bethroned upon the duck chair must not be interrupted. They have a piece to say and it is, in that moment, of utmost importance. Crucially, once they have had their rant they're not allowed to mention it again for the rest of the day.

Sometimes, when we have visitors and we can see they are becoming increasingly animated, we suggest that they might like to have a little go on the duck chair. In fact, it's become a bit of a running joke amongst my friends, who will slam their glasses of sauvignon on the pub table with a dramatic flourish and shout 'BRING ME THE DUCK CHAIR!'

I have held forth in the duck chair on a variety of topics, including but not limited to: the various incidents of fuckwittery inflicted upon me by ex-partners; why people care so much what children wear; why people care so much what anyone wears; the hugely disproportionate amount of airtime given to unelected UKIP representatives during televised debates; Tunnock's teacakes and other synthetic-tasting disgustingness masquerading as chocolate; why education is undervalued in the West; climate change deniers; why nothing I've bought from Zara has ever survived a machine wash; people who attempt to board trains before those alighting have had the chance to disembark; why people assume that films with a predominantly black cast were made exclusively for a black audience; and why bras always have to have that stupid little silk bow perched between your breasts.

The best duck-chair rant I ever witnessed was when Mum was lamenting the demise of local, specialized shops and how corporate supermarket chains were swooping in and selling everything from DIY materials to fashion under one roof, whilst Dad quietly pottered around in

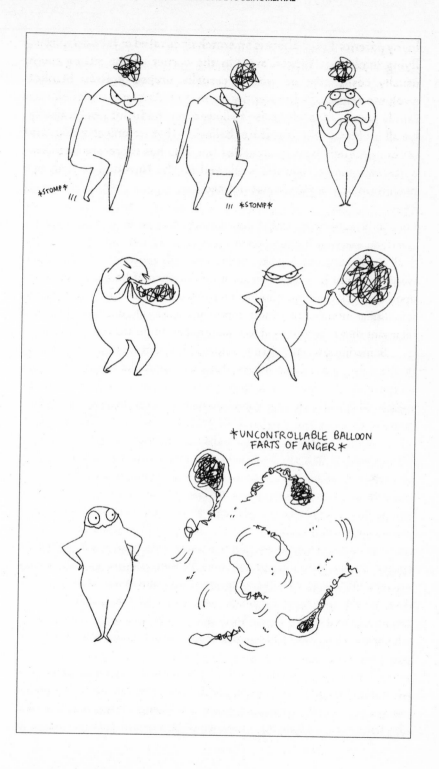

the immediate vicinity, picking up and pointing to various items that she had purchased from the same supermarket giants she was professing to hate. That's the thing about the duck chair – you're not shackled to logic and no one is allowed overtly to take the piss.

What my parents have shrewdly observed is that in order to build a cohesive community you must acknowledge that internalized anger damages the individual, but uncontrolled anger, flung around indiscriminately, damages everyone. Psychology tells us that anger with no outlet festers within us and is, over time, transformed into self-hatred. There is, therefore, evidence-supported therapeutic value in having a good old vent. The duck chair might have its tongue firmly in its cheek but it has served us well over the years.

For British people (especially the English who essentially have two modes: buttoned-up, passive-aggressive awkwardness or I've-had-a-pint-and-I'm-going-to-tell-you-what-I-really-think aggression) healthy anger is a difficult balance to achieve. In my experience, the biggest barriers are fear of recrimination and perceived rudeness.

A couple of years ago, I had the immense pleasure of going out for dinner with an American plus-size supermodel I had long admired. She had the innate ability all New Yorkers seem to possess whereby she can be totally direct and incredibly friendly simultaneously. (Scottish people also tend to have this talent, I've noticed.) Everyone I've met who has spent any length of time in that region can comfortably tell you to go fuck yourself with a smile, in such a way that you don't feel the slightest bit aggrieved.

During dinner, the model reached what I thought was the end of an anecdote and I said, 'Ooh, that reminds me of something that happened to me.' At which point she replied firmly but cheerfully, 'And I can't wait to hear it, but I'm not done ...'

Every British person I've told that story to has gasped and said, 'HOW RUDE!' as though the model had committed the ultimate faux pas. Yet the reason I impart the (wholly undramatic) incident in the first place is to show how people from other countries manage to assert themselves in what I consider to be a far healthier and more honest way.

If the altercation had happened in reverse I would have thought, 'I didn't reach the apex of my story, but I won't say anything.' The unused energy I had mustered with which to tell my tale would have lingered in my throat. My ability to concentrate on and enjoy the rest of the dinner conversation would have been impeded by a misplaced sense of resentment, which would then have been added to my personal savings account of self-hatred into which I have deposited every unfairness that has ever befallen me over the years. If the model and I had a long-term friendship, I might have developed a confirmation bias centring around a belief that she 'never lets me speak'. Each and every time I felt insufficiently heard in her presence, I'd have used that as evidence of my unfounded belief, until one day I'd be so overwhelmed by my self-created sense of the injustice of it all that I probably would have shouted at her for no reason whatsoever, potentially placing our relationship in jeopardy.

Emotions, like all energy, cannot be destroyed – they have to go somewhere. That means every time someone asked you to 'put it to the back of your mind,' what they were really saying was, 'Don't release this feeling into the ether, use it to create distress within the confines of your own psyche.'

Feelings are also like traffic lights. If you deal with them straight away, you've got a green. If you allow them to turn from amber to red you've restricted your ability to move forward.

The other barrier to healthy expression of anger is the fear that we will be held accountable for what we say, destined to have our words regurgitated and examined during subsequent altercations forever and ever until the sweet release of death. This is a self-perpetuating notion, since the less people practise using healthy manifestations of anger, the rarer rage becomes and the more we are encouraged to believe unconsciously that people must only show their frustration if they 'really mean it'.

This in turn leads to oscillation between two states: artificial tranquillity and toxic chaos. Victims of domestic abuse often experience the sharp end of this particular phenomenon, alternating between treading on eggshells and enduring the perpetrator's sudden outbursts of rage. Survivors have told me that the periods of quiet, where anger simmered below the surface without being articulated and they were left guessing what they had 'done', were often worse than the incidents of violence themselves.

Whilst this example might seem extreme, it strikes me that in making anger in all its forms socially unacceptable, a cultural situation is created whereby dangerous, venomous outbursts of anger are more likely. It's advantageous to get used to both expressing and being exposed to anger for that very reason.

The duck-chair episodes in my family home are undertaken on the understanding that the venter is entitled to have changed their mind regarding the thing about which they are ranting, the next day, month, year, or even mid-rant if they have the sudden realization that they're being silly.

We'd also never use the duck chair to address an issue with someone else present in the house – that would represent a hugely unbalanced way to have an argument. Yet I like to think that when those sorts of discussions need to take place (usually because I or one of my siblings needs to be bollocked about something), they can be conducted constructively and without fear, in no small measure because of the enduring presence of our duck chair.

## A BEGINNER'S GUIDE TO BEING ANGRY

Repeat after me: anger is not inherently bad. We all feel angry sometimes and if we do not have the means or opportunity to express it, harm is done to our self-esteem and our relationships with others, both of which are fundamental to our mental health.

Identify a cabal of close friends or family members who you can be angry with without the possibility of misinterpretation. Set some ground rules: anyone is allowed to vent if the mood so takes them, but it must be confined to a period of space or time that means it doesn't dominate everyone's day. Anger, like a recalcitrant puppy, needs boundaries.

If you are on the receiving end of a rant, understand that the person in front of you is just letting off steam. Don't extrapolate personal meanings from impersonal themes (when your friend says 'I hate the way the labels on scented candles will never peel off cleanly' it's probably not a euphemism for that time you got drunk and had ill-advised sexual relations). Don't internalize their anger and don't let it wind you up.

If you find yourself in a situation where you need to address a source of frustration with someone you love or who is a regular feature in your life, try to remove accusation from the narrative. Replace 'you made me feel' with 'when you do this, I feel . . .' in recognition of the fact that no one can actually make you feel anything and that they might not have done it intentionally. Believe that you are entitled to do this. You matter just as much and as little as everyone else.

Expressing anger in an appropriate way will, particularly if you're English, take practice. I find a good starting ground is politely yet firmly pointing out bad customer service. The first time I phoned a taxi firm and said, 'When your cabs are consistently twenty minutes late I feel I am not valued as your customer. Is that the case?' I felt empowered as fuck. Reassuringly, the world didn't implode, I wasn't immediately deported from The Land of Good Manners, and the matter was resolved to my satisfaction.

For those who aren't in the habit of being angry in a healthy way, the chances are there's quite a lot of rage stored up in your Anger Tank. This can be released through physical exertion (boxing is particularly good), singing loudly or thrashing around to angry music (I find anything by Children of Bodom does the trick) or, if circumstances permit, doing the clichéd thing of going to the middle of a field and screaming at the top of your lungs (which is also, coincidentally, what impersonating the lead vocalist in Children of Bodom involves).

My counsellor also taught me a nifty trick: on days when I arrive home carrying a particularly hefty wodge of pent-up frustration, I get a balloon and furiously blow all my unspent anger into it. Then I let it go. This both serves as a physical manifestation of letting go of my anger and also breaks the tension with all-important humour. Because I don't care who you are, no one can keep a straight face in the presence of a fart noise.

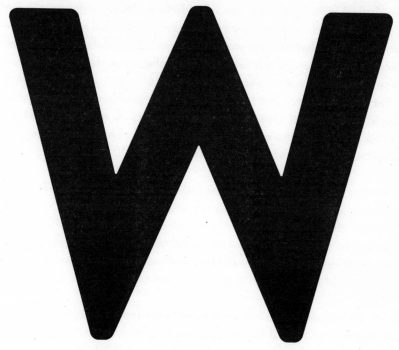

is for . . .

**WEED**

(and other non-prescription drugs)

I have written before about so-called recreational drugs and, possibly because my social silo is populated disproportionately by people who have mental-health issues, I wrote about them almost exclusively through the prism of addiction. Afterwards, people got in touch to tell me that they take drugs 'just for fun' and asking me to remember that not everyone 'has issues'. So, in deference to them and because I consider it respectful to believe people when they tell you about their own experiences, I want to begin by acknowledging that not everyone who takes drugs has a 'problem'. On the other hand, I am yet to meet anyone who admits to regularly smoking weed or taking cocaine who seemed happy. That isn't to say, of course, that such people don't exist.

I've observed that views on drug-taking differ dramatically between generations. Over the past decade, there has been a steady decline in the number of young people who drink alcohol and smoke tobacco, and this has been hailed as a victory in many quarters (not least of all by the Department of Health, whose policies of increasing the cost of alcohol per unit and enforcing plain packaging on cigarettes have occurred in conjunction with the downturn).

Yet millennials tend to view taking other types of recreational drugs as much less of a big deal than their parents. That's not to say that drug-taking is a new phenomenon, merely that what was once seen as the remit of rock musicians and movie stars is now much more socially acceptable. Whether that's because of increased availability, an unexpected and ironic result of soaring alcohol and cigarette prices, or simply because each generation wants to carve out a niche for itself that is different from that of its forebears is difficult to say.

I'm yet to see anyone deliver a class on drugs in a school that truly resonates with students, for that very reason. I was a teenager in the era of Leah Betts, who famously died after taking MDMA, a form of ecstasy, at a party. We were shown the same VHS virtually everyone my age has seen, featuring a reconstruction of the party and testimonials from Leah's devastated family. The message was very much 'if you take drugs you will definitely die or go to prison', and since none of us were aware of anyone who did, we believed that to be, irrefutably, the case.

Drug culture amongst young people has changed unrecognizably since then, and yet the education surrounding it remains broadly the same. Except now there is a 'truth gap'. Drug use is so public and so widespread that young people know they won't necessarily go to prison or die. Whilst mainstream, tabloid-style media still frowns on illegal drug use, in the confines of the media young people inhabit – the pages of online culture magazines and the videos of YouTube – it's discussed in a much more open and (arguably) balanced way.

All of the above musings are a convoluted way of saying that this chapter explores the worst-case scenarios. I am by no means a Peter Hitchens type figure, universally condemning anyone who comes within a two-metre radius of a spliff. I don't judge people who take drugs (although obviously some of the breaches of human rights that happen within the unregulated drug-production industry are appalling).

## CAUSE AND EFFECT

Avoiding drugs and minimizing alcohol intake is a professionally recommended form of self-care for almost every mental-health issue. This is primarily because they are likely to cause mood swings and can interfere with the efficacy of prescription medication. Alcohol and drugs of addiction flood the brain with dopamine. The correct balance of dopamine is critical for producing optimum mental wellbeing. An excess of dopamine is a disinhibitor, making us prone to risk-taking behaviours and cloudy thinking.

Marijuana and hallucinogens have been linked both to depression and to psychosis (see *P: Psychosis*). Yet correlation is not causation and we don't know for certain whether people who are in mental distress are simply more likely to smoke weed or take pills in a bid to distract, self-medicate and relax, or whether the drug can induce these kinds of symptoms in anyone who takes it. I tend towards the former theory, although I think there is probably a grain of truth in both.

It was controversially suggested during a debate in Parliament in 2016 that the primary reason a man kills himself in the UK every two hours is because men tend to have higher prevalence of drug and alcohol addiction, which can induce suicidal behaviours. What this theory fails to acknowledge is that mental illness is still perceived in traditional masculine culture as a sign of weakness, and therefore the cause of both the addiction and eventual reaching of crisis point is likely to be unarticulated distress. I explore this more in chapter *X: X Chromosome*.

What is undeniable is that drug and alcohol use exacerbate the symptoms of pre-existing poor mental health and make it more difficult to engage with therapeutic interventions. Again, however, the situation is not clear cut. Whilst most therapists refuse to treat a patient who is obviously intoxicated during their sessions, they will also acknowledge that in some cases alcohol and drug use is a survival strategy to deflect from emotional distress and that to immediately stop without an appropriate safety net might increase the risk of suicide.

Professor David Nutt (another 'tsar' who was also controversially sacked by the government) believes that, for some people, their amygdala is wired to overreact to stress (see *A: Anxiety*) and that these people will gravitate towards drugs and alcohol because they need something to take the edge off. This, along with low levels of dopamine giving rise to impulsivity, are two of the things that produce an 'addictive nature'. His findings indicate that addiction is an illness in the same way as depression is, rather than a side effect of drug use.

Again, there is a fundamental tension at the root of arguments around addiction. The idea that addictive substances cause addiction is increasingly unpopular. Most experts in the field now agree that a person who is an addict can become addicted to virtually anything. This might explain why there is a strong correlation between drug and alcohol addiction and bulimia nervosa, which is essentially an addiction to food with 'compensatory' behaviours (see *F: Food*).

Public understanding of addiction, which has always held that to try a drug like cocaine was automatically to become an addict, was challenged in 1981 when a study colloquially referred to as 'Rat Park' was finally published. The experiment was conducted during the 1970s at Simon Fraser University in Canada by Bruce K Alexander and his colleagues.

In a bid to prove that it was not substances in and of themselves but rather environmental factors that cause addiction, Alexander created 'Rat Park'. It was 200 times the size of a standard laboratory cage, contained amusements, plentiful food and sufficient space for mating. Johann Hari, author of *Chasing the Scream*, described it as 'rat Disneyland'. The rats were given a bottle of water laced with morphine, and a bottle of plain water. Unlike their counterparts who lived alone in standard laboratory cages, they showed very little interest in the morphine. The experiment showed it was not the substance itself, but the nature of the cage that was the crucial element in determining addiction.

It would seem that the formula for addiction is a natural proclivity in the form of an overactive amygdala and a lack of dopamine, plus a challenging environment (which would explain why drug use is higher in areas of economic deprivation). Psychologically, addiction is characterized primarily by two factors. The first of these is low-self-esteem. A belief of not being good enough results in attempts to try and distract from self-hatred or to 'fix' it through consumption. This is the model on which consumerist capitalism is based (see *C: Capitalism*). When, inevitably, the obtaining and imbibing of products and substances does not 'work', in that we are the same person with all the same issues as we were at the beginning of the process, we are conditioned to blame ourselves. The resultant shame feeds back into the low self-esteem, which ignites the entire cycle anew.

When framed in this way, addiction is in many ways a natural side effect of the way society is structured.

The second psychological component of addiction is what's known as a fractured sense of self. We all have the mask we present to the outside world and it is distinct from the 'real' us, but the further the distance between those two incarnations of self the more likely it is that mental-health issues, in particular addiction, will occur. As we know, acceptance and belonging are two key components of good mental health. If the way we behave under supervision is radically different to who we are when we are alone, or indeed how we feel inside, that indicates an internal conflict or self-hatred.

Knowing that most of us experience these thought processes, which are part of the mechanics of addiction, our tendency to 'other' people with addiction issues seems ludicrous. We talk about 'addicts' and 'junkies' as though they have nothing to do with us, whereas in fact they represent a group of vulnerable people who have been broken by elements of modern life in which we are all complicit.

That isn't to say that people with addiction issues can't be incredibly difficult to coexist with. All mental-health issues tend to involve an element of secrecy, and this will inevitably create the necessity to lie to people you love. When it comes to drug addiction, however, desperation tends to create behaviours that are deeply hurtful, if not criminal. It is this, I believe, which makes it so difficult for many people to empathize with addicts.

It is a cruel truth that often those who most desperately need our care are those who it is often hardest to love.

## A BEGINNER'S GUIDE TO WEED AND OTHER DRUGS

As a general rule, it's when you feel you 'need' a drink or a fix that you probably shouldn't have one. Alcohol, for example, provides momentary respite from anxiety or stress but it is a well-known depressant, meaning that the original symptoms will come back, magnified, to haunt you the next day. In the stress-bucket analogy outlined in chapter *S: Self-Care*, it represents a 'tap blocker' as opposed to a 'stress drainer'. I appreciate that this advice is much easier said than practised, which is why so many people with addictions to drugs and alcohol choose to follow the twelve-step programme as a way of controlling their behaviours.

If you are taking mental-health medication, remember that alcohol and drugs can interfere with its efficacy. It can also mean that you'll become incredibly drunk after about 3.5 sips of wine (as I discovered to my detriment when I first started taking Sertraline) or feel unusually bilious and vom all over your husband's rootin' tootin' snakeskin cowboy boots. For example.

If you are smoking weed or taking any other kind of drug regularly, or drinking more than four units of alcohol per day, you might find that mental-health services will refuse to see you until you are clean. This can present a problem if the reasons for drinking or drug-taking in the first place are mental illness. Ultimately, however, being intoxicated in whatever way will mean that therapy is less effective, so it might be that your recovery pathway involves a period of drying out before psychotherapy can commence.

Illegal drugs are never completely 'safe'. But statistically the greatest danger is addiction. If accessing a different reality feels like the only way to escape the one you inhabit, know that you and your circumstances will still be waiting for you when you come back down.

is for . . .

# X CHROMOSOME

**Even the most cursory glance at mental-health statistics will show distinct and obvious divides according to sex.**

If you are a woman, you are three times more likely to be diagnosed with anxiety or depression than if you are a man. Some people (and by 'people', I mean *Daily Mail* columnists) have a tendency to take this statistic in isolation and use it in an attempt to diminish the notion that mental illness is real. They play on stereotypes around the 'melodramatic' nature of women and use them to suggest that the 'fact' that there is less prevalence in men means the epidemic we face is one of women whingeing unnecessarily, rather than a genuine emotional or medical need. For example, here is Sarah Vine (partner of former Education Secretary Michael Gove) writing for the *Daily Mail* in response to a government-commissioned report stating that British young people are in the grip of a burgeoning mental health crisis, particularly prevalent amongst teenage girls experiencing depression:

> Forgive me if I don't join in the chorus of self-flagellating
> concern. Whilst I've no doubt that life for young British girls
> in the 21st century is hard work, let's face it, it's not Aleppo ...
> Yes, the small number of girls and boys who suffer genuine
> mental illness deserve every sympathy. But surely asking a
> 14-year-old girl if she's unhappy is a bit like asking a dog if it
> wants to go for a walk.

And yes, in case you are wondering, I did have to cease typing to go and find various inanimate objects to punch at several junctures whilst copying out that paragraph.

One of the many crucial contextural considerations Vine has missed here is that depression is one of a range of different mental illnesses. Men are three times more likely to develop an addiction to drugs or alcohol, and are also far more likely to take their own lives. At the time of writing, three in four suicides in the UK are completed by men. Suicide is the single biggest killer of men under fifty in this country and the second biggest of boys aged ten to twenty-four. In 2015 alone, 4,621 British men ended their own lives – that's one man every two hours. Furthermore, 90 per cent of suicides occur as a result of undiagnosed depression or substance addiction, making the understanding Vine's argument is predicated on – that boys and men don't experience the illness – entirely bogus. It boils down ultimately to men being less likely to speak about or seek help for their health issues.

In this chapter, I want to examine what these types of statistics tell us about the relationship between gender and mental health. First, however, it's necessary for me to describe what I mean when I employ the term 'gender'.

In 2018, there's an exciting and occasionally terrifying debate happening in education, pop culture and within the various screeching echo chambers of Twitter about exactly what gender is and how it impacts our lives. I have spoken with scientists who believe passionately that men and women are destined to fulfil fundamentally different roles from the point of birth, that masculinity and femininity are laid into our genetic codes and that the very existence of transgender people bears this out (after all, they argue, you can't feel that you are born into the wrong body if there is no such thing as a male or female mind). Other experts I've met take the view that all perceived differences between men and women are a result of the socially constructed gender biases that are drummed into us from our earliest moments, thus becoming a self-fulfilling prophecy.

I have done countless activities with teenagers in schools exploring the stereotypical ideas that lurk in their subconscious minds when it comes to gender. Below are the words they most often associate with men and women (brace yourself):

**Men:** strong, big, muscular, hairy, smelly, powerful, stoic, rational, logical, scientific, sporty

**Women:** small, delicate, weak, pretty, emotional, irrational, needy, talkative, annoying, pink, shopping

These are ideas that, lest we forget, they have absorbed from the society in which they find themselves.

Neuroplasticity is a term used for the way the brain develops according to the activities in which we partake. If we perform the same skill over and over again, the part of our brain responsible for that skill will grow. Thus, our patterns of mind-evolution are directly impacted by what we do. Neuroplasticity creates a powerful partnership with gender bias when shaping our individual personalities as well as our social environment.

According to neuroscientist Jack Lewis, what we are encouraged to do from infancy is more a result of the gender bias of the adults around us than instinct. For example, an experiment was conducted where the traditional clothing of male and female babies was swapped – the girls were put in blue and the boys in pink. A group of adults, who did not know the babies, were brought in and their behaviour was observed.

The babies dressed in pink were picked up and touched more, comforted more readily and extensively when they cried, more eye contact was made with them and the adults talked to them in a higher voice register. The babies dressed in blue were challenged more. Each adult was asked to select a baby and place it on a slope based on the gradient they believed he or she was capable of crawling. The babies dressed in pink were placed on the gentlest slopes, whilst those in blue were placed on gradients that were, in fact, too steep for their abilities. So whilst the behaviour of the adults conformed to the archetypes traditionally associated with the genders they believed these babies were, it can't be argued that they were responding to any kind of signal from the infant.

According to Dr Lewis, there is absolutely no discernible difference at birth between the brain of a baby with a penis and one who has a vagina. By the time they have reached adolescence, male and female brains usually exhibit significant divergence. Psychologists have tended to assume that this is because men and women are just 'different'. Yet when we take neuroplasticity into account, it presents the possibility that at least some of the differences in average male and female brains have been manufactured and manipulated by their socio-cultural environment.

Primary-school-aged children who, as Dr Javid Abdelmoneim in his BBC documentary *No More Girls and Boys* taught us, by dint of their lack of hormones are not dramatically different from one another, but they already show distinct patterns that are likely to be a response to social cues. Girls are more likely to be labelled as having an emotional disorder, boys a behavioural one. I suspect that the feelings these children are experiencing are the same. It is the way they have been taught is acceptable to express them, and more importantly the way their behaviours are interpreted by adults, which are different.

Whilst some gender stereotypes are rooted in a truth we can usually recognize, it doesn't mean that they are inevitable or that, if they existed in a cultural vacuum, men and women would naturally each gravitate towards these designated behaviours. For example, whilst one study found that women say on average 13,000 more words per day than men, which would support the notion that they are inherently 'chattier', you have to wonder whether that's because girls are encouraged to articulate and communicate more, whereas men are taught to express themselves in other, usually more physical or even violent, ways. Furthermore, just because something might be broadly true 'on average', it doesn't make it universally applicable. I cannot assume that the woman in front of me wants to talk and the man doesn't, so this type of knowledge has limited usefulness.

I'm not implying that, left to their own devices in a world of infinite free choice, there wouldn't be some patterns in the things the average man and woman are interested in. What I am saying is that our environment is so weighted towards certain gender-based prejudices that at the moment we simply don't know. Everything we understand about what men and women are naturally 'like' psychologically is pretty much just conjecture.

As a feminist (by which I mean 'someone who believes in equality'), I'm passionate about giving everyone, regardless of their gender, freedom of choice. At the moment, our choices and behaviours are restricted by what is deemed 'normal' for our sex, and never is that more true than when it comes to our mental health. I also subscribe to the belief put forward by Dr Ben Hine, Senior Lecturer at the University of West London, when he said to me that 'the gender socialization processes are frequently more intense and restrictive for boys than for girls, which often results in narrower and more strictly enforced gender roles and stereotypes across childhood, adolescence and beyond'.

So let's examine the stereotypes and how they affect our wellbeing. A word before I begin: gender exists on a scale. When I speak about 'men' and 'women' I am talking in averages – the median point in a spectrum of possibilities. The generalizations I make below are very far from universally applicable.

## WOMEN ARE PRETTY

Endless arguments begin with the question of whether the pressure to conform to some abstract notion of beauty is self-imposed by 'bitchy' women, or whether the expectations to be 'sexy' arise from the whims of demanding men. The answer is actually neither.

It's true to say the often painful and always time-consuming requirements of the female beauty paradigm are patriarchal in their nature, in that they have been used as a means to disempower women. Susie Orbach wrote in her 1978 tome *Fat is a Feminist Issue* about the ways in which, throughout history, body ideals became more restrictive during times of female emancipation, almost as though women were seen as getting a little too big for their boots and needed to be taken down a peg or two. However, as I shall never tire of saying, 'the patriarchy' and 'men' are not the same thing.

The real issue is those multi-billion-dollar beauty, fashion and fitness industries. Not only do they profit from our insecurities, they actively create them. By inventing flaws that need to be fixed, they justify the existence of their products and create demand. Thus, ideals of beauty become more restrictive over time.

In this way, beauty has become a constant distraction and worry for most women in a way that can be anxiety-inducing, or at the very least detrimental to self-esteem. The Girlguiding* national attitudes survey found that girls as young as seven already believe that society values them more for how they look than for their achievements and character. Dr Jean Kilbourne, a global expert on advertising, speaks very eloquently about how the dual messages that physical 'perfection' is a necessity and that we are doomed to fail in our pursuit of it have a devastating impact on the way most women see themselves.

## MEN ARE BIG AND MUSCLY

It's very important to note, however, that body image-related anxiety is far from a female-only issue. Martin Seager, who worked for the NHS as a psychologist for thirty years, believes that whilst the female 'shame trigger' relates to beauty, in men it relates to concepts of strength. In the same way the average woman fears being seen as ugly, most men fear being perceived as physically weak. It therefore makes sense that, according to a tabloid investigation in 2015, 45 per cent of British men will experience an episode of so-called 'bigorexia' (an obsession with muscle building) at some point during their lifetimes.

I don't particularly care for the term 'bigorexia' because I believe it diminishes what can be an incredibly serious, life-destroying issue. The testimonials on the website of charity Men Get Eating Disorders Too, which amongst other things campaigns for parity between services for men and women seeking eating-disorder treatment, show the scope and extent of compulsive-exercising behaviours in men. What might begin as negative associations with being 'puny', or even a genuine desire to be healthier and fitter, can spiral out of control as largely unnecessary (unless you're a professional athlete) protein products, various chemical shakes, pills and powders, as well as a hugely restrictive diet are added to the regime.

---

*Girlguiding is a charitable organization and the UK's largest girl-only youth group. They teach girls and young women skills for life and have media ambassadors who speak about issues that affect them, including body image, mental health and sexism.

In addition to this, the beauty industry appears to be gaining more and more of a vice-like grip on the male market. The same arguments about low self-esteem and its relation to mental illness apply as in the section above, here. I can't help but think that when women said they wanted a more level playing field, the notion that men should also have their insecurities systematically magnified and exacerbated by capitalism represents an epic misinterpretation.

## WOMEN ARE TALKATIVE AND IRRATIONAL

The advantage of this stereotype if you are a woman is that it makes it far more socially acceptable for you to speak openly about your emotions and mental wellbeing. This means you are more likely to have an ongoing awareness of your own psychological state, which consequently makes it more likely you'll identify early signs of mental distress in yourself. It also means other people will be primed to spot those symptoms in you. This should, in theory, make women more prone to receiving early treatment.

Having said that, there is also a chance that mental illness can become normalized within female groups. If all your female friends are speaking about feelings of depression and anxiety, you'll probably conclude that they're simply part and parcel of the experience of being a woman. Perhaps, then, you will be less likely to seek help. You might also feel some guilt and shame because you believe that everyone else is coping with their psychological struggles, simultaneously functioning and speaking openly about them, whilst you are not.

The other disadvantage is that women's concerns about their mental health are, certainly in social and sometimes in medical circumstances, less likely to be taken seriously. We are conditioned to receive the words of women in a way that assumes they have applied some exaggeration or are being drama queens.

Whilst more men complete the act of suicide, more women attempt it. Often, the response is to dismiss the suicide attempt as 'just a cry for help'. For reasons discussed in chapter J: Just Attention Seeking, the use of the word 'just' in this sentence really troubles me, since it implies that the act of attempted suicide was somehow indulgent and not to be taken totally seriously. Yet, if someone is seeking attention it's because they desperately need some. My hunch is that so many women attempt suicide using methods they know to have a high probability of survival because they think it is the only way they can convey the depths of their despair and be taken seriously.

The preconceived notions that exist around women talking more also present a problem if you happen to be a woman who bucks that trend and isn't particularly chatty. We tend to believe that if women aren't articulating any distress, they're probably fine – a view that can impede the chances of the early intervention that we know can be so infinitely helpful to the recovery process.

## MEN ARE STOIC

Our socio-cultural definition of 'strength' is inextricably linked with stoicism and martyrdom. We believe that dealing with things by ourselves, not drawing attention to our problems and inconveniencing others and 'soldering on' in the face of adversity are representative of a 'strong' character. Most often, it is men who are expected to conform to this definition of strength.

From their earliest moments, our culture teaches little boys that they must never cry, that feelings – whether acknowledging your own or caring about those of others – are 'gay' (and that being gay is bad), and that violence is preferable to talking. This is reflected in the language the adults often around them use, the toys they are encouraged to play with and the role models that exist for them.

By the time I'm parachuted in to work with these boys during their adolescence, most of them have a distinct lack of what I would term emotional vocabulary. They know that they don't feel quite right but, in contrast to most girls, haven't had a lifetime of practice in identifying, naming and expressing their sense of unease. As you would expect, this makes it much more difficult for them to tell me what is wrong. The research I have conducted in schools has shown clear evidence of a fear young men have of ridicule and rebuke if they speak out about their feelings – and in many cases they don't even have the words anyway.

Boys also feed back to me that if they do speak in emotional terms they do not feel that the lexicon of words they instinctually use are necessarily understood or interpreted correctly by the people around them. This is, I believe, a self-perpetuating problem that has arisen out of the notion that men don't have mental-health issues, meaning more research is done with women and interventions are designed with women in mind.

Unable to articulate what is troubling them, or to be heard when they do, no wonder men so commonly self-medicate with drugs and alcohol or reach a stage where their pain has outstripped their resources for coping with it and they feel they have no option but to end their own lives.

## A BEGINNER'S GUIDE TO CHALLENGING GENDER STEREOTYPES

Where the majority of mental-health interventions aimed at men are getting it wrong is that the message at their core is 'Men – you need to start talking.' This presupposes that it's a straightforward matter of men being more willing to kill themselves than have a chat. It's essentially victim blaming. The same sort of logic is applied by health campaigners who say, 'Fat people – have you considered eating less?' If it were that simple, they would have done it already. Instead, what we should be doing is examining why men live in an environment that makes it nearly impossible for them to talk about their mental health, or to be understood when they do.

A few years ago, I conducted some research in an all-boys school in which I asked a group of sixth-formers where they felt most comfortable having feelings-based discussions. The gym came through strongly as a 'safe' environment for this kind of talk, as did being in a car. There was one particular teacher whom the boys felt very at ease confiding in. It transpired they would always walk across the playing fields whilst they talked.

The conclusion I reached is that there is a lot of truth in what pop psychologists say about your average male not wanting to make eye contact when discussing difficult topics. If one thinks about the office set-up of most counsellors with the benefit of this knowledge, it's little wonder a lot of men are put off. If your aim is to get someone who falls at the masculine end of the gender spectrum to talk openly, doing another activity alongside the talking takes away the intensity and removes one of your barriers.

I also passionately believe that we have to challenge our social definition of 'strength'. Think how men's behaviour might change if we said to them 'it is strong to talk,' 'it is proactive to seek help,' 'you can provide for the people around you by lending them your ear.'

Altering language and thereby the underlying ideological narratives is a total game-changer and it's one that we can use to break down erroneous and self-esteem-damaging beauty standards too. People who exist at the feminine end of the gender spectrum need to be reassured that they are more than the sum of their parts. Instead of concentrating our conversations on exterior and relatively unimportant fashion and beauty considerations, we should show the people around us that we understand, accept and admire them for aspects of their character and their actions. The next time you're tempted to say 'nice shoes', think about saying 'I like being with you. You're funny/kind/entertaining/astute/interesting/brave/talented/ inspiring/a good listener/really good at assembling furniture/weird in the best possible way.'

Of course, the way men and women are portrayed in the media can be, to put it mildly, very unhelpful. The impact of gender stereotyping is, quite rightly, being publicly discussed and dissected, led by such almighty game-changers as Caitlin Moran and Robert Webb. As individuals, however, the only thing we really need in order to bypass the restrictions of gender expectations is to stop being distracted by muscles, bums and breasts and to engage with the real human being in front of us.

is for . . .

**YOUNG PEOPLE**

I consider myself a spokesperson for young people (as well as the people who care for and teach them), both at government level and in the media. I write and speak for young people because under-25s have been punished disproportionately by austerity. I do it because under-18s often have needs and concerns distinct from the parents, but can't vote. I do it because, as elaborated on below, young people are the most vulnerable to mental illness, as well as inadequate service provision. I consider it essential that someone like me, who is fortunate enough to have a platform, stands up for the rights of the young.

This aspect of my job necessitates having to put my own sense of reality to one side and hurl myself wholeheartedly into theirs, so that I can accurately relay the challenges they face and the needs they have. In doing so, I've discovered a whole range of ideas that have in turn helped me to make sense of the world (including intersectional, fourth-wave feminism).

So-called 'millenials' get a lot of flack, with reports of their avocado-munching, self-obsessed, technology-preoccupied ways leaking into common parlance and providing a handy straw man to fuel the futile fury of columnists and pundits.

I was born in 1981, which technically means I cannot describe myself as a 'millenial' (it's defined as anyone born between 1985 and 2000), but I feel a lot of affinity with the way that generation defines itself. What has been dubbed 'weakness' and led to the commonly used insult 'snowflake', I perceive as the bravery to challenge the parameters within which the more toxic and damaging aspects of our society have been defined and to highlight structural and unconscious racism, sexism, homophobia and injustice. What some see as 'wanting to be famous on YouTube' I consider to be a direct reaction to the challenges associated with finding more traditional employment and making a decent wage, and a creative attempt to carve out a career in an increasingly digital age. Their famed taste for avocados I read as a responsible concern for their own health, the realization that processed food has a lot of crap in it, and a desire to properly nourish the fleshy house in which their soul resides.

Most of the young people I now work with were born after 2000, and they're fantastic, too. Each new batch seems to me to be paradoxically wiser, more tolerant and more emotionally literate than the one before. They see things like gender fluidity with a beautiful clarity that their parents often find difficult to grasp. I have, during my decade working in schools, colleges and universities, seen a revolution in ideology which I am proud to represent.

Having said all of that, this generation of young people are uniquely burdened. Before you start throwing your kitchen utensils (or whatever happens to be in your immediate vicinity) at the wall and screeching 'but they all have smartphones!' perhaps go back and read chapters *C: Capitalism* and *H: Happiness*. Stuff cannot make you happier. (As a side note, I'm not entirely sure how owning a phone somehow became an emblem of wealth. I was once about to go into a coffee shop with a friend when a thirsty homeless man asked me if I'd buy him a bottle of water. My friend whispered that I shouldn't because 'he's got a phone'. My reply was 'can he drink it?').

Additionally, young people are facing a plethora of (largely invisible) financial challenges. The average amount of debt a student will leave university with is, at the time of writing, £57,000. House prices and travel expenses are prohibitively massive, particularly in areas where there are jobs, like London. Unemployment has reportedly fallen, but that doesn't take into account those who are on zero-hours contracts or not being paid enough to sustain a basic standard of living.

The accepted guidance is that no more than 30 per cent of your total income should be spent on housing. The so-called 'living wage', what a young person at the bottom of the professional ladder will get if they are lucky, is £8.75 per hour. That's £1,225 gross income per month if you work a 35-hour week. After tax and national insurance, you'll take home about £1,100. The average rent is between £800 and £900 per month (outside London, where it's £1,560). That leaves approximately £50 per week for food, travel, phone rental (which is basically mandatory in any profession) and bills.

Economic situation has a measurable impact on mental health. Whilst being very wealthy doesn't make you happier, being able to comfortably meet your basic needs does. As does gaining the independence that allows you to form a strong sense of identity away from your parents, something that natural changes in our brain chemistry dictate we should be doing during adolescence and our early twenties (more on this below).

I'm really fortunate in that my parents, who were 'baby-boomers' and also entirely self-made, don't have that immensely annoying attitude of 'We managed, we made sacrifices you wouldn't be prepared to. We earned everything we have.' They understand that, whilst of course not everything was smooth sailing for them, they had opportunities that I and my siblings do not. Essentially, they are well versed enough in the history of economics to know that their generation had a party, the bill for which following generations are having to foot. (This, in turn, makes me more sympathetic to their situation, in which they are having to provide financial support to members of our family both older and younger due to inadequate planning for the number of pensioners medical advancements would create.)

Not all young people have such liberal and understanding forebears, however. For many, in addition to the seeming impossibility of stable employment, a decent wage, a reasonably priced education and modest home ownership, they're having to endure a constant barrage of accusation that they are lazy, work-shy and selfish.

I want to take a breather here to state that this isn't me having a go at older people. Most people at whatever age are, I still believe, well intentioned and doing their best. Yet I feel that unconscious bias about what young people are 'like' can be just as damaging and insidious as some of the stereotypes we carry about people of a particular gender, sexuality or race. I'm inviting us to challenge the picture that has been painted of young people, in the hope that it will make the environment they inhabit kinder, fairer and more conducive to their flourishing.

In particular, I cannot fathom where this notion of teenagers being 'selfish' comes from. Yes, scientifically speaking, our powers of empathy don't kick in until we are about twenty-two, but that doesn't mean young people are selfish. In fact, quite the opposite. In 2016, I had the honour of being made a Fellow of my former university in Aberystwyth. I was invited to give a short address to the psychology and politics students. I said:

> There are lots of people who will tell you that you have no
> experience of 'real' life and that makes you selfish. I don't
> agree. As you get older, your world view tends to narrow.
> You can become bogged down in the specific concerns of
> your family, your mortgage, how much tax you have to pay,
> or considerations like the inevitability of death . . . But people
> your age, in my experience, whatever your political persuasion,
> believe the things you do because you want everything to be
> fair. And fairness, justice, equality . . . well, they're the noblest
> and least selfish motivations you can have. So I want you
> to remember what you felt and believed on this day and,
> as you go through your life, to keep checking in with your
> former self.

## PERINATAL MENTAL HEALTH

It is never too early to begin thinking about mental health and that extends to the psychological wellbeing of parents while their child is in the womb. 'Peri' simply means 'around' and 'perinatal mental health' can encompass any mental-health condition that occurs during pregnancy or in the period shortly after birth.

Dr Andrew Mayers from Bournemouth University is an expert on this topic, which has attracted greater awareness over the past couple of years. The most common mental-health problem experienced by new mums, he told me, is postnatal depression, followed by the relatively rarer postpartum psychosis. Contrary to popular belief, these conditions are not caused by hormonal changes alone, but usually by a combination of factors, including a family history of mental illness. Additionally, the creation of a new human is momentous for the people involved and often brings back long-buried or traumatic memories from the parents' pasts.

If a mother with a postnatal mental illness has trouble forming an attachment bond with her baby, it can have a serious effect on the development of the child. As Dr Mayers explains: 'Poor attachment from infancy can lead to whole range of developmental problems for the child and, in some cases, into adulthood. In more severe illnesses, the mother may find it very hard to care for the infant appropriately . . . and in very extreme (and incredibly rare) cases, mothers may harm or even kill their baby.'

Whilst postnatal depression is at least a well-known condition, up until recently the father's mental health was not often talked about. Yet there is evidence to show that they too can experience periods of anxiety and depression both before and after the baby is born. Dr Mayers says, 'The impact on that father, and the developing infant, can be every bit as distressing as it is for the mother. Some evidence has shown that fathers are as much as 47 times more likely to take their own life at this time than at any other . . . Depression in fathers can have an impact on the attachment bond in the same way as it does with mothers.'

Other than increased psychological support for new parents, which has begun to emerge through charities and online forums in recent years, it is worth exploring structural, policy-led changes that might lessen the risk of perinatal mental illness. I'd suggest lessening the pressure, both social and economic, placed on new parents to get back to full-time work as soon as possible after the birth of their child, might be a good starting point.

A key element of this is paternity leave. This is essentially a feminist issue because, whilst women are successfully carving out a strong presence in the professional and corporate world, they continue to be seen as the primary caregivers. This not only means that there is an unconscious prejudice against employing women of child-bearing age (because they'll 'want time off' to cater to the needs of their existing or prospective offspring), it also robs a lot of dads/same-sex partners who have not done the birth-giving of the opportunity to properly bond with their children.

In Sweden, a (hugely unpopular at the time) law was introduced that gave what was essentially compulsory paternity leave to new dads. Ten years later, being a caregiver has been comfortably incorporated into that country's notion of masculinity. Which, from where I'm standing (to the left, in Britain), seems brilliant.

## EARLY DEVELOPMENT

There are many oft-used phrases that make my teeth itch. Amongst these are 'life's not fair, deal with it', 'real women' (most often used to describe women at the heavier end of the weight spectrum, presumably in the misguided belief that thin women are holograms) and, most pertinently for this section, 'school should prepare children for the realities of life'.

We know enough about child and adolescent psychology now to be assured that a developing brain is fundamentally different from a developed one. Therefore, the needs of adults are not the same as the needs of young people, and their environment should reflect that. Children are not ready for 'the realities of life' . That's why it's illegal for them to have a job, sign a legal contract, smoke, drink, drive or join the army. No one can dispute the importance of stimulating children intellectually and creatively, and encouraging them to the best academic performance they can muster. I disagree, however, that more rigorous testing in schools, as introduced by the much-decried new education policy of 2016, is the way to go about it.

Before the age of approximately seven, we are simply absorbing our environment, like a sponge. We do not yet have critical faculty, which is the ability to apply nuance and context to what we are seeing and hearing. This is why children tend to think in very black and white terms. Whilst they will ask you 'why' incessantly, they also generally cannot tell if you are lying. They have no concept of agenda. They don't understand that their dad is having a bad day and that's why he's grumpy. They take everything literally and assume everything that happens to them is a direct result of their actions.

Additionally, a young child's world view is confined to what is immediately in front of them. Children under seven are tiny mindfulness gurus, absorbed utterly in whatever they are doing (for about three seconds). They cannot multitask. If they're upset, they cry. If they're happy, they laugh. If they don't understand something, they ask. They respond to situations by manifesting with determination and confidence the emotion they're feeling. They get it out of their system and consign it to history. We should all be a bit more like six-year-olds.

Around the age of seven or eight, a child who is developing along the ordinary pathway will experience a 'zooming out' of their world view. They become aware that they are part of a community and a social hierarchy and will make attempts to carve out their own space within it. You'll often find rapid changes in friendship groups, as they work out who are their 'leaders'.

Shortly after this, adolescence rears its disruptive head (which, terrifyingly, is deemed by neurobiologists to begin at the age of nine). Between the ages of around nine and when the brain completes its development at around twenty-two, most people experience a spike in the chemical dopamine. We've looked at the effect of dopamine in relation to stress, addiction and its effect on mental wellbeing. Nature, however, gives young people the gift of extra dopamine because it makes us prone to risk-taking and it wants them to test boundaries. Only by challenging our pre-existing structures and belief systems in this way can we establish independence and ingratiate ourselves into social networks of our own age, rather than relying on our parents or carers to fulfil all of our emotional needs. But, as we've seen, an imbalance of dopamine can also impact mental health, which is why, experts believe, depression, anxiety, autistic-spectrum disorders, addiction and psychosis all have their peak onset during adolescence.

### SPECIAL EDUCATIONAL NEEDS

There is an established link between having a learning difficulty like dyslexia or a condition like autism and experiencing mental-health issues. I have heard much speculation as to why this is, but there seems to be a number of elements that increase vulnerability, amongst which, again, is the belonging need not being fulfilled.

Children with special educational needs (SEN) tend to be labelled early and often put into a different school. Their entire existence is defined by the ways they diverge from what is considered 'normal'. Of course, a small percentage of children have needs that can only be met in an environment specifically designed for them and need to be cared for by people with specialist knowledge. However, when it comes to milder spectrum disorders I am left with the sense that we're simply punishing people for not thinking in ways that we have defined as acceptable.

Whenever I have worked with young people with SEN I have been struck by how talented they are. Not because my expectations for them were low, but because they have often been gifted in a way that's objectively extraordinary.

A couple of examples spring to mind. I met a teenage boy with autism in a small school for bullied, traumatized and excluded children. He was so keen to compensate for what he believed to be his lack of social skills that he came across as aggressively, weirdly friendly, which resulted in him being badly bullied in his mainstream school. He showed me the science project he was working on and I couldn't even begin to fathom its intricacy, complexity and the hours of work he must have put into it.

Another time I was approached by the mother of a sixth-form 'fan' of mine who wanted to speak to me at an event, but was apparently worried because they had (unspecified) learning difficulties and weren't very good at making eye contact, sometimes didn't understand humour and didn't want me to think they were rude. I told her I'd be delighted to meet them and to send them over. We stood side by side to make the encounter less awkward and they started to tell me about their artwork. There was some displayed in the school and they asked if I wanted to see it. It was magnificent. Better than pieces I'd seen selling for thousands of pounds in art galleries. I bought some and they hang on my wall. Visitors always admire them.

Now, I appreciate that I might be viewing young people with SEN through rose-tinted glasses, but I think there is an opportunity here to question the machinations of the entire education system. Albert Einstein famously said 'if you judge a fish by its ability to climb a tree it will live its whole life believing it is stupid.' Whilst children with SEN are the most marginalized by the way education is structured, I think we all probably are, to an extent.

At its heart, the curriculum and the way it is taught hasn't really changed for a century. There have been endless directives and successive Secretaries of State trying to leave their stamp on the sector by making ill-thought-out, sweeping policy changes (I'm looking at you, Michael Gove) but pupils still sit in rows to learn pieces of information that they then have to memorize and regurgitate under exam conditions. Being good at exams isn't intelligence as such, it's really just having a good memory, which appears to be one of only a handful of quite specific skills that our education system rewards.

I passionately believe, for the future and wellbeing of young people (not to mention teachers), the school system needs a rethink.

## HORMONES

When we talk about hormones it's often with a dismissive hand gesture and a derisive tone. 'Ha! Look at that pregnant person gnashing around on the carpet in floods of tears! Hormones! Aren't they hilarious?' Yet their impact is incredibly powerful, as anyone who has ever been through the menopause will attest. Hormones, to a large extent, dictate our drives, emotions and behaviours.

In my experience, there is an unwillingness by doctors to concede that there is any relationship between mental health and hormones and this is principally because of their propensity for trying to make symptoms fit neatly into a set of diagnostic criteria, rather than acknowledging the limitlessly complicated person sat in their surgery.

We know the perils of trusting Dr Google, but a search for 'hormones mental health' will uncover a gargantuan swathe of people who have noticed a distinct link. I consulted Dr Tory Eisenlohr-Moul, who is a clinical psychologist with a PhD in the link between hormones associated with the menstrual cycle and our emotional/behavioural responses to them. I also sought the wisdom of Gabrielle Lichterman, former health journalist and founder of the website Hormonology.

They told me that, whilst a routine hormone check might not show anything unusual, some people have an in-built sensitivity to what are medically considered to be normal hormonal changes. These are referred to as 'reproductive mood disorders' and are mostly likely to be seen during adolescence, menstrual cycle, pregnancy or menopause. Additionally, hormone imbalances, whilst relatively rare, can also cause stress and anxiety, so the relationship is symbiotic.

It's erroneous, however, to suggest that some mental-health issues are hormonal by nature and therefore not as 'real' or vice versa. What should rather be borne in mind is that adolescence and pregnancy are both peak times during which hormone fluctuation can impact mental health.

## UNIVERSITY

Ask most people to conjure up an image of a student and they'll tell of unbridled hedonism, characterized by unprecedented intellectual and physical freedom, shagging, binge-drinking and generally having the time of your life. It is this stereotype that stops so many students speaking openly about or seeking help for their mental-health issues.

According to Rosie Tressler, chief executive of charity Student Minds, undergraduate students (who represent almost 50 per cent of young people) have lower levels of wellbeing compared with the rest of the population. She says:

> There is something about being at university in itself which is contributing to low wellbeing ... For many young people these are the first years they will live independently and spending time away from established networks and family support. In adjusting to student lifestyle, many students struggle to maintain healthy day-to-day routines. Key challenges have been identified as: housing and relationships, cooking and budgeting, homesickness, culture shock, peer pressure, balancing a busy lifestyle of academic work, employment, social life and anxiety about future prospects in the job market. It's no wonder that roughly a third of students report psychological distress.

Irregular sleeping patterns and poor nutrition, as well as the general shifting of the tectonic plates of a person's life caused by moving away from home for the first time, can all be triggers for mental illness. The problem is that, whilst Child and Adolescent Mental Health Services are grossly underfunded (we spend fourteen times more on adult services than on CAMHS, despite the peak onset age mentioned above), there is at least a defined pathway. When funding is allocated or strategies devised for 'young people' it is generally for under-18s. Adults services can be intimidating for students who are, whilst technically adults, still vulnerable. Young people who have been visiting CAMHS often drop out of the system at this point, for that very reason.

Another barrier to consider is that students tend to spend twenty-five weeks of the year on campus and the rest of the time at home. This can lead to misunderstandings and miscommunications between teams, as well as confusion as to whose responsibility it is to provide ongoing mental-health care, if it is needed.

Encouragingly, there does appear to be more awareness of the psychological needs of students in recent years. Many student unions have a 'Wellbeing Officer'. I have been invited to advise on campus wellbeing strategy, not only at my former home in Aberystwyth but also at Coventry University: London and University of East Anglia. The times, they are (fingers, toes and all other crossable appendages crossed) a-changing.

## A BEGINNER'S GUIDE TO IMPROVING
## THE MENTAL HEALTH OF YOUNG PEOPLE

Do not, whatever you do, say 'one day you'll look back on this and realize it doesn't matter'. This sort of statement is kindly meant, but usually delivered by people who reached the age of twenty-one and got immediate amnesia regarding anything they felt up until that point. When you are at school, it represents almost the entirety of your world. Your friends, the people you are randomly thrown into proximity with, are your tribe. There is hardly anything that exists outside of this and no other yardstick by which to measure your experiences.

The concerns of young people sometimes seem unimportant to adults but, going back to what we explored in chapter *U: Unjudgmental Listening*, pain is pain, grief is grief and all perspectives are valid.

Also bear in mind that for teenagers experiencing mental illness, they don't have a blueprint for illness-free adult life to measure their present state against. Imagine having depression or anxiety and thinking that was what 'being an adult' was and therefore how you are going to feel forever. Grim.

## A BEGINNER'S GUIDE TO BEING YOUNG

Below, in no particular order, are some nuggets I've harvested throughout my life that you might find helpful.

- Remember that no one knows what they're doing. Everyone is walking around thinking 'Argh! I don't have a clue! Why am I in charge of this thing? How am I allowed to have responsibilities?' The process of becoming an adult is simply the means by which we become more adept at hiding this. Don't fall into the trap of thinking you're the only one who hasn't figured everything out. No one has.

- Sometimes, you do know better than your parents. (There are ways of saying things, though.)

- Most parents are trying their best. (They are also extremely right about some things.)

- Use your power as a consumer of social media. Find role models who reflect the values you'd like to live by and design a network based on positivity and empowerment.

- Lose people who make you feel worse about yourself. Waiting for the moment when a friendship or relationship becomes 'worth it' or resolves itself is like standing on a never-ending escalator to nowhere. Some people take a lifetime to reach that conclusion. Don't be one of them.

- Try not to label yourself. You're not 'anorexic' or 'anxious' or 'depressed', you are a multi-faceted person who might be currently experiencing those things.

- Never be sworn to secrecy by a friend who is telling you about their mental illness. It is not your burden to carry, it is not your problem to fix, and if they are a danger to themselves (for example if they are suicidal) it is not a betrayal to tell someone.

- There is at least one member of staff in your school who will fight your corner if an unrealistic amount is being expected of you academically. Honest – I have seen and spoken with them. Get together a group of you who have identified specific problems, write them down and find that person.

- It's incredibly annoying when people tell you to 'love yourself the way you are' because it's a statement that only resonates if you already do. But I just want to tell you this – I'm not your mum, or a teacher, or someone else you might assume 'has' to tell you you're fantastic because they're biased and that's their job. Unequivocally, you deserve to be loved, appreciated and celebrated. Working with people your age has given me an immeasurable amount of knowledge, fulfilment and pleasure, and anyone who cannot recognize your brilliance is, in my (objective) opinion, missing out.

is for . . .

# ZERO FUCKS GIVEN

(or the art of having
high self-esteem)

**I am often described as a 'Self-Esteem Expert' during media appearances, which is a term so vague and open to interpretation that even I couldn't tell you definitively what it means.**

'Self-esteem' is one of those phrases that's thrown around with merry abandon, but will have an entirely different connotation depending on the mouth it has issued from and the ear it has entered. I've variously heard self-esteem described as 'the easiest thing to work on' and 'the most closely guarded element of the psyche'. I've interviewed educators who believe it is teachable and learnable at any age and psychologists who say that if you haven't acquired a sufficient amount of it by the time you're seven you might as well write yourself off.

I've met people who have credited increased self-esteem for their ability to stand up for themselves, as well as those who say it is responsible for their new-found aptitude for shutting the fuck up and listening. I've argued with pundits who believe that the term is nothing more than a weak excuse for anti-social behaviour and thought to myself that their apparent total lack of empathy might, ironically, be a result of low self-esteem.

I've spoken to experts who believe self-esteem is the key to everything, including but not limited to the gender pay gap, domestic violence, discrepancies in academic performance between different socio-ethnic groups, and the incessant need reality TV stars have to inflict their nakedness upon the world via highly Photoshopped selfies. I've interviewed others who dismiss self-esteem as yet another bogus notion invented to persuade the population to part with their cash in the misguided pursuit of it whilst ignoring the economic and cultural factors that truly create injustice – another cog in the consumer machine.

### GOOD BOX MENTALITY™

Andre Symeou, a leading Harley Street psychologist, told me his 'Good Box Mentality' theory – an analogy that neatly sums up self-esteem as a concept and ethos and that I've found countless uses for since.

Andre described a former patient who was a painter and decorator. During one session, he brought along a beautiful, ornamental trinket box and dropped it on the coffee table in front of him. Andre complimented the painter on the box and he revealed, rather proudly, that he had made it.

After his session, the painter was on his way to be paid by a client. He had a policy of giving a home-made trinket box to each of his clients after completing their decorating job, both as a thank-you for using his services and also in the hope that they would put it on display, perhaps visitors to the house would notice it and comment upon it, which would ultimately lead to a word-of-mouth recommendation. In this way he had rather cleverly turned his trinket boxes, which he enjoyed making as a hobby, into a way of potentially generating more business.

'That's one of my best,' the painter declared, pointing at the box between them.

At his next session, Andre asked if the client had liked her gift.

'No,' the painter replied, with a dismissive wave of his hand. 'She didn't like it. She gave it back. It wasn't a good box, that one, anyway.'

Ever since then, Andre has spoken of self-esteem in terms of 'Good Box Mentality'. After he had initially crafted the box, the painter had judged it to be 'one of his best'. It was, therefore a 'good box' as far as he was concerned. His client's subsequent assessment of it shouldn't be relevant.

In the same way, self-esteem should never be outsourced. If our confidence is derived from the validation of others, then it can be easily taken away. This is an incredibly precarious position to place oneself in.

I, for example, have an enduring psychological sore-spot that is pressed during times when I feel I have been wilfully misinterpreted or misunderstood. I can handle criticism, so long as it relates to something I have actually said or done. If the criticism relates to an imagined slight or a projection from the other person's blik, Nigel surfaces swiftly, cackling.

Ever since I heard Andre's story, when I have felt my self-esteem is under attack from a deliberate misinterpretation, I have remembered that I considered myself to be, ultimately, a good box.

The appeal of Good Box Mentality is that it places self-esteem within the realms of our control.

Whilst researching this chapter, I sought out people who, in diverse ways, appear to be living and breathing their own philosophies on self-esteem. I asked them each to define what self-esteem meant to them and whether they felt their arrival at a place of high self-esteem had been a 'journey'. What each of the responses had in common was a conscious moment of deciding to give zero fucks about the opinions of others, arbitrary social demands or circumstances over which they had no control.

### Chidera Egerue

Better known as 'The Slumflower', Chidera is a poet, motivational speaker and social-media influencer, boasting an impressive following and sharing messages about body acceptance, feminism and racial equality. I met her when we were both part of a panel on *Late Night Women's Hour* discussing self-esteem and its relevance to modern life. Chidera immediately struck me as one of those people who is simultaneously interested and interesting. She's apparently threatened by no one on a personal or professional level, but you're left in no doubt that if you attack her principles she'll have your bollocks on a silver platter. Her confidence is catching.

Her latest project, she told me, is #saggyboobsmatter, an online body-positivity movement started after a string of uninvited commentary from male social-media users attempting to convince her that she shouldn't 'go bra-less' and that her breasts were abnormally droopy for her age.

There are few people of any age who would possess the requisite self-belief to draw attention to and encourage scrutiny of something about them that society considers a physical flaw. When I asked her where she gets her impressive capacity for confidence from, she referenced the racism she faced as person of Nigerian heritage growing up in the UK and the unconsciously curated beliefs that were an unwelcome by-product: 'I used to believe my nose was too big. I believed that having dark knees and dark elbows meant I looked "dirty",' she told me. 'I believed my hair had to be straight in order for me to be taken seriously. Imagine thinking that you were created incorrectly. That's what it's like to grow up in a society that tells you that being black is bad.'

In a culture with a vested interest in highlighting so-called 'flaws' and then selling us 'solutions', I think most of us can relate to a vague sense of having been 'created incorrectly'. The difference between Chidera's experiences and those of a white person in the UK is that her most prominent socially defined 'flaw', i.e. the colour of her skin, was not something she could 'fix'. Whilst this is clearly contemptable racism, it perhaps brought Chidera to the conclusion that the problem is society, not her, faster than it might have done if she was a white person wasting time chasing theoretically achievable Caucasian beauty ideals.

She explained: 'Self-esteem to me is the belief that [whilst] I might not be anybody's idea of perfect I am my idea of perfect and that's all that matters.' So speaks someone with textbook Good Box Mentality.

Chidera is still in her early twenties, and has managed to work out far quicker than most (or certainly faster than I did) that self-esteem isn't some magic unknown quality that some have and others don't, but an ongoing process that, just like physical fitness, needs consistent work. She describes it as 'shedding the idea that I need to be liked in order to be valuable.'

## Chris Russell

Chris is a professional musician and author of the hugely popular young-adult fiction series *Songs About a Girl*. He is talented, stylish, articulate and handsome. I'm fortunate to count Chris amongst my friends, and whether he's entertainly telling an anecdote, or attracting admiring glances from every quarter of a crowded pub, or saying, 'Hang on . . . I think I can work out the chords,' before faultlessly striking up a song on guitar or piano so we can have an impromptu sing-along, I often find myself thinking, 'If I were you I'd be *so* arrogant.'

In doing so, I make the fundamental and oft-repeated mistake of misunderstanding the nature of arrogance. Arrogance, in contrast to what most people believe, is not characterized by having an excess of self-esteem, but rather the opposite. Arrogance feels a need to prove itself constantly and happens in the realms of the superficial ego.

I have been, I now understand, arrogant. It was when I was young, thin, what our culture would label as externally beautiful, with an apparently maximum-freedom, minimum-responsibility lifestyle, that I displayed the most traits of arrogance. I only know this because people say to me now 'God, you used to be a bitch.' They describe behaviour I can't recognize in myself, even in retrospect, like sitting in the corners of clubs with my nose in the air, clutching a flute of champagne, giving passers by the 'Essex once-over'. The funniest thing is that my overriding memory is of wondering why no one wanted to talk to me. My feelings were of being 'alien', of disenfranchisement and of not belonging. I used to look at the women on the dance floor, hair skew whiff, sweat sending rivulets of mascara down their cheeks, heads thrown back in laughter, arms joyfully thrown around one another, and wish, desperately, that I was them.

Arrogant people don't feel anything resembling the genuine confidence Chris is imbued with. He's also, I have discovered, not immune to moments of insecurity. 'Unfortunately, we live in a society fuelled by envy and the messages around us every day are ruthlessly engineered to make us feel inadequate,' he told me.

I have reflected on this. Whilst Chris' band, The Lightyears, do well enough to tour the world, they aren't Kings of Leon. Whilst his books have all been bestsellers in their categories, he isn't JK Rowling. If he were a different sort of person, it would be very easy for him to bemoan the fact that his talent and his hard work hasn't yet provided him with all the wealth and splendour the world has to offer. I asked him his secret to avoiding the jealousy vortex. He replied:

When I was a kid, my grandfather told me that if I could find a way to get paid for doing something I loved, I'd be happy. And he was right. It isn't easy and the old cliché of 'following your passion' certainly doesn't work for everyone. I know plenty of people who keep their passion for the weekends whilst working in a job that pays the bills, and many of them are as happy as puppies on a trampoline – but for me, stumbling upon my passion at an early age and not letting go has kept my self-esteem ticking over.

Again, Chris is demonstrating Good Box Mentality, here. As long as he can be proud of his output and has regular access to the creativity that he identifies as his raison d'être, his relative commercial success matters not a jot. This is significant insofar as many people resist pursuing something that has been a long-harboured ambition because they fear the public response. Their consequent resentment can fester and slowly erode self-esteem.

Chris has also identified his motivation, which is crucial. For some people, it is being able to establish and maintain a certain quality of life – being able to have a roof above their heads, buy an Xbox, afford a beer on a Friday night – that brings them genuine contentment and they'll pretty much do any job that provides them access to that lifestyle. There is absolutely nothing wrong with this. In fact, assuming they live in an economy which allows them to be paid a fair wage and to create a decent standard of living for themselves in return for a hard week's graft, they might be the happiest people there are.

### Joanna Rowsell Shand

Jo is a multiple world-record-breaking professional cyclist who has twice won a gold medal for Britain at the Olympics as part of the team pursuit. Jo has Alopecia Totalis (an immune-system-based condition that means she has no hair at all), and during the London Olympics in 2012 there was a huge media frenzy following her accepting her medal without a wig on. The attention was overwhelmingly positive, with Jo hailed as a brave pioneer for people affected by alopecia, as well as body confidence more generally.

I had the pleasure of co-authoring Joanna's autobiography *Full Circle* in the early part of 2017.

Professional athletes have a reputation for arrogance and single-mindedness, which initially made me cautious about taking on Jo's book.

The old adage tells us that nice girls finish last and this was a woman who has won a huge number of titles for her country. It took approximately five minutes of being in Jo's company for me to establish that she couldn't be further from the archetypal gold-medal-winning Olympian. She is almost unbelievably nice, to the extent that I was waiting for the moment when her facade would inevitably fall away.

Needless to say that didn't happen, and instead we discussed her reputation as being 'too nice' to succeed – something that has haunted her for the entirety of her career:

> I've learned that you don't have to have the stereotypical 'thick skin' to succeed. I've got better at accepting life's small injustices, but I'm still sensitive. I still worry about what other people think . . . [but] I like who I am, and my career has taught me there is a difference between arrogance and resilience – the latter is essential, the former isn't.

As I got to know Jo, I realized that it was something of a badge of honour for her that she hadn't sacrificed her 'niceness' or had to compromise her character, which is naturally introverted, in pursuit of professional success. There is a quiet steadfastness about her.

Jo also spoke at length about the 'brave' label which was applied to her after accepting medals on television without a hair piece. She told me:

> After a race, you're rushed beneath the velodrome and you have what seems like only a few minutes before you're on the podium. It would never occur to me to put a wig on during that time. I didn't think I was being 'brave' and I was surprised by all the media attention. Afterwards, I realized how much it had meant to other people who have alopecia and it was only then I started becoming involved with charities working in that area.

That's the other thing I discovered about Jo – she just does things. Her career began because a British Cycling talent-spotting team came into her school when she was in Year Nine and she thought she'd give it a go. It's not that she assumes she's better than anyone else, it's simply that she doesn't assume she is any worse. She instinctively grabs at opportunities and sees where they take her.

## Jonny Benjamin

Jonny is best known for channel 4 documentary *The Stranger on the Bridge* and accompanying social-media campaign #FindMike. To sum up his story in a hugely inadequate nutshell: in 2008, a man found Jonny on a bridge and talked him out of ending his own life. Afterwards, Jonny's internet campaign to find the stranger who had saved him went viral and within weeks he had identified 'Mike' (who was actually called Neil Laybourn).

Jonny has a diagnosis of schizoaffective disorder, which is a combination of schizophrenia and bipolar. He has made more than a hundred vlogs about his experiences, as well as travelling the world speaking about suicide prevention. In 2016, he launched 'ThinkWell', an initiative that brings workshops designed to break down stigma associated with mental illness into schools. The same year he was given an MBE for his services to awareness raising.

In short, Jonny is inspirational as fuck.

When I spoke to him about his own journey with self-esteem, Jonny talked about his identity as a Jewish man and how he believed that being gay in addition to having a diagnosis of schizophrenia would lead to him being shunned and excluded from his community.

He told me, 'At one point I couldn't even press the button to cross a road. I feared the drivers would be angry with me for disturbing their journey. I felt absolutely worthless within the world. I had developed social anxiety and was constantly blushing whenever I spoke to anyone.'

For Jonny, salvation came in the form of YouTube. He identified the need to talk, but 'didn't feel ready' to look into another person's eyes, unburdening himself instead to a camera and creating his vlogs. Over time, Jonny developed the confidence to come out, not only about his sexuality but also his mental health issues. He describes the 'incredibly supportive response' he got from his family and friends and the overwhelming relief he felt.

Jonny is wise and has a talent for phrasing complicated things in a way anyone could grasp. I remember watching a presentation he gave about ways in which discussions around mental health could easily be included in the National Curriculum. He said, 'We're told *Romeo and Juliet* is a love story but it's actually a story about two young people who kill themselves,' and I'm convinced that every single one of the three hundred-odd people in the audience had an 'Oh yeeeeeeeeah' moment.

For the past year Jonny has been having CFT (Compassion Focused Therapy), which involves the use of both meditation and continuous positive self-affirmation and has been instrumental in allowing him to like himself. 'I still struggle and have had relapses and hospitalizations in the past few years, but learning to accept and forgive myself when this happens has helped me immensely. Recently, I was able to look into the mirror, smile at myself, and feel a great sense of self-esteem.'

## Me

In the year 2000, something happened in our family that I'm not allowed, owing to terms of an ongoing harassment order I have in place against the perpetrator, to tell you about. However, I can tell you that it had an indelible impact on all of us and for a long time I believed it was my fault.

It took many sessions with my counsellor to unravel the complex, self-esteem-destroying web of beliefs that had been created by the incident, as well as the situations leading up to it and the enduring consequences. I began to realize that my conscious mind, the logical part of me that knows it couldn't possibly have been my fault, was at odds with my unconscious, a place where rationality doesn't hold dominion.

I harboured a belief, deep down, that I shouldn't become close to people because I was somehow 'dangerous' and that bad things would inevitably happen to them. I pushed people away, deliberately sabotaged friendships and romantic relationships and blamed myself when the net result was that I was lonely and sad.

You'd think if you were lugging around such a hefty and all-encompassing philosophy as a fundamental belief that you are unworthy of love and doomed to wander the planet alone and tortured for all eternity, like some sort of Incredible Hulk figure, that you'd know about it. Yet I genuinely didn't.

When you're experiencing life day by day, you don't tend to notice patterns in your behaviour. It's like when you're a kid and an auntie you haven't seen for ages remarks on how much you've grown. You always think 'have I?' If you live in your body and see it in the mirror every day, you don't notice the tiny, incremental gains in height that are noticeable to an outsider.

I was also, I think, afraid of what would happen if I totally left all the guilt and sorrow of my past behind. So much of my existence is still – almost thirty years after I was changing my little brother's nappies and being told what a 'good girl' I was – characterized by being 'useful' to other people. I like being needed. I enjoy the idea that I can make a positive difference. I think a miniscule yet powerful part of me believed that if I

didn't think I had to atone for the past I'd become selfish. (Spoiler: turns out that was a load of old arse.)

My 'lightbulb' moment in terms of self-esteem was the realization that it's a conscious choice. So often, self-esteem is spoken about as though it is an ethereal quality, that clicks into place and needs no attention thereafter. No one, I believe, ever attains self-esteem in this way. There is no 'secret' to it. In fact, that's a key element of the way the concept of self-esteem has been commodified, framed as something that can be chased and purchased and which will come upon us suddenly, wrapping around us like a faux-fur vintage-style coat.

The reality is, in my experience, far more subtle, nuanced and, crucially, conscious in its nature. I now recognize the voice that reproduces and twists the shadows of all my previous heartbreaks and humiliations, and every time it whispers in my ear I tell it to shut up. I remind myself that the past and the future do not exist. That the only incarnation of Natasha Devon who matters is the one in the present, in this precious second I am experiencing. And present Natasha Devon, I have now finally begun to authentically believe, is a really good box.

## A BEGINNER'S GUIDE TO GIVING ZERO FUCKS

It might be that you are dissatisfied with an aspect of yourself you have the power to change. Maybe you are too quick to judge or become angry. Maybe you have addiction issues. Maybe you did some things that need rectifying in order to redress your karmic balance. Whilst these can only be tackled by you, remember that the very fact you have the desire to change them in the first place means that you are a good box.

At the beginning of this book we explored the peculiar marriage of terror and liberty that characterizes the fact that you are the only person inhabiting your skull. In turn, this means that when the work of your day is done and you descend into silent contemplation there is only one person there to judge you: yourself.

Life has taught me that there are, in reality, very few objectively bad boxes. There are millions of imperfect boxes. There are ones that are slightly battered. Ones that are a bit smelly and fraying round the edges. Ones with pieces missing. Ones that have buried themselves in layers of shit for so long that they and the people around them have lost the ability to see they were once and could again be good boxes. But there's only a miniscule percentage who could be reasonably dismissed as fundamentally 'bad'.

The likelihood is that you are not amongst them.

# A–Z

## CONCLUSION

According to the Mental Health Foundation, black, Asian and ethnic minority (BAME) people are more likely to be diagnosed with mental-health problems and less likely to see a positive outcome from treatment. Afro-Caribbean people living in the UK have lower rates of diagnosed common mental-health issues, but are more likely to experience severe mental illness, in particular schizophrenia. Suicide rates are high in young Asian women, whilst alcohol-dependency rates are elevated in Indian men.

This isn't just about discrimination arising from visual difference – Irish people living in the UK have higher rates of depression and alcohol dependency and are at greater risk of suicide.

You might argue that there is less cultural acceptability in certain communities for speaking about mental health and accessing treatment, and that therefore issues that might otherwise have been addressed in their early stages are left until they are severe and less treatable. There is some value, I believe, in this argument and it's backed up by the fact that BAME people are more likely than any other ethnic group to be prescribed treatment through, for example, the police service than to seek it themselves. However, we can also consider that the chain of causation might work the other way around and that the way the law is enforced in some quarters causes trauma. I'd need another book to explore this properly.

As explored in chapter Q: Queer, LGBT+ people are four times more likely to experience depression. Some have speculated that to come out as LGBT+ requires calling on reserves of bravery and strength, so being open about mental-health struggles seems less of a big deal. It's a theory and I'm sure it's correct in some instances.

However, there still remains the fact of higher instances of both attempted and completed suicide amongst LGBT+ people. And that the age that an LGBT+ person will attempt suicide is inversely proportional to the levels of social stigma surrounding homosexuality in their community, i.e. the more discrimination you witness, the younger you are pushed towards crisis.

What is absolutely indisputable is that all of these communities living in the UK – BAME, Irish, LGBT+ – who are more vulnerable to poor mental health also experience higher levels of social disadvantage and prejudice. We can, therefore, perceive an empirical link between social-economic factors and mental illness.

Researching this book has led me to discover that the people who truly suffer disproportionately with mental-health issues are the people whom our current social structure is no longer benefiting, and that is an increasing number of us. I don't mean simply in economic terms. Ideologically, many of us are living in an environment that feels less safe, less kind, less healthy and less conducive to our needs.

The worst bigotry I have encountered has been predicated on an idea that there is no such thing as social inequality – that life is fair, that everyone has an equal chance to flourish, that all good fortune is the result of a willingness to 'work hard', and therefore the wealthy 'deserve' what they have and the people at the other end of the scale should simply try harder. To me, this is the most dangerous myth of them all.

Life is in some ways more overwhelming, harsher, more fraught with worry, unrealistic expectation and judgment than it ever has been, for almost everyone. Couple that with the relative lack of community – the fact that so many of us don't even know our neighbours' names, let alone feel like we are part of a supportive and loving real, human, fleshy network happening in the world of three dimensions – and it is little wonder the result has been a mental-health crisis.

In short, if so many of us are losing our minds, it probably means that society is fucked. Concerns about global warming, economic uncertainty, poverty, politics, the impact of poorly funded infrastructure, longer working hours, sleep deprivation, the draining effect of consumerist capitalism, the effects of SAD, caffeine addiction, technology addiction, drug addiction, stress and anxiety – these things make an appearance, in some form, in an average morning for me and, I suspect, most people. The factors that influence mental health are everywhere and none of us are immune.

The most difficult part of the whole process is that the more mental distress you are in, the narrower your perspective generally becomes. I wouldn't have been able to come to any of the conclusions I have in this book, and certainly not in the ways that I have, when my mental illnesses were at their most acute. Then, I carried around the paradoxical belief that not only was everything my fault (including things I had literally no agency over) but that all my misfortune was caused by other individuals who were apparently happier or more successful or luckier than I was.

That's why it's so easy to encourage people who are struggling to expend their energy squabbling amongst themselves. Division and hatred are perpetuated when you take an angry or miserable person and persuade them it's the fault of someone who is equally angry and miserable, when in fact both people should be looking upwards, at their puppet masters.

In this book, I hope I have explored some of the ways we can try to circumnavigate this process. Ultimately, it's all about balance.

We can understand that nutrition, exercise and relaxation all play a part in basic mental health whilst acknowledging that mental illnesses are serious and that the urgency they are shown should have parity with their physical equivalents.

We should be able to take medication that will help us function better day to day without judgment or guilt, whilst still understanding that there are likely wider, social factors involved in mental illness.

We have the right to expect compassionate and expedient care from medical professionals, whilst understanding how constrained they are by a poorly funded and structured healthcare system and that they might very well be experiencing mental-health issues themselves.

We can reframe our understanding of what 'attention seeking' is (attention needing).

We can know that, whilst eating disorders are serious psychological conditions, they are to some extent influenced by the seemingly 'superficial' considerations of media and fashion.

We can grasp that 'the media' as an entity can have agendas that are unhelpful or actively harmful, but that the industry is populated by many genuinely kind-hearted and well-intentioned individuals trying (and often succeeding) to make a positive difference.

We can know that what constitutes a symptom of poor mental health in one person is simply a facet of someone else's personality and that knowing the difference is not about trying to perform amateur diagnoses but establishing genuine connection.

We can understand that we can't fix the mental-health problems faced by our friends, but we can provide valuable support and be the bridge to the therapeutic care they may require.

Truth is all about nuance. Mental health isn't just one thing. Mental illness isn't attributable to a single cause with a universally effective cure. No one can ever be an ultimate authority, but I hope this book has given you some useful tips, some ideological fodder to wrangle with, and the clarity on language and terminology needed to start some vital conversations.

If you've ever asked yourself the question 'is it just me who is going mad?' or looked around and thought 'there must be a better way', I wrote this book for you.

# ENDNOTES

**All online material was last accessed in February 2018, unless stated otherwise.**

## Introduction
The one in four statistic that is so widely quoted is from a UK-wide, government-subsidised study on mental health back in 2004. However, most experts and charities I have consulted with now estimate the figure to be closer to one in three. There is a distinction to be made between a mental-health problem/symptoms of mental illness and a mental-health disorder/long-term mental illness. For the latter, the Mental Health Foundation's latest figures estimate the prevalence to be one in six.

Medical diagnostic criteria: World Health Organization, the ICD-10 Classification of Mental and Behavioural Disorders, Geneva, 1993, WHO. Available at: www.who.int/classifications/icd/en/bluebook.pdf?ua=1

Mental health at the forefront of our social agenda: this has been helped in no small measure by the intervention of Princes William and Harry with their 'Heads Together' campaign. In 2017, Heads Together were the official charity for the London marathon, the Duchess of Cambridge guest-edited an edition of the *Huffington Post* dedicated to mental health, and Prince Harry was a guest on Bryony Gordon's 'Mad World' *Telegraph* podcast, which in turn generated endless press coverage.

Public backlash: www.webtopnews.com/katie-hopkins-mocks-royals-talking-mental-health-4016-2017/

Self-described libertarian magazine *Spiked* also ran several pieces in 2017–18 with titles such as 'Blue Monday: why unhappiness is good for you' and 'We don't need a minister for loneliness'.

Here is an example: www.spiked-online.com/newsite/article/the-year-mental-illness-went-mainstream/

## A is for Anxiety
The average human spends approximately six and a half years of their life worrying: http://www.dailymail.co.uk/debate/article-1103754/As-survey-reveals-spend-6-5-years-lives-worrying-self-confessed-neurotic-says--STOP-WORRYING.html

Cognitive ability was fundamental to human survival and evolution, according to Dr David Bainbridge: Bainbridge, D: *Curveology: The Origins and Power of Female Body Shape*, London, 2015, Portobello Books

Anxiety disorders as fastest growing illness in young people: this statistic first came to my attention at an education and wellbeing conference in February 2016. It has since been corroborated by my own qualitative research in schools. www.theguardian.com/society/2016/apr/29/government-expert-warns-child-mental-health-crisis-worse-than-suspected

*Diagnostic and Statistical Manual of Mental Disorders* (DSM-V, last updated 2013), 2017, Washington, DC, American Psychiatric Association Publishing

Claire Eastham 'We're All Mad Here': www.allmadhere.co.uk

NHS Choices definition of Generalized Anxiety Disorder: www.nhs.uk/conditions/generalized-anxiety-disorder

## B is for Brain
R. M. Hare's 'blik' first seen in 'The Parable of the Lunatic', a response to Anthony Flew's 1971 *Symposium on Theology and Falsification*

Anil Seth TED Talk: Our brain hallucinates our reality: www.ted.com/talks/anil_seth_how_your_brain_hallucinates_your_conscious_reality

## C is for Capitalism

New research says that there is no such thing as free will: https://blogs.scientificamerican.com/mind-guest-blog/what-neuroscience-says-about-free-will

Ha-Joon Chang on 'free market': Chang, H. J., 23 *Things They Don't Tell You About Capitalism*, London, 2011, Penguin

Russell Brand on double standards around relieving distress: Brand, R., *Recovery: Freedom from Our Addictions*, London, 2017, Pan Macmillan (Bluebird)

Dr Jean Kilbourne's documentary *Killing Us Softly* is made by Margaret Lazarus, Renner Wunderlich, Patricia Stallone and Joseph Vitagliano detailing a lecture given by Dr Jean Kilbourne and distributed by Cambridge Documentary Films. The first version was released in 1979 but it has since been updated four times. The trailer for the most recent version is on YouTube: www.YouTube.com/watch?v=jWKXit_3rpQ&t=3s

## D is for Drugs

Report by the BBC following World Health Organization concerns over widespread prescription of antidepressants to teenagers: www.bbc.co.uk/news/health-35756602

NHS Choices on side effects of SSRIs: www.nhs.uk/conditions/ssri-antidepressants

It has been claimed that SSRIs initially put patient at greater risk of suicide: www.ncbi.nlm.nih.gov/pmc/articles/PMC4034101/

*Billion Dollar Deals and How they Changed your World* aired on BBC2 in September 2017 and was presented by Jacques Peretti. Expert: Allen Frances, a psychiatrist on the DSM-III taskforce.

Watters, E., *Crazy Like Us: The Globalization of the American Psyche*, New York, 2010, Simon & Schuster (First Free Press)

Blackpool has the largest amount of antidepressant use per capita in the UK and the highest levels of social deprivation. Findings from Exasol, a database analysis company, state that 2.11 antidepressant prescriptions were issued in Blackpool per person in 2016, compared with a national average of 1.16.

## E is for Endorphins

Laughter is the best medicine: in 2014, a study at Loma Linda University in California found that laughter improved short-term memory and reduced levels of cortisol (aka 'the stress hormone').

## F is for Food

Crilly, L., *Hope with Eating Disorders: A Self-Help Guide for Parents, Carers and Friends of Sufferers*, London, 2012, Hay House

According to statistics, eating disorders are more common in females: the National Institute of Mental Health states that between 5 and 15 per cent of people diagnosed with anorexia and 35 per cent of those with binge-eating disorders are male.

Eddie Izzard: from the recorded stand-up tour 'Sexie' in 2003, directed by Declan Lowney

Most people with bulimia have a 'normal' BMI or are slightly overweight: https://patient.info/health/eating-disorders/bulimia-nervosa

Dr Rachel Abrams on negative impact of 'inflammatories' on the mindset: from an interview I did with her in October 2017.

Latest research on nutrients that are helpful for mental wellbeing: B12 – www.psychologytoday.com/articles/200402/be-healthy-b12 Omega 3 – www.ncbi.nlm.nih.gov/pubmed/10232294

Turmeric – www.swinburne.edu.au/news/
latest-news/2016/04/swinburneresearch-
highlights-the-cognitivebenefits-of-
curcumin.php
Soluble Fibre – www.nutritionjrnl.com/
article/S0899-9007(15)00523-7/
fulltext

**G is for GP**
It has been shown that long-term
physical illness can increase your
chances of developing depression: www.
kingsfund.org.uk/publications/long-term-
conditions-and-mental-health

Kay, A., *This Is Going to Hurt: Secret
Diaries of a Junior Doctor*, London, 2017,
Pan Macmillan (Picador)

DoH and media reports critical of 2015
junior doctors' strike: The *Sun* describing
junior doctors as 'militant': www.thesun.
co.uk/news/1875009/militant-nhsjunior-
doctors-plotting-crippling-sevenday-
strike-after-crushing-court-defeat/
The *Daily Mail* suggesting strike
threatens '100 years of neutrality': www.
dailymail.co.uk/news/article-5318611/
Momentumbacking-medics-demand-
end-BMAneutrality.html

Screenshot of me interviewing
Jeremy Hunt: https://
twitter.com/_NatashaDevon/
status/958758152425623553

Follow Young Minds and Luciana
Berger to support campaigns: https://
youngminds.org.uk; www.lucianaberger.
com

**H is for Happiness**
UK came 23rd in United Nations
World Happiness Report 2016: http://
worldhappiness.report/ed/2016

'Hackschooling Makes Me Happy' Logan
LaPlante, TEDx Univeristy of Navada,
February 2013.

In 2011 researchers examined
components of genuine happiness

across the globe: Belic, R. (director),
*Happy*, 2011, Netflix (documentary
film with Marci Shimoff, Gregory Berns
and Richard Davidson)
www.thehappymovie.com

Neuroscientists have shown that singing
(particularly in groups) fires up the right
temporal lobe of the brain and releases
endorphins: www.creativityaustralia.org.
au/research/choir-research/

Classic portrayal of the 'perfect man'
debunked in 2017 'masculinity report'
Barry, J. and Daubney, M. 'The Harry's
Masculinity Report', 2017, Harrys in
partnership with University College
London. www.malepsychology.org.uk/
wp-content/uploads/2017/10/The-
Harrys-Masculinity-Report.pdf

US study on levels of happiness in
different earning categories: http://
faculty.weatherhead.case.edu/
clingingsmith/NEIW.pdf

**I is for Internet**
2016 Natasha Devon TEDx talk:
'Is Society Breaking Children's Brains?':
'Self/Less' TEDx Sir William Perkins
School, September 2016

2016 study investigating Facebook use
and poor body image/low self-esteem
in adolescents: www.sciencedirect.com/
science/article/pii/S0191886915300398

Evidence that 'prolific' smartphone use
can interfere with normal development
pathway of infant or adolescent brain:
www.sciencedirect.com/science/article/
pii/S0028393210003581

Social-media use compels us on
a neurological level to obsessively
compare ourselves with others and
in turn damages self-esteem: www.
sciencedirect.com/science/article/pii/
S0028393210003581

Dr Rachel Thomson suggests young
people see school and family time

as 'pauses' in their more 'real' online existence: professional lecture, available on YouTube.

Dr Aaron Balick on memory: from an interview I did with him in March 2015 for my *Cosmopolitan* column 'Are you a #FilterAddict?'

In 2016 Childline reported 82% increase in calls: www.bbc.co.uk/news/education-37296326

Coppafeel! is a charity working across education and media to encourage young people to check for signs of breast cancer. Find out more at www.coppafeel.org.

The 12-step Alcoholics Anonymous programme advises that a mentor should have completed the programme themselves: www.alcoholic.org/research/alcoholics-anonymous-aa-the-12-step-program

Beat: www.beateatingdisorders.org.uk

The Self-Harm Network: http://nshn.co.uk

*Porn on the Brain* was first aired on Channel 4 in 2013. You can watch the documentary and links to the Cambridge University studies used at www.yourbrainonporn.com.

Research shows that 52% of 12-year-olds and 97% of 16-year-olds have seen pornography online: more details can be found in this study from Plymouth University, undertaken by Dr Andy Phippen, published in 2012: http://impact.ref.ac.uk/CaseStudies/CaseStudy.aspx?Id=3894

**J is for Just Attention-Seeking**
Attention Seekers: Self-harm awareness training: http://satveernijjar.com

Of those who need hospitalization for self-harming behaviours, 63% are female: http://aimhs.com.au/cms/uploads/

MSP_Table_Feb17_FINAL.pdf

Men and boys provoke physical fights they know they can't win for no other reason than to feel pain: charity Self-Harm UK acknowledges this on their website, saying 'boys are more likely to engage in behaviours . . . [not] always recognized as self-harm [which] doesn't come to the attention of hospitals'.

Hospitalizations in the UK for eating disorders and self-harm in under-21s doubled in 2013–16: www.thetimes.co.uk/article/self-harming-up-by-70-among-young-teenage-girls-k73k2khvv

Satveer Nijjar: from an interview I did with her in September 2017.

People who stop self-harming without receiving support for underlying causes at increased risk of suicide: I learned this during my Mental Health First Aid instructor training in 2016. www.mhfaengland.org.uk.

The Self-Harm Network: http://nshn.co.uk

**K is for Knowing Me, Knowing You**
To find out more about the government's PREVENT scheme, visit www.gov.uk/government/publications/protecting-children-from-radicalisation-the-prevent-duty

Read the Youth Select Committee report on mental health by going to: www.parliament.uk/business/news/2015/november/youth-select-committee-report/

**L is for Low**
90% of suicides happen as a result of untreated depression or substance misuse. For more information visit the National Alliance on Mental Health website: www.nami.org/learn-more/mental-health-conditions/related-conditions/suicide

*Bridget Jones: The Edge of Reason*, 2004, Universal.

*Diagnostic and Statistical Manual of Mental Disorders* (DSM-V), 2017, Washington, DC, American Psychiatric Association Publishing. Grief was first added to the DSM IV, the subsequent and most recent edition does acknowledge the issue to be more complex.

In the UK, one in four women and one in ten men have had at least one episode of depression for which they have sought treatment: NICE (2004a) 'Depression: management of depression in primary and secondary care', p.41

Depression affects one in ten new mothers: For more information visit the Royal College of Psychiatrists website: www.rcpsych.ac.uk/healthadvice/problemsanddisorders/postnataldepression

SAD was first added to the DSM IV

To read the full MIND charity definition of SAD visit: www.mind.org.uk/information-support/types-of-mental-health-problems/seasonal-affective-disorder-sad/

Quote from Rosie's column 'Exploding the Myths about Mental Illness', *Eastern Daily Press*, August 15th 2017

Samaritans: www.samaritans.org, 116 123 (free calls 24 hours/365 days a year)

**M is for Media**
Girls School's Association annual conference keynote 'Three Key Skills for Mental Health', Principal Hotel, Manchester, 21 November 2017.

Headline example: 'Teachers ORDERED to Avoid calling Female Pupils "Girls" because it REMINDS them of their gender', *Daily Express*, 21 November 2017: www.express.co.uk/news/uk/882568/Teachers-female-pupils-gender-neutral-girls-ladies-Natasha-Devon

'Ex Mental Health Tsar's advice is Labelled "Nonsense", *Daily Mail*, 22 November 2018

BBC 2 *Horizon special*: 'Why Did I Go Mad?' (May 2017)

Bryony Gordon's 'Mad World' podcasts: www.bryonysmadworld.telegraph.co.uk

Metro Online's health desk: www.metro.co.uk/tag/mental-health/

Samaritans: www.samaritans.org, 116 123 (free calls 24 hours/365 days a year)

Beat: www.beateatingdisorders.org.uk

Mental Health First Aid England (MHFA): https://mhfaengland.org

To see the Mental Health Media Charter and a list of signees visit: www.natashadevon.com/the-mental-health-media-charter

**N is for Number 10 Downing Street**
To read more about mental health difficulties in BAME people visit: www.mentalhealth.org.uk/a-to-z/black-asian-and-minority-ethnic-bame-communities

Government campaign to 'improve' mental health in young people in 2015: www.independent.co.uk/news/uk/politics/government-launches-national-campaign-to-end-mental-health-stigma-a6703866.html

MindEd Trust Conference, 18 March 2016

*Guardian* exclusive interview following sacking as mental health tsar: www.theguardian.com/society/2016/may/13/sacked-childrens-mental-health-tzar-natasha-devon-i-was-proper-angry

To find out more about austerity measures after the 2010 election, read the Coalition Social Policy Record

ENDNOTES

2010–2015 at: www.sticerd.lse.ac.uk

2005 election: statistics as reported on Sky News, www.news.sky.com

The average local authority spends 1% of its overall budget on mental health: www.mind.org.uk/news-campaigns/news/charity-reveals-shocking-spend-of-less-than-1-per-cent-on-public-mental-health

Information on waiting times for therapeutic care for mental illness has been collated from NHS England, charities Young Minds and MIND, as well as anecdotal evidence from service users. At a rally at the House of Commons in March 2018, chair of the Labour Campaign for Mental Health and former Shadow Minister for Mental Health Luciana Berger stated that the average waiting time for an assessment in her Liverpool constituency had increased from 3 weeks in 2010 to 23 weeks in 2018.

For every £10 spent on mental health, £1,571 is spent on cancer: www.pharmaceutical-journal.com/opinion/comment/filling-the-gap-in-mental-health-research/2020022.article. For more information on mental health research and funding visit: www.mqmentalhealth.org

See notes in introduction for information on the prevalence of mental illness. Note that the number of people set to receive a cancer diagnosis is predicted to rise to an estimated 47% by 2020: goo.gl/8yJeCq

Government spending: www.gov.uk/government/news/new-investment-in-mental-health-services

Trident: https://fullfact.org/economy/trident-nuclear-cost/

After the first investment of £76 million 2015–16 to support mental-health services, only half of local authorities increased their spending on mental health in real terms: www.theguardian.com/healthcare-network/2016/may/09/mental-health-services-must-get-the-funding-they-need

Only 8% of people who have had a severe episode of psychosis manage to reclaim some vestige of the life they had before in the form of employment: ReThink Mental Illness 'Lost Generation' Report, May 2016

**O is for Obsessive Compulsive Drive**
Dr Nancy Adreasen's 1987 study at University of Iowa: www.ncbi.nlm.nih.gov/pmc/articles/PMC3181877/

Illnesses associated with psychosis are connected to higher ability for creative thinking: https://web.stanford.edu/group/cosign/Sussman.pdf

Crilly, L., and Devon, N., *Fundamentals: A Guide for Parents, Teachers and Carers on Mental Health and Self-Esteem* London, John Blake Publishing, 2015

Osgood, K., *How to Disappear Completely: On Modern Anorexia*, New York, Overlook Press, 2013.

**P is for Psychosis**
An episode of psychosis can affect anyone, and most people recover fully: Picchioni, M.M., Murray, R.M., 'Schizophrenia', BMJ, 2007

People who have a parent affected by psychosis are more likely to develop it themselves: Picchioni, M.M., Murray, R.M. (2007) Schizophrenia, *British Medical Journal*, 335: 91-95

A good overview of evidence that cannabis use is linked to psychosis can be found at: www.rcpsych.sc.uk/healthadvice/problemsanddisorders/cannabis/aspx

Debate on whether personality disorders count as 'mental illness' or are conditions in their own right: http://bjp.rcpsych.org/content/180/2/110

**Q is for Queer**
Statistics on transgender people and suicide: www.ncbi.nlm.nih.gov/pmc/articles/PMC5178031/

Depression LGBT+: https://www.nami.org/find-support/LGBTQ

Mental health at Stonewall: www.theguardian.com/commentisfree/2017/may/12/lgbt-mental-health-sexuality-gender-identity

Being a victim of bullying doubles your risk of developing depression in later life: www.livescience.com/51056-teen-bullying-doubles-adult-depression.html

There are huge discrepancies in statistics on the number of people who are LGBT+. A book by Kinsey Roberts published in 1948 called *Sexual Behaviour in the Human Male* stated it to be around 1 in 10 and this has been quoted widely since because (in my opinion) it feels about right. Another US poll in 2011 by Gallup estimated the number at 1 in 4. The most recent ONS 'Integrated Households' Survey has 93.5% of people self-identifying as straight. However, stigma and cultural expectation undoubtedly plays a role in self-identification and for this reason the percentage of LGBT+ people living the UK is almost certainly higher than the figure on the Office for National Statistics website, which is 1 in 64

Men and Boys Coalition: www.menandboyscoalition.org.uk

Williams, C., *Sugar and Slate*, 2002, Northbridge, Planet Books

**S is for Self-Care**
Mental Health First Aid England (MHFA): https://mhfaengland.org

2017 All-Party Parliamentary Group on Arts, Health & Wellbeing report on psychological benefits of creative activities in education: www.artshealthandwellbeing.org.uk/APPG

**T is for Therapy**
Information on average waiting times for therapeutic care for mental illness gathered from charities Young Minds, Mental Health First Aid England and also the Care Quality Commission.

Government green paper: Department of Health/Department for Education, 'Transforming Children and Young People's Mental Health Provision', published 4 December 2017, www.gov.uk/government/consultations/transforming-children-and-young-peoples-mental-health-provision-a-green-paper

For more information about CAMHS visit: https://youngminds.org.uk/find-help/your-guide-to-support/guide-to-camhs

Improving Access to Psychological Therapies (IAPT): www.england.nhs.uk/mental-health/adults/iapt/

Counselling Directory: www.counselling-directory.org.uk

**U is for Unjudgmental Listening**
Dr Stephen Jacobi studied English Literature at St Catharine's College Cambridge, before going on to get a PhD at London University and an MA in screenwriting. He has taught English in schools all over the world and is a Royal Literary Fellow at Warwick University.

Curtis, R. (director) *Love Actually*, 2003, Universal

Dr Andrew Curran: quote from a Mental Health First Aid training video – 'Brain Development by Dr Andrew Curran'

Simon Sinek quote from lecture 'Learn to Listen' available on Youtube: www.youtube.com/IP_UbJu7xWE

'For what do we live if not to make sport for our neighbours and laugh at them, in our turn?' Austen, J., *Pride and Prejudice*, London, 1813

**W is for Weed**
Decline in past decade in numbers of young people who drink alcohol and smoke tobacco: Health Survey for England, published by NHS Digital, December 2016

Hitchens, P., *The War We Never Fought*, London, 2012, Bloomsbury

Nutt, D., *Drugs – Without the Hot Air: Minimising the Harms of Legal and Illegal Drugs*, Cambridge, 2012, UIT Cambridge Ltd
Read Professor David Nutt's blog 'Addiction: a life long illness not lifestyle choice' here: www.profdavidnutt. wordpress.com/2011/02/28/addiction-a-life-long-illness-not-lifestyle-choice/

'Rat Park' addiction study1: Alexander, B. K., Beyerstein, B. L., Hadaway, P. F. and Coambs, R. B. 'Effect of early and later colony housing on oral ingestion of morphine in rats', *Pharmacology, Biochemistry & Behavior*, 1981, 15, 571–576

Hari, J., *Chasing the Scream; The First and the Last Days of the War on Drugs*, London, 2015, Bloomsbury

**X is for X Chromosome**
Mental health statistics from Mental Health First Aid England Youth Instructor Manual. www.mhfaengland.org.uk

Sarah Vine: 'Calm down dears! British teenager girls have always been angst-ridden but they don't exactly live in Aleppo', *Daily Mail*, 24 August 2016
Report referenced by Sarah Vine: www.gov.uk/government/publications/improving-the-mental-health-of-children-and-young-people

Jack Lewis: Lecture at 'He and She' Campaign Event by Hobbs Consultancy, London, June 2016

Dr Javid Abdelmoneim's documentary: *No More Boys and Girls: Can Our Kids Go Gender Free?* (BBC2, August 2017)

The study that found women say 13,000 words per day than men was conducted by the University of Maryland and published in the journal *Neuroscience* in February 2013: Bowers, M., Perez-Pouchoulen, M., McCarthy, M., 'Foxp2 Mediates Sex Differences in Ultrasonic Vocalisation by Rat Pups and Directs Order of Maternal Retrieval'

Dr Ben Hine, from an interview I did with him in January 2018.

Orbach, S., *Fat Is a Feminist Issue*, London, 1978, Random House (Arrow Books)

Girlguiding national attitudes survey: you can download the most recent version of the survey at goo.gl/6VfjGT

Dr Jean Kilbourne on physical perfection: from her documentary *Killing Us Softly*, made by Margaret Lazarus, Renner Wunderlich, Patricia Stallone and Joseph Vitagliano detailing a lecture given by Dr Jean Kilbourne and distributed by Cambridge Documentary Films. The first version was released in 1979 but it has since been updated four times. The trailer for the most recent version is on YouTube: www.YouTube.com/watch?v=jWKXit_3rpQ&t=3s

Martin Seager on female and male 'shame triggers': from an interview I did with him in July 2016 when researching material for my classes in schools

Bigorexia: http://www.dailymail.co.uk/news/article-2396498/Doctors-warn-rise-number-men-suffering-bigorexia.html

Men Get Eating Disorders Too charity: https://mengetedstoo.co.uk

More men complete the act of suicide, but more women attempt it: source: MHFA England

Caitlin Moran and Robert Webb on gender stereotyping as detailed in their books: *How To Be a Woman, Moran, C*, London, Ebury Publishing, 2011. *How Not to Be a Boy*, Webb, R, Edinburgh, Canongate Books, 2017.

**Y is for Young People**
Statistics on average student debt: www.bbc.co.uk/news/education-40493658

Information on Living Wage: www.livingwage.org.uk

Information on average rent: www.telegraph.co.uk/finance/ property/11984097/London-rents-now-a-record-108pc-higher-then-rest-of-uk.html

Dr Andy Mayers on postnatal depression: from an interview I conducted with him in December 2017

More rigorous testing in schools: www.bbc.co.uk/news/education/35907385

Dr Tory Eisenlohr-Moul's work on role of hormones associated with menstrual cycle and our emotional/behavioural responses to them: Ph.D in Clinical Psychology, University of Kentuky, 2008.

Gabrielle Licterman, founder of Hormonology® www.myhormonology.com

Rosie Tressler on student life and mental health: From an interview I did with her in November 2017. Rosie is Chief Executive of Student Minds – www.studentminds.org.uk

**Z is for Zero Fucks Given**
Chidera Eggure's latest book of poetry will be published in July 2018: Eggure, C., *What a Time to Be Alone: The Slumflower's Guide to Why You are Already Enough'*, London, 2018, Quadrille Publishing Limited

First instalment in Chris Russell's trilogy: Russell, C., *Songs About a Girl*, London, 2016, Hodder Children's Books

Rowsell-Shand, J., *Full Circle*, London, 2017, John Blake

Jonny Benjamin: 'The Stranger on the Bridge', Channel 4, 2015 (documentary), and book *The Stranger on the Bridge*, London, 2018, Pan Macmillan (Bluebird)

**A–Z Conclusion**
To read more about mental health difficulties in BAME people visit: www.mentalhealth.org.uk/a-to-z/black-asian-and-minority-ethnic-bame-communities.

# ACKNOWLEDGEMENTS

**Words cannot express how grateful I am to everyone who supported me, either emotionally or intellectually, whilst I wrote this book . . . but I'm going to try anyway.**

Thank you to my agent, Anna, for your hours of toil, keeping it real and reminding me I'm not Eddie Izzard and therefore can't get away with huge, meandering footnotes. Thank you also to the team at Bluebird, especially Katy, Henry and Carole, whose serenity and positivity is a gift to anyone within radius of it.

Ruby, thank you for sprinkling the pages of this book with your creative genius.

Thanks to everyone who contributed their expertise, including Dr Andy Mayers at Bournemouth University, Dr David Bainbridge at Cambridge University, Dr Ben Hine from University of West London, Martin Daubney from the Men & Boys Coalition, Caroline Hounsell and everyone at Mental Health First Aid England, Rosie Tressler at Student Minds, Amie Sparrow and the team at Counselling Directory, Dr Adam Kay, Satveer Nijjar, Tory Eisenlohr-Moul, Gabrielle Lichterman, Martin Seager, Andre Symeou and 'Self-Care Queen' Georgia Dodsworth. Thanks to Chidera Eggerue, Chris Russell, Joanna Rowsell Shand and Jonny Benjamin for trusting me to recount their precious, intimate memories in the *Z: Zero Fucks Given* chapter.

Thanks also to James O'Brien, 'The Voice of Liberal Britain' for your endorsement. I shall remember you calling this book a 'masterpiece' forever.

Thank you to all the people who have shared their knowledge and experiences with me over the past decade to inform my research. Special shout out to all the teachers: you are heroes.

Thanks to all the people who let me natter unremittingly in their lugholes as I oscillated wildly between elation that this book is happening and deadline panic. Particular thanks to fellow writers Claire Eastham and Kelsey Osgood for being there to sympathise and not chastising me when I compared writing a book to childbirth (especially since Kelsey actually gave birth in the same year I wrote this). Thanks to my mates Karen, Amy, Adrian and Simon for your incessant, affectionate piss-taking which will ensure that, for as long as you are around, my ego will remain in check.

Finally, thanks to my brilliant family. I literally couldn't love you bunch of leftie, sweary, multi-coloured eccentrics more.